Volume 32

EXPLORING THE DIGITAL FRONTIER

Advances in
Librarianship

Volume 32

EXPLORING THE DIGITAL FRONTIER

Advances in
Librarianship

Edited by
Anne Woodsworth

New York, USA

United Kingdom • North America • Japan
India • Malaysia • China

Emerald Group Publishing Limited
Howard House, Wagon Lane, Bingley BD16 1WA, UK

First edition 2010

Reprints and permission service
Contact: booksandseries@emeraldinsight.com

British Library Cataloguing in Publication Data
A catalogue record for this book is available from the British Library

ISBN: 978-1-84950-978-7
ISSN: 0065-2830

Emerald Group Publishing
Limited, Howard House,
Environmental Management
System has been certified by
ISOQAR to ISO 14001:2004
standards

Awarded in recognition of
Emerald's production
department's adherence to
quality systems and processes
when preparing scholarly
journals for print

INVESTOR IN PEOPLE

Contents

Education and Training in the Digital World

Library and Information Science Education in the Digital Age   77

Heting Chu

E-Government and Public Access Computers in Public Libraries   113

Diane L. Velasquez

Knowledge Organization, Management and Policy Issues

Social Semantic Corporate Digital Libraries: Joining Knowledge Representation and Knowledge Management   137

Wolfgang G. Stock, Isabella Peters and Katrin Weller

Planning Strategically, Designing Architecturally: A Framework for Digital Library Services   159

Steven Buchanan

Recent Trends in EU Information Policy: Toward Greater Transparency in the Information Society   181

Debbie Rabina and Scott Johnston

Contributors

Numbers in parantheses indicate the pages on which the author's contributions begin.

Steven Buchanan (159), Department of Computer and Information Sciences, University of Strathclyde, Glasgow, UK

Heting Chu (77), Palmer School of Library and Information Science, Long Island University, Brookville, NY, USA

Scott Johnston (181), McPherson Library, University of Victoria, Victoria, British Columbia, Canada

Dirk Lewandowski (35), Fakultät Design Medien Information, Department Information, Hamburg University of Applied Sciences, Hamburg, Germany

Terrance S. Newell (55), School of Information Studies, University of Wisconsin-Milwaukee, Milwaukee, WI, USA

Isabella Peters (137), Department of Information Science, Heinrich-Heine-University, Düsseldorf, Germany

Debbie Rabina (181), School of Information and Library Science, Pratt Institute, New York, NY, USA

Chirag Shah (3), School of Communication and Information, Rutgers, The State University of New Jersey, New Brunswick, NJ, USA

Wolfgang G. Stock (137), Department of Information Science, Heinrich-Heine-University, Düsseldorf, Germany

Diane L. Velasquez (113), Graduate School of Library & Information Science, Dominican University, River Forest, IL, USA

Katrin Weller (137), Department of Information Science, Heinrich-Heine-University, Düsseldorf, Germany

Preface

As a new editor faced with a short deadline, it was gratifying to receive a large number of outstanding submissions in the past 6 months. This volume focuses on topics that push the edge in our increasingly electronically driven world. Not only is the field of library and information science awash in changes wrought by rapidly evolving technologies but so are almost all sectors that touch our daily lives. From e-banking to movies delivered through Wii and to smart phones with webcams and GPS applications, we face complexities that can paralyze us or make us embrace the digital environment. As our information environment becomes enriched, so do the challenges of keeping current as individuals and as librarians and information scientists. The most troublesome quandary is how we can learn from these early days of becoming digital to plan and accept changes in our work, our learning environments, and our personal and family lives. Just as industrialization changed the world a century ago, the digital explosion is causing another radical shift in our world.

In many ways the digital environment is a stressor that has the potential to both isolate people and yet provide more opportunities to network, particularly through social networks such as LinkedIn and Facebook. At the same time, both in learning and at work, we rely more and more on collaboration and team work, which can be assisted and supported by new information technologies. The need for speed in information-seeking processes and the need to obtain valid and accurate information call for those of us in the information and library fields to learn as much as we can so that we can in turn educate and train those who are less informed.

This volume explores aspects of digitization from a broad perspective. It takes a look at information seeking in collaborative settings; changes in library and information sciences teaching and learning; how videogames impact learning; how online public access catalogs can be improved to manage information, e-texts, and knowledge; and how we deal the impact of e-government on library users—all explorations of the digital frontier. Several of the authors (Newell and Velasquez) present studies that cover topics on which little prior research has been done. The remaining authors present thoughtful and well-grounded positions and theoretical approaches to emerging problems.

The first part of this volume, entitled "Information Seeking and Searching," approaches the digital frontier through the eyes of collaborative information seeking, the changing face of library and information science education, and the lessons that can be learned by libraries by emulating search engine technology. The first chapter by Chirag Shah, assistant professor at Rutgers University, provides an exhaustive literature review about collaboration in general and then turns to discussions about how best to provide support for information seeking by groups or teams of people. Too often, such information-seeking tasks are hampered by search systems that were designed for use primarily for individuals. Dr. Shah identifies and synthesizes core issues in this field, including how best to evaluate systems and collaborative tools. The key lessons from the literature review are summarized, and gaps in research are identified to enable further research.

In Chapter 2, Dirk Lewandowski, professor at Hamburg University of Applied Science in Germany, outlines how search engine technology can be used to improve library catalogs and to help improve users' experiences with searching them. A review of current online public catalogs determined that they are as not user-centered as they should be. Furthermore, they present results in a manner that is not highly sophisticated compared with online search engines. Use of rankings in catalogs is recommended as it helps find out more specifically what user intentions are. The ranking systems discussed include relevance, freshness, popularity, and locality. The chapter concludes with recommendations from which libraries and library systems vendors can learn how to improved library online public access catalogs.

The third chapter focuses on a different sector of information, namely the use of videogames in information skill development. The author, Terrance S. Newell, assistant professor in the School of Information Studies at the University of Wisconsin-Milwaukee, used qualitative research to obtain empirical knowledge about the information resources that players use in three genres of videogames—shooters, action/adventure, and role playing. His analysis of the content concluded that there are seven strata of information used to generate solutions for problem solving in games. Knowing these will help librarians, particularly in schools, to design instructional modules based on videogames and help gamers to apply problem-solving solutions to other domains such as schools, their communities, and every day problem solving.

The next two chapters provide a look at the digital world through the lens of higher education and through public libraries. Professor Heting Chu, Long Island University in Brookville, NY, presents research and a literature review of the first decade of library, and information science education in the 21st century has particular focus on how curricula have adapted in response to changes in the digital environment. She also examines the organizational changes that have occurred including the repositioning of schools within their institutions and school closures. The emergence of iSchools and the chasm between education and practice are also covered with the conclusion that library and information science education will thrive in the digital age. The author of the other chapter in this part is Diane L. Velasquez, assistant professor in the Graduate School of Library & Information Science at Dominican University in River Forest, IL. Her research explored the impact of governmental shifts to use of e-documents and its impact on access to information in public libraries that serve populations of 25,000–100,000 in the United States. Through a mixed-methods questionnaire administered to library staff, she discovered that there is a knowledge gap about access to and use of e-government information, not just on the part of the public but also on the part of librarians. She characterized the shift to digital government information as an unfunded mandate that places additional burdens on already thinly stretched public library staff members.

The last three chapters discuss knowledge from the point of view of knowledge organization systems, knowledge management systems, and recent policy trends in the European Union. Chapter 6 by Professor Wolfgang G. Stock and Researchers Isabella Peters and Katrin Weller (all from Hienrich-Heine University in Dusseldorf, Germany) provide a thorough theoretical review of how different knowledge organization systems can support corporate knowledge management systems or digital libraries. They discuss folksonomies, nomenclatures, classification systems, thesauri, and ontologies and consider how to handle persons as "documents" in such systems along with traditional documents. The research questions they explore include which knowledge representation methods are best for mapping explicit and implicit information and whether or not all information documents or knowledge containers are of equal importance in knowledge management systems and digital libraries, particularly in the Web 2.0 environment.

Chapter 7, by Steven Buchanan, senior lecturer at the University of Strathclyde, UK, argues that digital libraries have changed libraries from a support role to a strategic one. This, he indicates, calls for integrated planning for information technology that encompasses all elements of multidimensional elements beyond the technology and takes into account people, processes, requirements, and relationships. With such integrated and strategic planning, libraries will be able to evolve or at least keep pace with change and alternative information providers. Without it, digital libraries as enterprises risk being buffeted by external forces that could make them obsolete and misunderstood.

In the last chapter, Debbie Rabina (assistant professor at Pratt Institute, NY) and Scott Johnston (Graduate Studies Librarian at the University of Victoria, Canada) trace attempts on the part of policy makers in the European Union to adopt proactive and anticipatory measures in the digital information sector to create an information society that will enable economic and industrial competiveness. Their analysis covers not only attempts to achieve transparency in the policies but also the tensions derived from privacy and open access to information in the digital world.

The chapters in this volume will assist in unraveling the marvelous digital universe we are experiencing. They point out problems from many perspectives, yet they also point to practical and pragmatic solutions. I want to thank the authors who contributed their talents to this volume, not just for their contributions but also for their timely responsiveness to editorial suggestions and comments. Also needing acknowledgment are members of the Editorial Advisory Board who were stalwart in reviewing submissions and giving me their wisdom and experience: Barbara A. Genco, editor of Collection Management, *Library Journal*, New York, NY; Tula Giannini, dean of the School of Information and Library Science, at Pratt Institute, Brooklyn, NY; Kenneth Haycock, Follett chair in Library and Information Science at Dominican University, River Forest, IL; Maureen L. Mackenzie, associate professor of Management and Leadership at Dowling College, Oakdale, NY; Pat Molholt, Columbia University (Retired), New York, NY; W. David Penniman, executive director of Nylink, Albany, NY; Marie L. Radford, associate professor, Rutgers University, Newark, NJ; and Robert A. Seal, dean of Libraries at Loyola University Chicago, IL.

I would also like to thank Jim Walther, Emerald's US Publishing Adviser, for introducing me to Emerald. It would be remiss of me not to express my gratitude to Diane Heath, Mary Miskin, and other staff at the Emerald Group for being willing to "break in" a new editor in a period of short time. I truly look forward to working with them on future volumes.

Anne Woodsworth
Editor

Information Seeking and Searching

Collaborative Information Seeking: A Literature Review

Chirag Shah

School of Communication and Information, Rutgers, The State University of New Jersey, New Brunswick, NJ, USA

Abstract

Collaboration is often required for activities that are too complex or difficult to be dealt with by a single individual. Many situations requiring information-seeking activities also call for people to work together. Often the methods, systems, and tools that provide access to information assume that they are used only by individuals working on their tasks alone. This review points to the need to acknowledge the importance of collaboration in information-seeking processes, to study models, and to develop systems that are specifically designed to enable collaborative information seeking (CIS) tasks. This chapter reviews the literature from various domains including library and information science, human–computer interaction, collaborative systems, and information retrieval. Focus of the review is on the extent to which people work together on information seeking tasks and the systems and tools that are available for them to be successful. Since CIS occurs in the broader context of collaboration in general, a review of literature about collaborations is first undertaken to define it and place it into context with related terms such as cooperation and communication. A more focused review of research follows relating CIS to systems that have attempted to support such interactions. Included are identification and synthesis of a number of core issues in the field and how best to evaluate systems and collaborative tools. Key lessons learned from the review are summarized, and gaps in the literature identified to spur future research and study.

I. Introduction

Collaboration is a useful and often necessary component of complex projects. It is in human nature to collaborate with others when the task at hand is difficult or cannot be carried out by one individual. It began when man hunted for food (Lee and DeVore, 1968) to modern office environments (Hansen and Jarvelin, 2005). Recognizing this, many libraries are undergoing renovations and expansion to provide spaces in which students and

EXPLORING THE DIGITAL FRONTIER
ADVANCES IN LIBRARIANSHIP, VOL. 32
© 2010 by Emerald Group Publishing Limited
ISSN: 0065-2830
DOI: 10.1108/S0065-2830(2010)0000032004

faculty can work together, moving away from the 1950's and 1960's models using single carrels.

In many social situations, it is also common to collaborate. These situations span cultural, gender, and age differences. Large *et al.* (2002) in a study of web searching in a Canadian grade-six classroom found that participants often wanted to collaborate on search tasks. Similarly Morris' (2008) survey of knowledge workers found that the majority of them wanted to work collaboratively. Morris (2007) also proved that collaboration in many situations is vital to the success of the task at hand.

When it comes to a search for information, collaboration could be a wise choice. Twidale and Nichols (1996) pointed out a problem, however, in that "The use of library resources is often stereotyped as a solitary activity, with hardly any mention in the substantial library science and information retrieval literature of the social aspects of information systems" (p. 177). They argued that introducing support for collaboration into information retrieval (IR) systems would help users to learn and use the systems more effectively. Levy and Marshall (1994) noted that "support for communication and collaboration is . . . important for information-seeking activities, and . . . indeed, support for the former is needed to support the latter" (p. 164). On the basis of their extensive study of patent office workers, Hansen and Jarvelin (2005) concluded that the assumption that IR is a solitary one needs to be reconsidered. Twidale *et al.* (1997) showed that users often desire to collaborate on search tasks and argued that browsing is a collaborative process unlike how it is presented by a majority of search engines, that is, a single-user process. To them a truly user-centered system must acknowledge and support collaborative interactions between users. Morris (2007) proposed that four features of exploratory search experience—coverage, confidence, exposure, and productivity—could be enhanced by providing explicit support for collaborative searching and subsequent sense-making processes.

Recognizing the increasing importance of group, team and/or project, and learning environments for students and library users in general, this chapter presents a review and synthesis of related literature. The chapter is primarily divided into two parts with the first providing an overview of the concept of collaboration as studied in various fields. The second part presents a description of different aspects of collaborative computer information seeking (CIS) behavior while identifying the issues and challenges involved in building and evaluating CIS systems. In the conclusion there is a review of lessons learned from the literature and suggestions for future research.

A. Definitions and Models of Collaboration

Most people have an intuitive understanding of what it means to collaborate. As its Latin roots "com" and "laborate" suggest, *collaboration* indicates, "to work together." London (1995) interpreted this meaning as *working together synergistically*. Gray (1989) defined collaboration as "a process of joint decision-making among key stakeholders of a problem domain about the future of that domain." Roberts and Bradley (1991, p. 209) called collaboration "an interactive process having a shared transmutational purpose."

People use the word collaboration in various contexts and interchangeably with terms such as coordination and cooperation. It is important therefore to define collaboration here. Denning and Yaholkovsky (2008) said that coordination and cooperation are weaker forms of working together, yet all these activities require sharing information with others. Taylor-Powell *et al.* (1998) added another component—contribution—and concluded that for effective collaboration, each member of the group has to make a contribution to the collaborative. Using communication, contribution, coordination, and cooperation as essential steps toward collaboration, they showed how a true collaboration requires a tighter form of integration, moving from simple communication to higher levels of coordination, cooperation, and collaboration.

On the basis of these two works, a model of collaboration is synthesized and presented in Fig. 1. This model has five components: communication (information exchange), contribution, coordination, cooperation, and collaboration. It shows which activities support others. For example, coordination is a subset of collaboration, which indicates that for a meaningful collaboration, there has to be coordination of people and events. These five sets are described below in more detail with examples.

1. *Communication.* This is a process of sending or exchanging information, which is one of the core requirements for carrying out collaboration, or maintaining any kind of productive relationship. For example, a message on a public library bulletin board about a book sale is a way for the library to communicate with visitors.
2. *Contribution.* This is an informal relationship by which individuals help each other to achieve their individual goals. For example, Mark has some old books that he no longer needs, and he asks the library if they would take them. Upon the library's approval (communication), Mark donates the books.
3. *Coordination.* This is a process of connecting different agents together for a harmonious action. This often involves bringing people or systems under one umbrella at the same time and place. For example, a secretary setting up a meeting of computer, library, and university administrators to plan for future technology enhancements is undertaking a task of coordination.

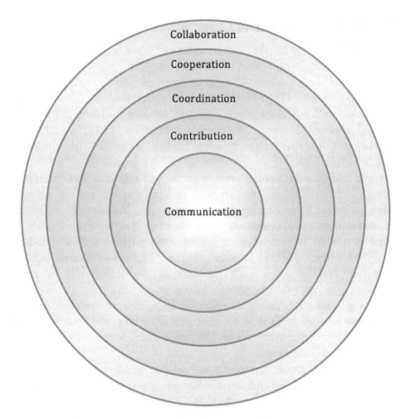

Fig. 1 A set-based model of collaboration. An inner set is essential to or supports the outer set.

4. *Cooperation.* This is a relationship in which different people with similar interests take part in planning activities, negotiating roles, and sharing resources to achieve joint goals. In addition to coordination, cooperation involves following some rules of interaction. An example in a library setting might be a reference librarian working with a cataloger to develop finding guides for a donation of personal papers.

5. *Collaboration.* This is a process involving various individuals who may see different aspect of a problem. They engage in a process that goes beyond their own individual expertise and vision to complete a task or project. In contrast to cooperation, collaboration involves creating a solution or a product that is more than the sum of each participant's contribution. Authority is vested in the collaborative rather than in an individual entity or organization. For example, in the library world, consortia and networks such as OCLC are built collaboratively by member libraries to provide broader and deeper access to information.

A collaborative solution tends to be better than one made by one individual. (Surowiecki, 2004). Chrislip and Larson (1994) defined collaboration as a "mutually beneficial relationship between two or more parties [agents] who work toward common goals by sharing responsibility, authority, and accountability for achieving results" (p. 5). Similarly, according to Gray (1989), collaboration is "a process through which parties [agents] who see different aspects of a problem can constructively explore their differences and search for solutions that go beyond their own limited vision of what is possible" (p. 5).

The difference among these five activities can be summarized using the variables, which are depicted in Fig. 2.

1. *Interaction.* While communication is at the center of other activities, it is possible to have little/no interaction while communicating. For example, a system administrator sending an email to a user may not require any further interaction. Collaboration, however, requires high levels of interactions among the participants.
2. *Intent.* Similar to interaction, a collaborative project requires much stronger intent compared to those tasks that merely need coordination of events or one entity cooperating with another.
3. *Trust.* To have an effective and mutually beneficial collaboration, participants need to establish trust, which is not required for coordinating or cooperating.
4. *Human involvement.* Communication may not require much human involvement. For instance, posting a message on a notice board is an act of communication, but seldom requires interactive communication or involvement. Collaboration, on the contrary, requires participants to be actively engaged with one another other.
5. *Symmetry of benefits.* The kind of collaboration considered here is, by definition, mutually beneficial. Thus, it benefits everyone involved in the process. The amount of benefit may vary depending on participants' roles and responsibilities. For example, a person gathering literature

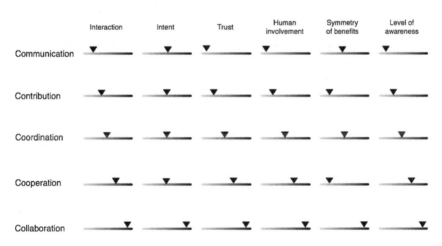

Fig. 2 Distinguishing communication, contribution, coordination, cooperation, and collaboration using different variables. A variable is represented with a bar going minimum to maximum from left to right.

for someone is performing an act of contributing to (cooperating) another's task such as writing a report. Co-authorship, on the contrary, is an act of collaboration, benefiting all the participants.

6. *Level of awareness.* For an interactive, intentional, and mutually beneficial collaboration to be successful, it is imperative that all the participants be aware of each other's actions and contributions. This also helps to establish trust among participants. Such awareness may not be a requirement for coordination or cooperation.

B. Principles

Let us now look at the principles or conditions for an effective collaboration. Most researchers agree that an effective collaboration must be *democratic* and *inclusive*, that is, it must be free of hierarchies of any kind, and it must include all of the stakeholders (London, 1995).

Regarding democracy in collaboration, Flora *et al.* (2004) pointed out that "without community empowerment and broad participation in agenda setting, the decision-making process of discussion, debate, and compromise is relatively meaningless" (p. 273). Osborne and Gaebler (1992) also expressed their views against hierarchies by noting that centralized and hierarchical associations tend to be divided up into many layers and boxes. This makes communication across units and between layers difficult, thus inhibiting the real potential of collaboration.

There is also a general agreement about the inclusiveness in collaboration. Theobald (1987) argued that all leadership in a community must be involved, whether participants fit traditional definitions of leaders or not. Chrislip and Larson (1994) concurred, reporting that all the successful collaborations that they studied involved participants from affected sectors, such as government, business, and community groups. Gray (1989) also claimed that collaboration could only be meaningful if the stakeholders were interdependent, stating that "collaboration establishes a give and take among the stakeholders that is designed to produce solutions that none of them working independently could achieve" (p. 11).

To spell out what situations could create a meaningful collaboration, Surowiecki (2004) presented four conditions for a successful collaboration.

1. *Diversity of opinion.* Each person should have some private information, even if it is just an eccentric interpretation of known facts.
2. *Independence.* People's opinions are not determined by the opinions of those around them.
3. *Decentralization.* People are able to specialize and draw on local knowledge.
4. *Aggregation.* Some mechanism exists for turning private judgments into a collective decision.

Collaboration, in many situations, is a process that ties people of varying opinions and abilities together. However, the process may not necessarily lead to agreement on all issues. Gray (1989) acknowledged that not all collaborations lead to consensus, but added that when agreements for action are reached, they are always done so through consensus. Denning and Yaholkovsky (2008) also noted that it is solidarity, not software, which generates collaboration.

C. Process

Following are questions compiled by London (1995) that need to be considered before starting a collaborative process.

1. What are the structural relationships between the parties and the possible power issues inherent in the collaborative arrangement?
2. Is there a clear understanding among all the parties of the respective goals of the other participants?
3. What form of leadership is required to facilitate the process?
4. Does the project have some form of integrating structure, such as a cross-section of steering committees, to facilitate and coordinate decision making and implementation?
5. Will the project be more effective with a neutral, third party mediator?
6. Should the media be involved?
7. Does the project have enough time, money, and staff support?

Such questions are important to answer since collaboration may incur costs and since the problem and circumstances may not call for collaboration.

Collaboration is typically a complex process involving a number of phases, various interactions, and other sub-processes. Gray (1989, pp. 57–74) identified three major phases of collaboration.

1. *Pre-negotiation or problem-setting phase.* This phase is often the most difficult, and involves six issues.
   a. The parties must arrive at a shared definition of the problem, including how it relates to the interdependence of the various stakeholders.
   b. The parties must make a commitment to collaborate.
   c. Other stakeholders must be identified whose involvement may be necessary for the success of the endeavor.
   d. The parties must acknowledge and accept the legitimacy of the other participants.
   e. The parties must decide what type of convener or leader can bring the parties together.
   f. The parties must determine what resources are needed for the collaboration to proceed.
2. *Direction-setting phase.* During this phase, the parties need to identify the interests that brought them together, determine how they differ from the interests of the others, set directions, and establish shared goals. This phase is characterized by six steps.
   a. Establishing ground rules.
   b. Setting the agenda.
   c. Organizing subgroups (especially if the number of issues to be discussed is large or the number of stakeholders exceeds the 12–15 member limit for effective group functioning).

    d.   Undertaking a joint information search to establish and consider the essential facts of the issue involved.
    e.   Exploring the pros and cons of various alternatives.
    f.   Reaching agreement and settling for a course of action.
3. *Implementation phase.* During this final phase, the participants go through the following steps.
    a.   Participating groups or organizations deal with their constituencies.
    b.   Parties garner the support of those who will be charged with implementing the agreement.
    c.   Structures for implementation are established.
    d.   The agreement is monitored and compliance is ensured.

Similar to these three phases defined by Gray (1989), Denning and Yaholkovsky (2008) provided three main stages of solving a complex problem: design, collaboration, and follow-through. They defined five specific stages of collaboration: (1) declare, (2) connect, (3) listen to and learn all perspectives, (4) allow a "we" to develop, and (5) create together.

D. Limitations

As was noted earlier in many situations collaboration is a natural choice, especially for solving complex problems (Denning, 2007). However, the costs and benefits associated with a collaborative process must be understood to evaluate the usefulness and the effectiveness of a particular collaboration.

London (1995, p. 9) identified the following limitations of a collaborative process.

1. Collaboration is a notoriously time-consuming process and is not suitable for problems that require quick and decisive action.
2. Power inequalities among the parties can derail the process.
3. The norms of consensus and joint decision-making sometimes require that the common good take precedence over the interests of a few.
4. Collaboration works best in small groups and often breaks down in groups that are too large.
5. Collaboration is meaningless without the power to implement final decisions.

Gray (1989) listed four circumstances under which it is best *not* to collaborate: (1) when one party has unchallenged power to influence the final outcome; (2) when conflict is rooted in deep-seated ideological differences; (3) when power is unevenly distributed; and (4) when constitutional issues are involved or legal precedents are sought, and when a legitimate convener cannot be found.

Sometimes collaboration is forced upon a group of people. Such examples might include the merger of two companies or an instructor using forced groupings in a class. In these situations, collaboration may start with acts of cooperation, in which participants merely follow a set of rules for working together. Later, it may or may not result in collaboration depending on responses to the previously mentioned factors and questions.

Disparity of workload and benefits is another limitation. Having diversity in collaboration could lead to success (Surowiecki, 2004), but as Aneiros and Estivill-Castro (2003) point out, roles according to positions (manager vs. knowledge workers) can create constraints in collaborative information seeking (CIS). They advised against a master/slave model of collaboration and proposed instead to have unconstrained co-browsing with asymmetric roles. Grudin (1994) also talked about disparities in benefits and responsibilities among participants. He claimed that it is almost impossible to have a groupware system in which every participant does the same amount of work and/or benefits the same. Owing to such inequality, a groupware application may become less useful over time and may even stop being used.

The kind of collaboration that is considered here (intentional and mutually beneficial) is slightly different than Grudin's notion of groupware, and CIS systems are considerably different than the groupware systems Grudin discussed. However, several of the issues he identified are relevant, and several are explored further in Shah (2009).

Grudin's recommendation for a system developer was to ensure that the system benefits all participants. At the same time, he pointed out difficulties in so doing because, while managers or higher authorities gain more benefits, they are the decision makers and pleasing them is equally, if not more important, than pleasing participants who have to do more of the work.

E. Collaboration in the Context of LIS

To understand the model of collaboration presented earlier (Fig. 2) in the context of information science, the five sets from that figure are enlisted in Table 1 with examples. Sending an email or instant messaging (IM) is a form of communication, but these communications may or may not be part of a collaborative project. Morris (2008) in fact established that email is one of the most frequently used methods of communication in a collaborative project. While communication tools to exchange contributions, there are specialized tools and places for so doing. Popular ones include, online support groups and social Q and A sites, such as Yahoo! Answers. The askers and answerers (contributor) on these sites are not truly collaborating however. One user is merely helping the other with his/her information need. To make such a process more effective and explicit, people use traditional/video conference calls or net meetings, which require coordinating agents (people as well as systems). Once again, such a coordinated event might/might not be a part of a collaborative project.

Table 1
Various Group Activities and Examples

Activity	Definition	Examples
Communication	Exchanging information between two agents	Email, chat
Contribution	Offering of an individual agent to others	Online support groups, social Q&A
Coordination	Connection different agents in a harmonious action	Conference call, net meeting
Cooperation	Agents following some rules of interaction	Wikipedia, second life
Collaboration	Working together synergistically to achieve a common goal	Brainstorming, co-authorship

As stated before, coordinated contribution needs a set of rules that the participating agents need to follow, and Wikipedia is a good example of cooperation. Its participants not only contribute in a coordinated fashion, but are governed by rules that need to be followed. For example, in cases of a disagreement, there are guidelines for how to make interactions work.

Let us look back to the terms coordination and cooperation and see how they fit around this understanding of collaboration expressed in Table 1. Austin and Baldwin (1991) noted that while there are obvious similarities between cooperation and collaboration, with the former involving pre-established interests, while the latter involves collectively defined goals. Malone (1988) defined coordination as "the additional information processing performed when multiple, connected actors pursue goals that a single actor pursuing the same goals would not perform" (p. 5). While this definition is close to the one given previously, it could be argued that it still fits in the model described in Fig. 2 since it says nothing about creating solutions.

From the definitions and models described earlier, we can synthesize that to have a successful collaboration while seeking information, we need to create a supportive environment where:

1. The participants of a team come with different backgrounds and expertise;
2. The participants have opportunities to explore information on their own without being influenced by the others, at least during a portion of the whole information seeking process;

3. The participants should be able to evaluate the discovered information without always consulting others in the group; and
4. There has to be a way to aggregate individual contributions to arrive at the collective goal.

One important requirement for successful collaboration is the kind of tasks being undertaken, but this has not been mentioned in the literature. As Morris and Horvitz (2007b) hypothesized, it is tasks that are exploratory in nature, which are most likely to benefit from collaboration.

F. Lessons for Collaborative Information Seeking

On the basis of the lessons learned from the general notion of collaboration, this subsection proposes (1) a set of conditions under which collaborative information seeking is useful and (2) a set of guidelines for building a successful CIS environment. The conditions under which collaboratively seeking information is useful are given below. They are not very different from those of any other kind of collaborative process.

1. *Common goal and/or mutual benefits*. For the most part, this is not a function of a system. A system can provide support for people with a common information goal who want to collaborate but does not typically initiate the collaboration. People do. A few systems can connect visitors to the same web sites in order for them to potentially collaborate, such as the one described by Donath and Robertson (1994). These systems are based on the assumption that the people browsing the same web sites may have the same information needs.
2. *Complex task*. Denning and Yaholkovsky (2008) recognized the benefit of collaborating while solving "messy" or "wicked" problems. While listing the conditions under which it is not useful to collaborate, London (1995) argued that if a task is simple enough, there is no point in collaborating.
3. *High benefits to overload ratio*. Often, a simple divide and conquer strategy could make collaboration successful. However, such a process may carry overhead due to phases preceding and following the process of information seeking. London (1995) noted that collaboration is only useful if such overhead is acceptable for a given situation. Fidel *et al.* (2004) showed that collaboration induces an additional cognitive load, which they referred to as collaborative load. For the collaboration to be viable, it has to meet or exceed benefit expectations with the cognitive load that it brings.
4. *Insufficient knowledge or skills*. A common reason to collaborate is that one individual has insufficient knowledge or skills to solve a complex problem.

The guidelines for building successful CIS systems are as follows:

1. They should provide effective ways for the participants to communicate with each other;
2. They should allow, and encourage, each participant to make an individual contribution to the collaborative information search;

3. They should coordinate participant actions, information requests, and responses to have an active and interactive collaboration either synchronously or asynchronously whether co-located or remote;

4. They should ask participants to agree and follow a set of rules. For example, if participants disagree on the relevancy of an information object, they should have a way in the system in which to discuss and negotiate a mutually agreeable solutions; and

5. They should provide mechanisms to let participants not only to explore their individual differences but also to negotiate roles and responsibilities.

II. Collaborative Information Seeking

While this author uses CIS, readers should be aware that there are many related and interchangeable terms in use such as collaborative information retrieval (CIR) (Fidel *et al.*, 2000), social searching (Evans and Chi, 2008), concurrent search (Baecker, 1995), collaborative exploratory search (Pickens and Golovchinsky, 2007), co-browsing (Gerosa *et al.*, 2004), collaborative information behavior (Reddy and Jansen, 2008; Talja and Hansen, 2006), and collaborative information synthesis (Blake and Pratt, 2006).

Despite the lack of agreement on terminology, following is an attempt to examine CIS in the context of space-time and user-source-time.

Foster (2006) defined collaborative IR as "the study of the systems and practices that enable individuals to collaborate during the seeking, searching, and retrieval of information" (p. 329). Shah (2008) referred to CIS as a process of information seeking "that is defined explicitly among the participants, interactive, and mutually beneficial" (p. 1). There is still lack of a universally accepted definition. Focus here is not only on retrieving or browsing but also on performing information seeking in collaboration. As we saw earlier, information seeking goes beyond searching and retrieving information.

A. Space and Time

The classic way to organize collaborative activities is based on two factors: location and time (Rodden, 1991; Hansen and Jarvelin, 2005; Golovchinsky *et al.*, 2008). Fig. 3, inspired by Twidale and Nichols (1996) depiction, shows various activities, methods, and environments on these two dimensions.

As we can see from this figure, the majority of collaborative activities in conventional libraries are co-located and synchronous (e.g., face-to-face meetings, reference interviews), whereas collaborative activities relating to digital libraries are more often remote and synchronous (e.g., digital referencing, virtual meetings). Social information filtering, or collaborative filtering, a process benefiting from other users' actions, is asynchronous and

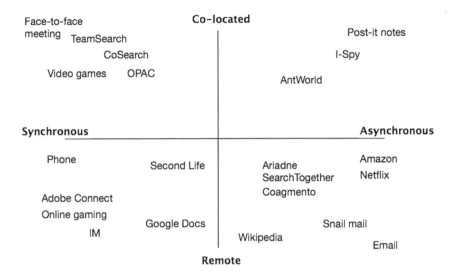

Fig. 3 Looking at collaboration with space and time dimensions.

mostly remote. Email also serves as a tool for doing asynchronous collaboration among users who are not co-located. Chat or IM (represented as "internet" in the figure) enables synchronous and remote collaboration.

Adobe Connect[1] facilitates online meetings in which the participants can share and discuss information and falls under synchronous-remote collaboration in Fig. 3. This environment needs (1) a way to connect remote participants, (2) a shared space for exchanging information, and (3) a communication channel to provide real-time message passing among the participants.

B. User-Source-Time Configurations

Another way of looking at how different systems fit into a broad spectrum of collaboration is to consider user(s), source(s), and time as shown in Table 2.

- *Single-user mode search.* This is a typical search. A user issues a query to a search engine and receives a ranked list. Relevance is found by considering various factors about individual documents, the whole collection, and links (Brin and Page, 1998; Kleinberg, 1999). Relevance feedback (Buckley *et al.*, 1994) and personalization (Teevan *et al.*, 2005) are common ways to improve searches in this mode.
- *Multisource search.* No search engine has full coverage of the web (Sullivan, 2005) so issuing the same query to different search engines typically yields different sets of results.

[1]http://www.adobe.com/products/acrobatconnect/

Table 2
Different Scenarios of Collaborative Information Processing

User	Source	Time	Examples
Single	Single	–	Typical search
Single	Multiple	Asynchronous	Multisource search
Single	Multiple	Synchronous	Meta-search
Multiple	Single	Asynchronous	Collaborative filtering, collaborative navigation, collaborative IR
Multiple	Single	Synchronous	Collaborative navigation, collaborative IR
Multiple	Multiple	Asynchronous	Collaborative filtering, collaborative IR
Multiple	Multiple	Synchronous	Collaborative navigation, collaborative IR

- *Meta-searching.* Instead of a user issuing a query to different search engines, a system can do so simultaneously by combining results obtained from a set of search engines, re-ranking them, and presenting a single ranked list to the user (Aslam and Montague, 2001). Examples are *Dogpile* and *Clusty.*
- *Collaborative filtering or recommender systems.* If multiple users are using the same source for information, the source can keep track of what users are looking for and what they find. On the basis of tracking statistics, the source can make recommendations to other users who are looking for the same or similar information. *Amazon.com* is an example of such a system.

Two other systems to consider are CIR and collaborative navigation, both of which are discussed later.

C. Control, Communication, and Awareness

Three components specific to group-work or collaboration that are highly predominant in the literature are control, communication, and awareness. Understanding these factors are helpful in various design stages of CIS systems.

1. Control

Rodden (1991) identified the value of control in computer-supported cooperative work (CSCW) systems and listed a number of projects for implementing control. For example, the COSMOS project (Wilbur and Young, 1988) had a formal structure to represent control in the system. They used roles to represent people or automatons and rules to represent flow and processes. Roles of people could be supervisor, processor, or analyst. Rules could be a condition that a process needs to satisfy to start or finish. Rodden classified these control systems as procedural-based systems.

To express control in a collaborative environment, early CSCW systems used various mechanisms to pass around messages. These messages were often referred to as structured definition language (SDL) messages. In the most basic sense, these were email messages sent back and forth among participants. SDL provided support for collaborative projects by imposing a structure to messages, incorporating additional fields of information that were used to filter and distribute messages appropriately. For example, Malone *et al.* (1987) proposed an *Information Lens* framework, in which messages carried additional information (some of which was automatically generated), which could be used to filter and classify the messages to suit individual needs within a group.

Later Malone extended this framework to *Object Lens* (Malone and Lai, 1988), in which the participants could create not only messages to pass information around but also any kinds of objects. Each objects had a similar structure imposed on it to guide control and distribution processes. Object Lens also allowed people create links among the objects formed. Malone pointed out that this was similar to hypertexts on the world wide web.

2. Communication

Communication is one of the most critical components in any form of collaboration. In fact, Rodden (1991) identified message or communication systems as the class of systems in CSCW that are most mature and most widely used. Donath and Robertson (1994) presented a system that allowed users to know that others were viewing the same webpage and to communicate with them to initiate a possible collaboration or at least a co-browsing experience.

Using four multidisciplinary design situations in the USA and Europe, Sonnenwald (1996) identified 13 communication roles. He explained how these roles can support collaboration, among other aspects of information seeking process, such as knowledge exploration and integration, and task and project completion, by filtering and providing information and negotiating differences across organizational, task, discipline, and personal boundaries.

3. Awareness

Several related terms and definitions are used in the literature to refer to awareness in collaborative projects. For example, Dourish and Bellotti (1992,

p. 107) defined awareness as "an understanding of the activities of others, which provides a context for your own activity" (p. 107). Dourish and Bly (1992) provided the following definition for awareness:

> Awareness involves knowing who is "around," what activities are occurring, who is talking with whom; it provides a view of one another in the daily work environments. Awareness may lead to informal interactions, spontaneous connections, and the development of shared cultures—all important aspects of maintaining working relationships which are denied to groups distributed across multiple sites. (p. 541)

A set of theories and models for understanding and providing awareness emerged in the early literature. Gaver (1991) asserted that an intense sharing of awareness characterizes focused collaboration in which people work closely together on a shared goal. He further claimed that less awareness is needed for division of labor and that more casual awareness can lead to serendipitous communication, which can turn into collaboration. He proposed a *general awareness* model that incorporates and supports all such activities. Bly *et al.* (1993) also identified the importance of general awareness saying, "When groups are geographically distributed, it is particularly important not to neglect the need for informal interactions, spontaneous conversations, and even general awareness of people and events at other sites" (p. 29).

4. Importance of control, communication, and awareness

Empirical observations and other studies of usability testing relating to control, communication, and awareness indicate that an effective collaborative system should have the following attributes:

1. A flexible mechanism to incorporate structured message passing;
2. A way of facilitating control among the participants as well as with automaton components; and
3. Facilities to present awareness of various objects, processes, and people at any given time to everyone in the group.

Several systems such as *SearchTogether* (Morris and Horvitz, 2007b) and *Coagmento* (Shah, 2010) incorporate support for chat or IM. Some works have also tried to provide other sorts of communication channels in collaborative workspaces, such as audio chat, video conferencing, and bulletin board support. While chat is an obvious choice for synchronous communication, email still prevails when it comes to providing asynchronous communication Morris' (2008). Given the importance of email, and the level of familiarity and comfort that most people have with it, an effective collaborative search system should provide support for passing such messages among the participants. In addition, there needs to be some kind of structure imposed on messages such as time stamps, tags, and associated processes. This can be helpful in distributing the messages with some sort of filtering and/or following rules and roles of a system. Pickens *et al.* (2008) demonstrated a collaborative video search system where one of the participants was responsible for issuing queries (prospector), and the other participant was responsible for going through the results looking for relevant information (miner).

Since users of a collaborative search system work with different sources, documents, queries, snippets, and annotations, everyone in the group should be aware of all such objects as they are collected and modified. In addition to this, it is important to show attributes associated with an object, for example, that a document has already been viewed.

Several systems supporting collaboration have identified control, communication, and awareness as critical to their design. For example Farooq *et al.* (2009) used such a collaborative design for *CiteSeer*, a search engine in computer and information science disciplines. On the basis of a user survey, they identified four mandates for redesigning the *CiteSeer* collaboratory: (1) visualize query-based social networks to identify scholarly communities of interest, (2) provide online collaborative tool support for upstream stages of scientific collaboration, (3) support activity awareness for staying cognizant of online scientific activities, and (4) use notification systems to convey scientific activity awareness.

D. Co-browsing or Collaborative Navigation

Co-browsing or collaborative navigation is a process that allows participants to navigate or browse, and share information with a possible intermediate interface. Root (1988) introduced the idea of social browsing to support distributed cooperative work with unplanned and informal social interaction. He described a "social interface," which provided direct, low-cost access to other people through the use of multimedia communications channels. The design of his conceptual system, called *CRUISER*, incorporated three basic concepts: social browsing, a virtual workspace, and interaction protocols. His premise was that by integrating all digital media into a richly interconnected workspace, the context of workgroup activities would be significantly extended and enriched. Root's idea of facilitating informal and effortless interaction among a group of people was continued by Donath and Robertson (1994) with *The Social Web*. This allowed a user to know what others were concurrently viewing and to communicate with them. They worked on the assumption that users accessing the same page are likely to share similar interests.

Cabri *et al.* (1999) unveiled a system for synchronous cooperative browsing that permitted users within a workgroup to share information and work toward a common goal. This was done using a proxy without changing browsers on the user's end. Gerosa *et al.* (2004) had a similar idea with proxy-based co-browsing in e-learning. They called this *Symmetric Synchronous Collaborative Navigation*, a form of social navigation, in which users shared a virtual web browser. They provided a symmetric, proxy-based architecture that did not need a special browser. This allowed users to merge into a collaborative environment with as little effort as possible. Esenther (2002), with his collaborative web browsing (CWB) system, targeted casual (nontechnical) users allowing them remotely to synchronize pointing, scrolling and browsing of uploaded content in their web browsers.

Another example of a collaborative browsing application is *AntWorld* by Menkov *et al.* (2000). This tool was developed to make it easier for the members of a common-interest user group to collaborate in searching the web. *AntWorld* harnesses the expertise of members of a common interest group as displayed by their evaluation of documents encountered while searching. It stores users' judgments about documents they found and uses this information to guide other users to pages that might be useful.

Sometimes it is not just the web pages that people want to browse and share, but other objects such as bookmarks. Keller *et al.* (1997) provided *WebTagger*, a social bookmarking service similar to *del.icio.us*, which allowed a group of users to tag and share webpages. *WebTagger* enables users to supply feedback on the utility of resources that they bookmarked relative to their information needs, and provides dynamically updated rankings of resources based on incremental user feedback.

Several other systems used their own interfaces rather than relying on a web browser. For instance, *GroupWeb* (Greenberg and Roseman, 1996) is a browser that allows group members to share and navigate world wide web pages visually in real time. Its groupware features include document and view slaving for synchronizing information sharing, telepointers for enacting gestures, and "what you see is what I see" views to handle display differences. *GroupWeb* also incorporated a groupware text editor that lets groups create and attach annotations to pages. Similar is *GroupScape* (Graham, 1997), which was a multiuser HTML browser to support synchronous groupware applications and browsing of HTML documents on the web. Yet another architecture to support multiuser browsing is *CoVitesse* (Laurillau and Nigay, 2002), a groupware interface that enabled collaborative navigation of the web based on a collaborative task model. This system represented users navigating collaboratively in an information space made of the results of a query submitted to a search engine. In contrast to these systems, which are primarily designed for remotely located participants, *CoSearch* (Amershi and Morris, 2008) provides multidevice support for collaborative browsing among co-located participants.

E. Collaborative IR

As discussed earlier, if and when a problem in IR is difficult to solve, a carefully executed collaboration can help. Smyth *et al.* (2003) argued that one way would be to connect users to information that is difficult to find by collaboration in the search phase of an information-seeking process. They showed how collaborative searches could act as a front-end for existing search engines and could re-rank results based on the learned preferences of a community of users. Smyth *et al.* attempted to demonstrate this concept by implementing the *I-Spy* system (Freyne *et al.*, 2004).[2] *I-Spy* captures queries and related results for a given workgroup and uses that information to provide filtered, and presumably more relevant, information to users. Thus, *I-Spy* acts more as a collaborative filtering process than as synchronous collaborative searching.

While I-Spy attempts to extend content-based filtering techniques by incorporating communities, several collaborative systems have been developed by extending a traditional IR model to incorporate multiple users. However, such extension is often ineffective or nontrivial. For instance, Hyldegard (2006), in studies of information seeking and retrieval in a group-based educational setting, found that people in a collaborative group to some extent demonstrated cognitive experiences similar to individuals in Kuhlthau's information search process (ISP) model (Kuhlthau, 2005). However, these experiences did not result only from information-seeking activities but also from work-task activities and intragroup interactions. Her later work also indicated (Hyldegard, 2009) that group-based problem solving is a dynamic process that shifts between a group perspective and an individual perspective. Such a finding calls for a thorough investigation into CIS that is not simply an extension of a traditional IR system. As stated by Olson *et al.* (1992) "The development of schemes to support group work, whether behavioral methods or new technologies like groupware, should be based on detailed knowledge about how groups work, what they do well, and what they have trouble with" (p. 347).

Unlike co-browsing, where the applications are aimed toward web browsing, works on collaborative IR are often focused on specialized domains

---

[2]This has been transposed to HeyStaks (http://www.heystaks.com/).

for searching. For example, Twidale and Nichols (1996) provided the *Ariadne* system, which allowed users to collaborate with an information search expert remotely and synchronously over a library catalogue. The authors saw the importance of supporting social aspects of searching for information and showed how it can be addressed. *Ariadne*, however, did not support asynchronous collaboration.

Morris and Horvitz (2007b) introduced *SearchTogether* that allowed a group of remote users to collaborate synchronously or asynchronously. It focused on supporting awareness, division of labor, and persistence in collaboration. Awareness was provided using per-user query histories, page-specific metadata, and annotations. Division of labor was implemented using integrated IM as well as a recommendation mechanism, by which a participant could recommend a page to another participant. *SearchTogether* also provided "Split Search" and "Multi-Engine Search" options for automatic division of labor. Finally, persistence was implemented by storing not only information about all sessions, but automatically creating a shared artifact that summarized the results of a collaborative search.

MUSE (Krishnappa, 2005) supports synchronous, remote collaboration between two people who are searching a medical database. *MUSE* lets its users perform standard single-user searches, with a provision of chat and the ability to share metadata about the current database results with the other user. Another example is S^3 (Morris and Horvitz, 2007a) which is not so much a CIS system, but it does enable sharing of retrieved results asynchronously among a set of users.

Research produced by the CIR group at University of Washington, studied situations where members of a work-team were seeking, searching, and using information collaboratively and showed how such processes can be realized in a multiteam setting. This started with Fidel *et al.* (1999), who defined collaborative IR (CIR) "as any activity that collectively resolves an information problem taken by members of a work-team regardless of the nature of the actual retrieval of information" (p. 2). They used a cognitive work analysis framework in a field study that examined social, organizational, cognitive, and individual characteristics of information seekers, and then focused on collaborative situations (Fidel *et al.*, 2000). From their studies involving two design teams working in collaboration, they found (Bruce *et al.*, 2003) that the nature of the task and the structure and the culture of the organization in which tasks are performed are important factors that determine CIR behavior. Later Poltrock *et al.* (2003) found that any IR activity may be performed by an individual on behalf of a team, by an ad-hoc group, or by the team working together in a meeting. They also concluded that technologies intended to support teamwork could be more effective by recognizing and supporting collaboration in the activities that comprise IR and their coordination.

F. Realization of a Collaborative Environment

There are several ways in which a collaborative environment can be realized. People are familiar with using tools such as telephones and email for collaborating with remotely located users, both asynchronously and synchronously. These tools, however, are not specifically designed to handle collaboration. Effective collaboration may require a different set of tools. To understand the issues in implementing a collaborative system, three important aspects can be identified: processes, content, and devices. Following is a brief description of each of these aspects along with related works.

1. Processes

Several realizations of a collaborative environment have focused primarily on systems. These typically present algorithmic ways of combining multiple instances of search requests, result lists, or other interactions from different users to perform implicit "collaboration." For example, a good deal of work in implementing a collaborative search system has focused on reformulating search requests of a user based on other users' search requests on the same/ similar search goals. Fu et al. (2007) showed how different queries from a set of users for the same information goal can be combined for better retrieval performance.

2. Content

A simple way of taking advantage of collaboration is dividing the content among the users for viewing, judging, or manipulating. With *WebSplitter*, Han et al. (2000) demonstrated how a unified XML framework could support multidevice and multiuser web browsing. Similarly, Maekawa et al. (2006) developed a page partitioning method for collaborative browsing, which divides a web page into multiple components. They also designed and implemented a collaborative web browsing system in which users can search and browse their target information by discussing and watching partial pages displayed on multiple devices.

3. Devices

Typically, in a CIS environment, by system, we are referring to computers, but several works have tried to extend information access and distribution to other forms of devices to enable collaboration among users in various work places. For instance, Maekawa *et al.* (2006) presented a collaborative web browsing system in a mobile computing environment. Their motivation for using collaboration in the mobile device environment was to overcome the issue of low functionality that restricts the services provided for mobile users. Amershi and Morris (2008) presented *CoSearch*—a collaborative browsing interface to be used on computers, and introduced *CoSearchMobile*, designed to provide similar functionalities on mobile devices. The *CoSearch* system leverages readily available devices such as mobile telephones.

Blackwell *et al.* (2004) described a tangible interface for collaborative IR. The purpose of this interface was to allow multiple users to interact simultaneously to refine a query. Morris *et al.* (2006) presented *TeamSearch* system, which used an interactive table for a small group of co-located participants in searching for digital images to use in a report. Mitsubishi Electric Research Lab (MERL) has developed *DiamondTouch* (Smeaton *et al.*, 2006b), an interface device that supports direct user collaboration on a tabletop. Such an interactive tabletop is ideal for multimedia searches done collaboratively. Smeaton *et al.* (2006a, c) reported video searching in collaboration using *DiamondTouch* interactive tabletop devices. Among other things, the authors found about a 10% increase in the level of user-interaction as the users moved from their first search to the last one.

G. Evaluation

Evaluating a collaborative information searching environment can be a huge challenge due to its complex design involving users, integrated systems, and a variety of interactions. While a CIS system can be measured using typical measures of IR as did Smyth *et al.* (2005) additional measures for evaluating collaborative information search systems are needed. To date, evaluating various factors in CIS behaviors and results can be summarized as measuring (1) retrieval performance of the system, (2) effectiveness of the interface in facilitating collaboration, and (3) user satisfaction and involvement.

Baeza-Yates and Pino (1997) presented work on a measure that could extend evaluation of a single-user IR system to a collaborative environment based on retrieval performance. Aneiros and Estivill-Castro (2005) proposed evaluating the "goodness" of a collaborative system through its usability. Baeza-Yates and Pino (1997) treated the performance of a group as the summation of the performances of the individuals in the group. In short, the majority of the work on evaluation has addressed the usability of the collaborative interfaces. For example, Morris and Horvitz (2007b) tested their *SearchTogether* system with a user study to evaluate how users used various tools offered in its interface and how those tools affected the act of collaboration. While they showed the effectiveness of their interface in letting people search together, there was no evaluation of the learning that took place in the group due to collaboration. Laurillau and Nigay (2002) for their *CoVitesse* system, did evaluations for the user interface as well as various network-related parameters, but not on its effects on retrieval performance.

Some of the application designers also let "real" users use their systems and evaluated the effectiveness of their system based on users' feedback and/or their success in solving their "real" problems with it. For instance, Twidale *et al.* (1995) invited volunteers to bring an existing problem to solve. Students from a wide range of academic backgrounds (including Psychology, Computing, Women's Studies, Chemistry, Religious studies, and Environmental Science) used their *Ariadne* system. The typical case was that they were about to write an extended essay, dissertation or group project and needed to do a literature search. The testing informed the iterative development of the system. Smyth *et al.* (2003) tested their I-Spy system with leave-one-out evaluation methodology. From 20 users, they left one user as a *testing user* and used the other 19 users as the *training users*.

Prekop (2002) presented a qualitative way of evaluating CIS studies. He proposed this by measuring *information-seeking patterns*. These patterns describe prototypical actions, interactions, and behaviors performed by participants in a collaborative endeavor. The three patterns that the author described were information seeking by recommendation, direct questioning, and advertising information paths. Along similar lines, Olson *et al.* (1992) analyzed behavior and patterns of users by studying 10 design meetings from four projects in two organizations. The meetings were videotaped, transcribed, and then analyzed using a coding scheme that looked at participants' problem solving and the activities they used to coordinate and manage themselves. The authors also analyzed the structure of their design arguments. The authors claimed that the coding schemes developed might be useful for a wide range of problem-solving meetings other than design.

Wilson and Schraefel (2008) analyzed an evaluation framework for information seeking interfaces in terms of its applicability to collaborative search software. Extending Bates' tactics model (Bates, 1979) and Belkin's model of users (Belkin *et al.*, 1993), they showed that the framework can be just as easily applied to collaborative search interactions as individual information seeking software, but pointed out that there are additional considerations about the individual's involvement within a group that must be maintained as the assessment is carried out.

III. Conclusion

While exploring the notion of collaboration in general, and the motivations behind it, it was discovered that there are a variety of definitions of collaboration in the literature, and that the term t is often used interchangeably with coordination and cooperation. For purposes of this review, a working definition a definition of collaboration was deemed to be a "group of participants intentionally working together in an interactive manner for a common goal." The second part of the review was devoted specifically to research, literature, and products in the fields of library and information science and related domains. Several key issues for designing and implementing collaborative information search systems, user behavior, and evaluation in these environments were identified and synthesized.

To summarize, the following key points were derived from the review of the literature.

1. Collaboration involves people working together for a common goal or solution; simply working together or interacting is not enough.
2. Collaboration is intentional and interactive.
3. The value of collaboration in information seeking depends on the kind of task involved, that is, people may not find it useful to collaborate in simple known-item, fact-finding tasks.
4. Collaboration may help an individual participant to achieve what he could not accomplish working in solitude.
5. A careful collaboration can help a team produce something that is more than the sum of individual participants' contributions.
6. Collaboration involves certain overhead and an additional cognitive load. These factors need to be considered when evaluating CIS environments.
7. Information exchange and filtering may be necessary conditions for collaboration, but they are not sufficient conditions of and by themselves.
8. Collaboration among the users can occur at various levels during information-seeking processes: (1) while formulating an information request, (2) while obtaining results, and (3) while organizing and using the results. All these levels should be supported to create an effective collaboration environment.
9. A successful collaborative system needs to have support for control, communication, and awareness to help participants be more efficient and be actively engaged in the collaboration.
10. A deeper understanding of how collaboration as well as information seeking works is required to accommodate multiuser environment, going beyond the single-user IR systems and environments.
11. A holistic approach is needed, along with models that can measure and evaluate collaborative information systems and environments which beyond traditional single-user IR paradigms.

From a review of relevant literature, it is clear that there are still several missing pieces in the field of CIS systems and environments as follows:

- While there is a fairly good understanding of why people collaborate, motivations are not always identified in the context of situations in which collaborative information searches occur.
- The literature provides a list of tools and methods that are used in collaboration, but the relative merits of these tools and methods are not clear. Too often, tools not specifically designed for collaboration are being used for carrying out collaborative tasks.
- The literature about computer-supported collaboration identifies three major issues in information seeking/searching systems and environments: control, communication, and awareness. Control is domain specific, and communication is system specific. Awareness, however, may depend on a number factors, including task, distribution of responsibilities among the collaborators, roles of the collaborators, nature of the final product, need for privacy versus sharing among the collaborators, and the nature of their collaboration (synchronous vs. asynchronous, co-located vs. remote). Since the issue of awareness is highly understudied in the literature a better understanding of how to support for awareness in a collaborative search system would add considerable value to them in both theory and practice.
- Several suggestions are made for evaluating a collaborative information systems as well as users' performance while working with such systems. However, it remains unclear what factors should be measured and how. Therefore, a taxonomy of evaluation metrics for information seeking in different collaborative environments is indicated.
- The literature to date includes a number of works that try to understand people working with collaborative systems and their behavior in both online communities and social networking sites. A link that connects these two is missing. A better understanding is needed of how to leverage people's engagement in social networking sites to promote collaboration and to support various social activities within collaborative systems.
- Finally, there is need to develop models that extend or augment single-person information-seeking systems and information-seeking behaviors into collaborative environments.

The above issues are at the core of the CIS domain. Given the shift to teamwork and group-driven projects and information gathering, further study and research would enable development of better and more supportive collaborative information systems.

References

Amershi, S., and Morris, M. R. (2008). CoSearch: A system for co-located collaborative web search. In *Proceedings of ACM SIGCHI Conference on Human Factors in Computing Systems*, pp. 1647–1656, Florence, Italy.

Aneiros, M., and Estivill-Castro, V. (2003). Foundations of unconstrained collaborative web browsing with awareness. In *Proceedings of the IEEE/WIC International Conference on Web Intelligence*, pp. 8–25, Beijing, China.

Aneiros, M., and Estivill-Castro, V. (2005). Usability of real-time unconstrained www- co-browsing for educational settings. In *Proceedings of the IEEE/WIC International Conference on Web Intelligence*, pp. 105–111, University of Technology, Compiegne, France.

Aslam, J. A., and Montague, M. (2001). Models for metasearch. In *Proceedings of the Annual ACM Conference on Research and Development in Information Retrieval (SIGIR)*, pp. 276–284, New Orleans, LA.

Austin, A. E., and Baldwin, R. G. (1991). *Faculty Collaboration: Enhancing the Quality of Scholarship and Teaching.* Jossey-Bass, San Francisco, CA.

Baecker, R. M. (1995). *Readings in Human-Computer Interaction: Towards the Year 2000.* Morgan Kaufmann, San Francisco, CA.

Baeza-Yates, R., and Pino, J. A. (1997). A first step to formally evaluate collaborative work. In *Proceedings of ACM Group Conference*, pp. 56–60, Phoenix, AR.

Bates, M. J. (1979). Information search tactics. *Journal of the American Society for Information Science* 30(4), 205–214.

Belkin, N., Marchetti, P., and Cool, C. (1993). Braque: Design of an interface to support user interaction in information retrieval. *Information Processing and Management* 29(3), 325–344.

Blackwell, A. F., Stringer, M., Toye, E. F., and Rode, J. A. (2004). Tangible interface for collaborative information retrieval. In *Proceedings of ACM SIGCHI Conference on Human Factors in Computing Systems*, pp. 1473–1476, ACM Press, Vienna, Austria.

Blake, C., and Pratt, W. (2006). Collaborative information synthesis I: A model of information behaviors of scientists in medicine and public health. *Journal of the American Society for Information Science and Technology* 57(13), 1740–1749.

Bly, S. A., Harrison, S. R., and Irwin, S. (1993). Media spaces: bringing people together in a video, audio, and computing environment. *Communications of the ACM* 36(1), 28–46.

Brin, S., and Page, L. (1998). The anatomy of a large-scale hypertextual web search engine. *Proceedings of the Seventh World Wide Web Conference*, Brisbane, Australia. Retrieved from http://ilpubs.stanford.edu:8090/361/

Bruce, H., Fidel, R., Pejtersen, A. M., Dumais, S. T., Grudin, J., and Poltrock, S. (2003). A comparison of the collaborative information retrieval behaviour of two design teams. *The New Review of Information Behaviour Research* 4(1), 139–153.

Buckley, C., Salton, G., and Allen, J. (1994). The effect of adding relevance information in a relevance feedback environment. In *Proceedings of the Annual ACM Conference on Research and Development in Information Retrieval (SIGIR)*, pp. 292–300, Springer-Verlag, New York, NY.

Cabri, G., Leonardi, L., and Zambonelli, F. (1999). *Supporting Cooperative WWW Browsing: A Proxy-Based Approach.* University of Modena, Modena, Italy.

Chrislip, D. D., and Larson, C. E. (1994). *Collaborative Leadership: How Citizens and Civic Leaders Can Make a Difference.* Jossey-Bass, San Francisco, CA.

Denning, P. J. (2007). Mastering the mess. *Communications of the ACM* 50(4), 21–25.

Denning, P. J., and Yaholkovsky, P. (2008). Getting to "we". *Communications of the ACM* 51(4), 19–24.

Donath, J. S., and Robertson, N. (1994). The sociable web. In *Proceedings of the World Wide Web (WWW) Conference*, CERN, Geneva, Switzerland.

Dourish, P., and Bly, S. A. (1992). Portholes: Supporting awareness in a distributed work group. In *Proceedings of ACM SIGCHI Conference on Human Factors in Computing Systems*, pp. 541–547, ACM Press, Toronto, Ontario, Canada; New York, NY.

Dourish, P., and Bellotti, V. (1992). Awareness and coordination in shared workspaces. In *Proceedings of the Conference on Computer-Supported Cooperative Work (CSCW)*, pp. 107–114, Toronto, Ontario, Canada.

Esenther, A. W. (2002). Instant co-browsing: lightweight real-time collaborative web browsing. In *Proceedings of the World Wide Web (WWW) Conference*, pp. 107–114, Honolulu, HI.

Evans, B. M., and Chi, E. H. (2008). Towards a model of understanding social search. In *Proceedings of JCDL 2008 Workshop on Collaborative Exploratory Search*, Pittsburgh, PA.

Farooq, U., Ganoe, C. H., Carroll, J. M., and Giles, C. L. (2009). Designing for e-science: Requirements gathering for collaboration in CiteSeer. *International Journal of Human Computer Studies* 67, 297–312.

Fidel, R., Bruce, H., Dumais, S. T., Grudin, J., Poltrock, S., and Pejtersen, A. M. (1999). *Sollaborative Information Retrieval (Technical Report)*. University of Washington, Seattle, OR. Retrieved from http://projects.ischool.washington.edu/cir.

Fidel, R., Bruce, H., Pejtersen, A. M., Dumais, S. T., Grudin, J., and Poltrock, S. (2000). Collaborative information retrieval (CIR). *The New Review of Information Behaviour Research* 1, 235–247.

Fidel, R., Pejtersen, A. M., Cleal, B., and Bruce, H. (2004). A multidimensional approach to the study of human-information interaction: A case study of collaborative information retrieval. *Journal of the American Society for Information Science and Technology* 55(11), 939–953.

Flora, C. B., Flora, J. L., and Fey, S. (2004). *Rural Communities: Legacy and Change*. Westview Press, Boulder, CO.

Foster, J. (2006). Collaborative information seeking and retrieval. *Annual Review of Information Science and Technology (ARIST)* 40, 329–356.

Freyne, J., Smyth, B., Coyle, M., Balfe, E., and Briggs, P. (2004). Further experiments on collaborative ranking in community-based web search. *Artificial Intelligence Review* 21, 229–252.

Fu, X., Kelly, D., and Shah, C. (2007). Using collaborative queries to improve retrieval for difficult topics. In *Proceedings of the Annual ACM Conference on Research and Development in Information Retrieval (SIGIR)*, pp. 879–880, Amsterdam, Netherlands.

Gaver, W. W. (1991). Sound support for collaboration. In *Proceedings of European Conference on Computer Supported Cooperative Work (ECSCW)* (L. J. Bannon, M. Robinson and K. Schmidt, eds.), pp. 293–308, Dordrecht Kluwer, Amsterdam, Netherlands.

Gerosa, L., Giordani, A., Ronchetti, M., Soller, A., and Stevens, R. (2004). Symmetric synchronous collaborative navigation. In *Proceedings of the 2004 IADIS International WWW/Internet Conference*, pp. 1–7, Madrid, Spain.

Golovchinsky, G., Pickens, J., and Back, M. (2008). A taxonomy of collaboration in online information seeking. In *Proceedings of JCDL 2008 Workshop on Collaborative Exploratory Search*, Pittsburgh, PA.

Graham, T. C. N. (1997). GroupScape: Integrating synchronous groupware and the World Wide Web. In *Proceedings of INTERACT*. Chapman and Hall, Sydney, Australia.

Gray, B. (1989). *Collaborating: Finding Common Ground for Multiparty Problems*. Jossey-Bass, San Francisco, CA.

Greenberg, S., and Roseman, M. (1996). GroupWeb: A WWW browser as real time groupware. *Proceedings of ACM SIGCHI Conference on Human Factors in Computing Systems*, pp. 271–272, ACM Press, Boston, MA.

Grudin, J. (1994). Groupware and social dynamics: Eight challenges for developers. *Communications of the ACM* 37(1), 92–105.

Han, R., Perret, V., and Naghshineh, M. (2000). WebSplitter: A unified XML frame-work for multi-device collaborative Web browsing. *Proceedings of Computer Supported Cooperative Work (CSCW)*, pp. 221–230, ACM Press, New York, NY.

Hansen, P., and Jarvelin, K. (2005). Collaborative information retrieval in an information-intensive domain. *Information Processing and Management* 41, 1101–1119.

Hyldegard, J. (2006). Collaborative information behaviour-exploring Kuhlthau's Information Search Process model in a group-based educational setting. *Information Processing and Management* 42, 276–298.

Hyldegard, J. (2009). Beyond the search process—exploring group members' information behavior in context. *Information Processing and Management* 45, 142–158.

Keller, R. M., Wolfe, S. R., Chen, J. R., Rabinowitz, J. L., and Mathe, N. (1997). A bookmarking service for organizing and sharing URLs. *Computer Networks and ISDN Systems* 29, 1103–1114.

Kleinberg, J. M. (1999). Authoritative sources in a hyperlinked environment. *Journal of the ACM (JACM)* 46(5), 604–632.

Krishnappa, R. (2005). *Multi-User Search Engine: Supporting Collaborative Information Seeking and Retrieval*. Master's thesis, University of Missouri-Rolla, Rolla, MO.

Kuhlthau, C. C. (2005). Towards collaboration between information seeking and information retrieval. *Information Research* 10(2). Retrieved from http://informationr.net/ir/10-2/paper225.html

Large, A., Beheshti, J., and Rahman, T. (2002). Gender differences in collaborative web searching behavior: An elementary school study. *Information Processing and Management* 38, 427–433.

Laurillau, Y., and Nigay, L. (2002). CoVitesse: A groupware interface for collaborative navigation on the WWW. In *Proceedings of the ACM conference on Computer Supported Cooperative Work (CSCW)*, pp. 236–240, New Orleans, LA.

Lee, R. B., and DeVore, I. (eds.) (1968). *Man the Hunter*. Aldine, Chicago, IL.

Levy, D. M., and Marshall, C. C. (1994). What color was George Washington's white horse? A look at assumptions underlying digital libraries. In *Proceedings of Digital Libraries*, pp. 163–169. Retrieved from http://www.csdl.tamu.edu/DL94/paper/levy.html

London, S. (1995). *Collaboration and Community*. Retrieved from http://scottlondon.com/reports/ppcc.html

Maekawa, T., Hara, T., and Nishio, S. (2006). A collaborative web browsing system for multiple mobile users. In *Proceedings of IEEE Conference on Pervasive Computing and Communications (PERCOM)*, Pisa, Italy.

Malone, T. W. (1988). *What is Coordination Theory?* Technical Report SSM WP 2051-88. Massachusetts Institute of Technology, Boston, MA.

Malone, T. W., and Lai, K. (1988). Object lens: A spreadsheet for cooperative work. In *Proceedings of the Conference on Computer-Supported Cooperative Work (CSCW)*, Portland, OR.

Malone, T. W., Grant, K. R., Turbak, F. A., Brobst, S. S., and Cohen, M. D. (1987). Intelligent information sharing systems. *Communications of the ACM* 30(5), 390–402.

Menkov, V., Neu, D. J., and Shi, Q. (2000). AntWord: A collaborative web search tool. In *Proceedings of Workshop on Distributed Communities on the Web (DCW)*, Quebec City, Quebec, Canada.

Morris, M. R. (2007). Interfaces for collaborative exploratory web search: Motivations and directions for multi-user design. In *Proceedings of ACM SIGCHI Conference on Human Factors in Computing Systems 2007 Workshop on Exploratory Search and HCI: Designing and Evaluating Interfaces to Support Exploratory Search Interaction*, pp. 9–12, San Jose, CA.

Morris, M. R. (2008). A survey of collaborative web search practices. In *Proceedings of ACM SIGCHI Conference on Human Factors in Computing Systems*, pp. 1657–1660, Florence, Italy.

Morris, M. R., and Horvitz, E. (2007a). S³: Storable, shareable, search. In *Proceedings of INTERACT*, Rio De Janeiro, Brazil.

Morris, M. R., and Horvitz, E. (2007b). SearchTogether: An interface for collaborative web search. *ACM Symposium on User Interface Software and Technology (UIST)*, pp. 3–12, Newport, RI.

Morris, M. R., Paepcke, A., and Winograd, T. (2006). TeamSearch: Comparing techniques for co-present collaborative search of digital media. *First IEEE International Workshop on Horizontal Interactive Human-Computer Systems (TABLE-TOP '06)*, pp. 97–104, Adelaide, Australia.

Olson, G. M., Olson, J. S., Carter, M. R., and Storrosten, M. (1992). Small group design meetings: An analysis of collaboration. *Human-Computer Interaction* 7(4), 347–374.

Osborne, D., and Gaebler, T. (1992). *Reinventing Government*. Addison-Wesley, Reading, MA.

Pickens, J., and Golovchinsky, G. (2007). Collaborative exploratory search. *Proceedings of Workshop on Human-Computer Interaction and Information Retrieval*, Computer Science and Artificial Intelligence Laboratory (CSAIL), pp. 21–22, Masschusetts Institute of Technology, Cambridge, MA.

Pickens, J., Golovchinsky, G., Shah, C., Qvarfordt, P., and Back, M. (2008). *Algorithmic Mediation for Collaborative Exploratory Search*. Paper presented at Annual ACM Conference on Research and Development in Information Retrieval (SIGIR), Singapore, China.

Poltrock, S., Grudin, J., Dumais, S. T., Fidel, R., Bruce, H., and Pejtersen, A. M. (2003). Information seeking and sharing in design teams. In *Proceedings of ACM Group Conference*, pp. 239–247, Sanibel Islands, FL.

Prekop, P. (2002). A qualitative study of collaborative information seeking. *Journal of Documentation* 58(5), 538–547.

Reddy, M. C., and Jansen, B. J. (2008). A model for understanding collaborative information behavior in context: A study of two healthcare teams. *Information Processing and Management* 44(1), 256–273.

Roberts, N. C., and Bradley, R. T. (1991). Stakeholder collaboration and innovation: A study of public policy initiation at the state level. *The Journal of Applied Behavioral Science* 27(2), 209–227.

Rodden, T. (1991). A survey of CSCW systems. *Interacting with Computers* 3(3), 319–353.

Root, R. W. (1988). Design of a multi-media vehicle for social browsing. In *Proceedings of Conference on Computer-Supported Cooperative Work (CSCW)*, pp. 25–38, ACM Press, Portland, OR, New York, NY.

Shah, C. (2008). Toward collaborative information seeking (CIS). In *Proceedings of JCDL 2008 Workshop on Collaborative Exploratory Search*, Pittsburgh, PA. Retrieved from http://workshops.fxpal.com/jcdl2008/submissions/tmpE1.pdf.

Shah, C. (2009). Lessons and challenges for collaborative information seeking (CIS) systems developers. *Group 2009 Workshop on Collaborative Information Behavior.* Sanibel Island, FL. Retrieved from http://www.personal.psu.edu/sap246/Shah_CIB_Workshop.pdf.

Shah, C. (2010). *Coagmento—A Collaborative Information Seeking, Synthesis and Sense-Making Framework.* Demonstration at Computer Supported Cooperative Work (CSCW), Savannah, GA.

Smeaton, A. F., Foley, C., Gurrin, C., Lee, H., and Givney, S. M. (2006a). Collaborative searching for video using the Físchlár system and a DiamondTouch table. In *Proceedings of TableTop2006—The 1st IEEE International Workshop on Horizontal Interactive Human-Computer Systems,* pp. 149–156, Adelaide, Australia.

Smeaton, A. F., Lee, H., Foley, C., and Givney, S. M. (2006b). Collaborative video searching on a tabletop. *Multimedia Systems Journal* 12(4), 375–391.

Smeaton, A. F., Lee, H., Foley, C., Givney, S. M., and Gurrin, C. (2006c). Físchlár-DiamondTouch: Collaborative video searching on a table. In *Proceedings of SPIE electronic imaging—Multimedia Content Analysis, Management, and Retrieval (6073),* pp. 8–19, SPIE Publications, San Jose, CA.

Smyth, B., Balfe, E., Briggs, P., Coyle, M., and Freyne, J. (2003). *Collaborative Web Search.* Paper presented at International Joint Conference on Artificial Intelligence (IJCAI), Acapulco, Mexico, Morgan Kaufmann, San Francisco, CA, pp. 1417–141.

Smyth, B., Balfe, E., Boydell, O., Bradley, K., Briggs, P., Coyle, M., and Freyne, J. (2005). *A Live-User Evaluation of Collaborative Web Search.* Paper presented at International Joint Conference on Artificial Intelligence (IJCAI), Edinburgh, Scotland.

Sonnenwald, D. H. (1996). Communication roles that support collaboration during the design process. *Design Studies* 17(3), 277–301.

Sullivan, D. (2005). *Search Engine Sizes.* Retrieved from http://searchenginewatch.com/showPage.html?page = 2156481.

Surowiecki, J. (2004). *Wisdom of Crowds: Why the Many are Smarter than the Few and How Collective Wisdom Shapes Business, Economies, Societies and Nations.* Anchor Books, New York, NY.

Talja, S., and Hansen, P. (2006). *Information Sharing.* Springer, New York, NY.

Taylor-Powell, E., Rossing, B., and Geran, J. (1998). *Evaluating Collaboratives: Reaching the Potential.* Technical Report G3658-8. University of Wisconsin-Extension, Madison, WI. Retrieved from http://www.empowerment.state.ia.us/files/annual_reports/2001/Collaboration.pdf

Teevan, J., Dumais, S. T., and Horvitz, E. (2005). *Personalizing Search Via Automated Analysis of Interests and Activities.* Annual ACM Conference on Research and Development in Information Retrieval (SIGIR), Salvador, Brazil, pp. 449–456.

Theobald, R. (1987). *The Rapids of Change.* Knowledge Systems, Houston, TX.

Twidale, M. B., and Nichols, D. M. (1996). Collaborative browsing and visualisation of the search process. *Aslib* 48(7–8), 177–182.

Twidale, M. B., Nichols, D. M., and Paice, C. D. (1995). Supporting collaborative learning during information searching. In *Proceedings of Computer Supported Collaborative Learning (CSCL),* pp. 367–374, Bloomington, IN.

Twidale, M. B., Nichols, D. M., and Paice, C. D. (1997). Browsing is a Collaborative Process. *Information Processing and Management* 33(6), 761–783.

Wilbur, S. B., and Young, R. E. (1988). The COSMOS project: A multi-disciplinary approach to design of computer supported group working. In *EUTECO 88: Research into Networks and Distributed Applications* (R. Speth, ed.). Vienna, Austria.

Wilson, M. L., and Schraefel, M. C. (2008). *Evaluating Collaborative Search Interfaces with Information Seeking Theory.* Workshop on Collaborative Information Retrieval, Pittsburgh, PA.

Using Search Engine Technology to Improve Library Catalogs

Dirk Lewandowski

Fakultät Design Medien Information, Department Information, Hamburg University of Applied Sciences, Hamburg, Germany

Abstract

This chapter outlines how search engine technology can be used in online public access catalogs (OPACs) to help improve users' experiences, to identify users' intentions, and to indicate how it can be applied in the library context, along with how sophisticated ranking criteria can be applied to the online library catalog. A review of the literature and the current OPAC developments forms the basis of recommendations on how to improve OPACs. Findings were that the major shortcomings of current OPACs are that they are not sufficiently user-centered and that their results presentations lack sophistication. Furthermore, these shortcomings are not addressed in current 2.0 developments. It is argued that OPAC development should be made search-centered before additional features are applied. Although the recommendations on ranking functionality and the use of user intentions are only conceptual and not yet applied to a library catalogue, practitioners will find recommendations for developing better OPACs in this chapter. In short, readers will find a systematic view on how the search engines' strengths can be applied to improving libraries' online catalogs.

I. Introduction

For some years now, libraries' online public access catalogs (OPACs) have been competing with, if not threatened by, Web search engines. Although it has not yet been agreed which way this threat should be answered, it is certain that search engines will now remain a rival of libraries and their catalogs. As a consequence, some libraries have taken advantage of search engines by outfitting their OPACs with this new technology to provide and maintain quicker access to desired content.

This technical improvement, however, is only one side of the coin. It should also be mentioned that despite the technological advantage and the improved content in the library catalogs, there is no guarantee that users

EXPLORING THE DIGITAL FRONTIER
ADVANCES IN LIBRARIANSHIP, VOL. 32
© 2010 by Emerald Group Publishing Limited
ISSN: 0065-2830
DOI: 10.1108/S0065-2830(2010)0000032005

will acknowledge that the OPAC as their primary or, indeed, only instrument for their search for academic content. To achieve this, it would be necessary not only to train the users sporadically but also to establish systematic information literacy programs. Although it is not the focus of this chapter, it is nevertheless an important issue to mention at the outset to make clear that there cannot be only a technical solution for the "OPAC problem."

Now, what can be done from a technical standpoint? To identify any technical requirements, it is necessary to examine the user. Apart from the OPAC, where else does academic research take place? General Web search engines rank first (Google being the most widely used). Others include academic search engines, interdisciplinary databases, professional databases, academically oriented social software, as well as the listings of publishers and online booksellers.

It is clear that the OPAC is merely one alternative among many and that if the OPAC is to remain relevant for more than mere stock retrieval of individual titles, it will clearly have to take position beside its rivals in the future.

During the process of digitalization and in the case of "digital only," definition of library material has frequently been requested. Libraries, which until now have defined themselves by their physical stock, are experiencing problems defining exactly what belongs to their collections. Should only printed stock be included? Should they include academic content that is freely available on the Web or only the licensed databases? Here, libraries are primarily asked which search path the users wish to follow. Do they want to begin searching in the local materials and then expand to additional collections when required? Would they prefer a "top-down approach" whereby the users initiate their search in a library before being guided to the locally available stock in a subsequent step? The answer to this is crucial: it means we are dealing either with an OPAC approach or with that of an academic search engine, which would naturally significantly influence the assembly of the system.

In this chapter, the OPAC system is compared to some well-known Internet search engines. It is especially important to take Web search engines into consideration because they define the standards upon which other information systems (i.e., not only the library search systems) will have to act to remain accepted by the users.

On the one hand, it can be said that, due to their assembly and by responding to the user's characteristics, search engines educate their users toward a "bad" user's attitude. On the other hand, the search engines have shown that even simple requests can be answered satisfactorily by means of elaborate ranking systems. In this respect, search engines are role models because they cater to the actual search behavior of their users (i.e., their research knowledge) in an attempt to optimize the results.

The influence of Web search engines on the users' search behavior should not be underestimated. Nevertheless, there is another reason why they should be compared to library-based methods: Web search engines such as Google have developed services aimed at the core of the libraries, for example, Google Books and Google Scholar. These services use search-engine technology and elaborate ranking systems for searches in "library contents." Specialized search engines, however, are not the only source of inspiration for library services. An examination of the ranking of general Web search engines is recommended.

The next section begins with an overview on the stage of development of modern OPACs. It provides a description of the existing deficiencies of current OPACs and how far they can be improved in terms of a search engine orientation. It is argued that OPACs can only become a competitive alternative when they can impress with a mature and user-friendly ranking. Furthermore, it is shown which factors can be used for such a ranking. Finally, suggestions for future OPAC advancement in research and practice are given.

II. OPACs Current State of Development

In this chapter, it is assumed that the OPACs provide the central access to libraries' contents. I then deal with the domains' spectrum of content, catalog enrichment (and user participation), and discovery.

As a general rule, the spectrum of content of a library is not fully represented in its catalogs (Lewandowski, 2006). This is due to the prevalent lack of journal articles, articles from anthologies, and contents of the library-licensed databases within the libraries' catalogs. Newer OPACs tackle this problem by adding further titles (articles) and an automatic search expansion to additional databases. The user remains unaware, however, of the collections he is searching and the amount of information covered. For instance, it is not clear to users during a regular query which journal articles are covered. Are they effectively presented with the articles of all existing journals within the library? With the articles of all library-licensed electronic journals? Or is it an entirely self-contained collection independent from the library, which neither covers the collection completely nor is limited to it? Although the idea of adding results from additional sources to a search is surely a good idea, we can see that it is executed insufficiently. What would be needed is a systematic expansion of the library catalog with regard to the library's holdings of articles.

With regard to external databases, the result is similar: here, there is an attempt to integrate further data sources by means of a federated search and, more recently, the establishment of "complete indices." The first case, however, only interrogates a limited number of databases and accounts only for a strongly limited number of results per database. The second case tries to avoid these issues as well as the performance problems that accompany the federated search. This concerns a seminal approach although the index assembly can only be achieved with great effort, which is not the least due to problems dealing with licensing rights.

When it comes to the catalog enrichment, two sources can be generated, which support the admission of titles. On the one hand, additional information is selectively purchased or complemented during the process of compiling catalog data, and on the other hand, library users themselves are urged to generate additional "user-generated content" for the titles. Although the first case mainly deals with indexes, blurbs, and possible reviews, it is the users who must amend ratings and reviews. As is known from all systems dealing with *user-generated contents*, the crucial factor remains the achievement of a critical group of users who are actually willing to contribute to the content. It has to be said here that only a fraction of those users wishing for user-generated content agree on generating it themselves. Taking this into consideration, it is strongly recommended that data be exchanged between a preferably large number of libraries instead of relying on their individual and limited users.

The expression "discovery" signifies an exploration of databases, which integrate both searching and browsing approaches. While the user is searching for information, it is not yet clear if he is specifically *searching* or merely browsing through the collection. The distinction is questionable in many cases. Here, the act of searching must be seen as alternating searching and browsing. This means that users at some points enter search terms while at other times they sift through the set of results, influenced by the system. This phenomenon is known as an "exploratory search."

Search systems offer so-called drill-down menus, which help the user explore the set of results. For instance, results are refined by media type, key word, year of publication, and so forth. This provides the user with a simple means to limit the number of hits from the initial query to achieve a manageable number of results. Furthermore, a great advantage is provided by the suggestions offered in the drill-down menus generated from the initial pool of results, which means they constitute a dynamic reaction on the original set of results, as opposed to static browsing, which draws upon predetermined classifications and tables of contents.

Additional information from the enhanced catalog supports the user in validating the received results. Furthermore, enhanced descriptions of the results aid users evaluations, reducing the need to evaluate entire texts. When these two functions are connected with a list/shopping cart, they facilitate the explorative search for literature and display a clearly added value compared to sole searching and browsing approaches.

An overview of modern OPAC developments in Europe indicate that they (Community Walk, forthcoming) generally support the users well when it comes to the refinement of results sets as well as the screening of the received results. However, most of their problem lie with incomplete support of the target-oriented search and therein predominantly with ranking of the given results. Although the more recent OPAC approaches orientate themselves toward the users, they stay bound to the traditional idea of information search through an information professional particularly in one regard. They assume the user to be capable of (and to acknowledge the necessity of) constricting the results set to receive a manageable number of results that are then fully screened. However, Web search engine-trained behavior shows that users tend to rely strongly on the order of the results produced by the search engine, instead of implementing a further refinement of the results set by themselves. Studies on selective behavior within the results set show a strong focus on the results that rank first. Another influential factor, next to position, is any emphasis within the result description (see later for more information on selective behavior). Users demand quick access to the results and are not willing to think about formulating the request for long. The initially generated results list becomes important in terms of it being the basis for the decision of if, and how, the search is to be continued. This makes it essential to design the initial results list in such a way that the first positions already display relevant results. Moreover, for a significant number of requests, the results list is sufficient to find answers.

Considering the pros and cons of the OPAC searches compared with Web search engines (Table 1), it can be seen that the strengths of the OPACs lie in the areas relevant for elaborate research by information professionals, whereas the search engines are strong in all areas related to broadly untrained users. Accordingly, OPACs offer a wide number of functions that can be used for the specific query but also require advanced knowledge of refinement techniques and search languages. Search engines, however, contain only a very limited number of functions for a broader search. Some of the functions are even restricted in terms of their operational reliability (Lewandowski, 2004; Lewandowski, 2008a). The second strength of the OPAC lies in the existence of metadata in the database that can be utilized during the search. Nevertheless, this metadata (as shown earlier) is used to support browsing rather than for specific research. Here, a real opportunity for improving the systems can be seen.

Table 1
Comparison of the Strengths and Weaknesses of OPACs and Search Engines

	OPAC	Search engine
Simple searches	Weak, order of results sorted by date	Strong because of good ranking
Expanded searches	Range of functions	Marginal number of functions, faulty functions (!)
Order of results/ ranking	Bad, sorted only by date	Good due to mature ranking and diversity within results lists
Presentation of results	Sparsely flexible due to author/title/ year	Result description with static and context-related elements
Collection	Only part of the library offering	Integration of all collections provided by the search engine
Metadata	High-end quality data	Metadata is barely used; no own production

III. Query Types and Search Intentions

The evaluation of search systems should always be oriented toward the queries that are put to this special type of search system. To test and optimize an individual system, it is helpful to use actual queries for an evaluation. Furthermore, it is essential to use different query types in tests to cover the different search intentions of the users. The analysis of those queries in terms of the (potential) search intention and optimization of the system toward these intentions can be seen as the key to successful responses to queries.

In information science, a differentiation is made between a *Concrete Information Need* (CIN) and a *Problem-Oriented Information Need* (POIN) (Frants *et al.*, 1997). CIN asks for factual information and is satisfied with only one factum. In the case of document retrieval, this means it is satisfied with only one document containing the required factum. In contrast, POIN requires a smaller or larger number of documents for satisfaction. Table 2 sums up the distinctive features of CIN and POIN.

Table 2
Concrete Information Need vs. Problem-Oriented Information Need

CIN	POIN
Thematic boarders are clearly defined	Thematic boarders are not clearly definable
It is possible to express the formulation of the query in exact terms	The formulation of the query allows a variety of terms
One fact information is usually enough to cover the requirements	Usually a diversity of documents must be found. It remains open as to whether the information need is covered
The information problem is solved when the fact information has been transmitted	The transmission of literature information is possible to modify the information problem or generate a new need

Source: Translated from Stock, 2007, p. 52.

When applying the problem-oriented and the concrete information needs to the search with OPAC, one can distinguish between a thematic search on the one hand and an item-specific search on the other. The second case is also known as *known-item search* (Kantor, 1976) because it is already known that the corresponding title *exists*. It remains merely to be found in the system.

Broder (2002) differentiates between three different types of intentions when querying Web search engines: informational, navigational, and transactional. Navigational queries aim at a Web page that is already known to the user or which he assumes exists, for example, homepages of companies (e.g., DaimlerChrysler) or people (e.g., John von Neumann). Such queries normally terminate in one correct result. The information need is satisfied when the requested page is found.

In contrast, informational queries require more than one document (POIN). The user wishes to be informed about a topic and therefore reads several documents. Informational queries aim at static documents to acquire the desired information, which makes further interaction on the Web page unnecessary.

Transactional queries, however, aim at Web pages offering the possibility for a subsequent transaction, such as purchasing a product, downloading data, or searching a database.

Broder's (2002) differentiation is also applicable to OPACs. Here too exist different search intentions that have to be responded to satisfactorily by the same information system. Whereas the navigational query equals the known-item search, and the informational query corresponds to the topic

Table 3

Applicability of Query Types According to Broder (2002) to Library OPACs

Query type according to Broder	Analog query type in the OPAC	Example query	Explanation
Informational	Topic search	Collaborative tagging	Search for literature toward a certain topic, requesting a variety of documents
Navigational	Known-item search	Wolfgang Stock Information Retrieval	Search for evidence of a certain title; only one title is accepted
Transactional	Search for sources	Database of Court decisions	Search for a source/ database in which the research can be continued

search, the transactional query correlates with the search for an adequate source to do further research (Table 3). Today's OPACs are not attuned to this diversity of queries, and the types of queries are not being discerned during evaluation, which differs from the evaluation of search engines (Lewandowski, 2010; Lewandowski and Höchstötter, 2007). In the course of a more user-oriented approach, the future development of the OPACs should be conducted with regard to the different types of queries. Furthermore, the differentiation between the query types is essential for an appropriate ranking; knowing the user's intention is of tremendous importance for the accentuation of adequate documents. In other words, a successful ranking is impossible without acknowledging the user's intention!

This raises the question as to how far we can gain access to the user's intention and the query types. Generally, libraries carry out user-specific studies such as surveys and smaller laboratory investigations (e.g., qualitative opinion polls, search tasks under observation, and focus groups). In my opinion, these methods are barely adequate to produce the required data. Even more so, it is necessary to investigate and continuously monitor internal log files. Indeed, logfile investigations for library catalogs have taken place in the past (Hennies and Dressler, 2006; Lown and Hemminger, 2009; Obermeier, 1999; Remus, 2002). However, they have concentrated primarily on the lengths of queries, the usage of field search and amplified search functions, or, in the case of Lown and Hemminger, on the usage of drill-down menus. The analysis of the queries was not a priority in these investigations.

A. Ranking Systems as a Central Means for Information Search

This section deals circumstantially with the search and selection behavior of users when they employing Web search engines. Again, it is assumed that the search behavior of users is applied to other types of information systems and that these systems then need to adjust to the given behavior, rather than requesting a too demanding adjustment to the respective system. Afterwards, the typical ranking factors applied to Web search engines are discussed and the efficiency for library OPACs is questioned. A set of suitable ranking factors is suggested as is general problem of ranking, that is, repeated bias toward the same results. For this problem, a solution is also offered based on Web search engines.

The user behavior toward Web search engines can be characterized as follows:

- Queries in most cases contain only a few words with the majority consisting of one word, followed by two-word queries. The average length of German queries is one to seven words (Höchstötter and Koch, 2008), whereas English queries are longer due to specifics of individual languages. A shift in the user behavior toward longer queries cannot be detected.
- Studies have shown that user behavior concerning query formulation and length does not differ between library catalogs and Web search engines (Hennies and Dressler, 2006). Whereas Web search engines admittedly are adjusted to this query behavior to a great extent (Lorigo et al., 2008; Bar-Ilan et al. 2009), five conventional OPACs display very long results lists that are only sorted according to the age of the data.
- Selection behavior within the search engine results lists show explicitly how much users rely on the engine-based ranking (Granka et al., 2004; Joachims et al., 2005; Lorigo et al., 2008). Not only do a significant number of users limit themselves to screening the first page of results (Höchstötter and Koch, 2008), they also focus heavily on the top results.

Despite the fact that not only the position of the result is crucial but also the description of the result within the results list (Lewandowski, 2008b). Studies during which the order of the results sets was manipulated have shown that the presentation of low-ranking results does not have a great impact on the selection behavior (Bar-Ilan et al., 2009; Keane et al., 2008).

The characterization of the most important aspects of user behavior toward Web search engines and the related expectations toward other information systems show the importance of an adequate ranking within the results list. This is true not only for success in the sense of efficiency and effectiveness of modern information systems but also for their acceptance by the user. Commercial providers of search systems have known this for years and have adjusted their information systems to these conditions. Examples are *Google Scholar* and Elsevier's *Scirus*. Both systems administer very large databases and offer the user intelligently sorted results lists without neglecting possibilities of a complex research. In this respect, academic search engines can be seen as a role model for search applications in libraries (Lewandowski, 2006).

Also, regarding the factors used in the ranking, Web search engines can act as role models for other information systems. Although it is true that the insight gained from the ranking of Web contents is not applicable one-on-one to other content, the broad preliminary stages from this context can nevertheless help to improve the rankings in other contexts.

B. Applying Ranking to Library Materials

Already at an early stage, an attempt was made to apply ranking to a library-based inventory of titles. Buckland *et al.* (1993) state that in online catalog, "the computer could be programmed to provide any one or combination of a variety of orderings" (p. 313). Nevertheless, most of the OPACs that rank the results are still limited to *text matching* and field weighting today (Dellit and Boston, 2007). Some library catalogs go beyond this and experiment with, for example, popularity factors (Flimm, 2007) as well as copy data and lending data (Mercun and Zumer, 2008; Sadeh, 2007). All of these experiments tried to integrate individual factors without systematically verifying adequacy and practical use.

Meanwhile, the core of the ranking problem has evolved from merely matching queries and documents (i.e., text matching) to quality evaluation of the potentially relevant documents gained through text matching. Considering the Web context, this can be explained by the sheer mass of documents that respond to a typical query on the one hand and the very limited quality evaluation in the course of indexing on the other hand. Web search engines already try to discard so-called SPAM documents and duplicates during this process. This cannot, however, be compared to a quality-evaluation process, through the selection of a title, as implemented in libraries.

In the field of search engines, three sections of quality evaluation have developed, which can serve as evidence for the improvement of ranking within library catalogs (Lewandowski, 2009).

1. Popularity

The popularity of a document is referenced for its quality evaluation. For example, the number of user accesses and the dwell time on the document is measured as well as the linking of a document within its Web graph, which is decisive for the ranking of Web documents. For this purpose, not only the number of clicks and links respectively is crucial but weighted models are also implemented that enable a differentiated evaluation. These models are well documented in literature (Culliss, 2003; Dean *et al.*, 2002; Kleinberg, 1999; Page *et al.*, 1999), and their main elements are applicable to document evaluation in library catalogs.

2. Freshness

The evaluation of freshness is important for Web search engines in two respects. Firstly, it is a matter of finding the actual or rather relative publication and refresh dates (Acharya *et al.* 2005). Secondly, the question is in which cases is it useful to display fresh documents preferentially. Whereas the first point is omitted with regard to library content, the second point is highly relevant when it comes to different professional cultures. Whereas fresh literature would be favored in quickly changing disciplines such as the sciences, such a preference cannot be useful in historically oriented disciplines such as history and philosophy. Therefore, the use of freshness should be limited.

3. Locality

Although essential for search engines, evaluating documents according to their proximity to the user has not often been taken into consideration in the library context (Lewandowski, 2009). Proximity can be seen here as the physical location of the user such as in the library, on campus, or at home, as well as the physical location of the item such as a central library, or a branch library, the item's availability or unavailability, and total lack of a physical location in case of items that are available online.

Concerning library contents, a strong quality evaluation takes place due to selection of items by the library. However, a quality-oriented ranking is essential when it comes to responding to queries that are strongly oriented toward the *precision* of the results—like a user who is searching for relevant titles to collect basic information about a certain field.

C. Misunderstandings Concerning Ranking Systems

The considerations reviewed so far show that quality as the aim of ranking has only been defined by means of auxiliary constructions such as weighted popularity. This might be lacking on the theoretical level, but as a pragmatic approach, it is a sustainable way of evaluating quality. It should be taken into consideration that a ranking system never changes the total quantity of results but merely gives them a certain order. Therefore, a ranking system provides an *additional* benefit compared to previously existing systems and does not limit the possibilities in any way for professional users in particular.

Unfortunately, there exist some misunderstandings concerning ranking systems and not only in libraries. For instance, the argument is brought forward that one sole, clear, and understandable sorting criterion is better than an elaborate ranking. It can be countered that without taking into consideration the user's appraisal of either system, further sorting possibilities, in addition to relevance ranking, can be offered without a problem.

Another misunderstanding is the idea that hitherto, OPACs work without a ranking. This assumption appears correct only at first sight. The question arises as to how far one should speak of a ranking system that sorts according to the year of publication. When ranking is considered simply as a non-random order of results though, sorting according to the publication date must also be seen as a form of ranking. In this case, one has to ask whether this form of ranking is the best solution for the user.

A third misunderstanding consists of the neglect of relevance ranking because it does not work well. Naturally, it is hard to define "relevance" dependant on context. Nevertheless, this cannot obscure the fact that ranking according to *assumed* relevance is at least capable of offering a satisfactory order of results. The criterion for evaluation of such generated results lists of course can only be identified through the user.

The last misunderstanding is based on the exact opposite opinion to the third, that ranking is seen as solvable in an artless way. As a rule, standard processes of text matching by means of Term Frequency/Inverted Document Frequency (TF/IDF) are implemented here. This cannot lead to satisfactory results.

D. Factors Appropriate to Ranking Library Materials

I have shown that Web search engines go far beyond the limits a solely text-based ranking and that such a ranking is not at all likely to be successful. Library catalogs and their scant bibliographic data present us with a similar problem. Text-based ranking needs to be amended with appropriate factors that are aimed at particular qualities of the documents. The relevant factors that can be employed are demonstrated in the following sections. Focus is on four groups of ranking factors: text statistic, popularity, freshness, and locality. Subsequent sections refer to OPAC-specific ranking factors that cannot be summarized in one of these sections. Table 4 summarizes all ranking factors as mentioned in the following text.

Table 4
Ranking Factors for Library Catalogs

Group	Ranking factor	Note
Text statistic	Terms – within bibliographic data – within enriched data – within full text	Bibliographic data does not contain enough text for a good term-based ranking The amount of text per catalog listing varies drastically, meaning that the same ranking algorithm cannot be applied to all three terms
	Field weighting	Appearance of search term is weighted differently according to the field
	Availability of text – review – table of contents – full text	The existence of additional information alone can lead to a better rating of an item
Popularity	Number of available local copies	Based on the individual item
	How often has the item been viewed?	Based on the individual item
	Circulation rate	Based on the individual item
	Number of downloads – author – publisher – book series – user ratings – citations	Based on the individual item Based on either the individual item or a group of items
Freshness	Publication date	Based on the individual item (could also be measured by its relationship to a group of items to which it belongs, e.g., systematic group/compartment)
	Accession date	Based on the individual item (could also be measured by its relationship to a group of items to which it belongs, e.g., systematic group/compartment)

Table 4. (*Continued*)

Group	Ranking factor	Note
Locality	Physical location of the user (home, library, campus)	Location could be derived from IP address of a certain user
	Physical location of the item — central library — library branch — electronically available (i.e., no physical location important to the user) Availability of the item — available as a download — available at the library — currently unavailable	
Other	Size of item (i.e., number of pages)	
	Document type (monograph, edited book, journal article, etc.)	Could be related to the importance of certain document types within certain disciplines
	User group (e.g., professors, students, graduate students)	

Source: Modified from Lewandowski (2009).

1. Text Statistic

Text-statistic systems normally use standard processes such as TF/IDF. They can be successfully implemented within collections of text that have already gone through quality control when being accepted into a database (e.g., newspaper databases). Here, library catalogs have a problem in that the items are generally too short to enable a successful ranking in accordance with a text-statistic system. The sole employment of text-statistic systems, however, leads to unsatisfactory results. Unfortunately, ranking is often likened to text-statistic ranking and thus it is assumed that the latter is generally not qualified for OPACs (e.g., in Beall, 2008).

Partly enriched catalog data results in the problem of a highly diverse range of items and this makes ranking by means of the same system impossible. Even more so, a diagnosis of additional information is necessary in advance. The documents are thus only consolidated into a concerted ranking after the initial ranking has taken place. Apart from the analysis of text, the sole existence of text can be regarded as a ranking factor. This way, items possessing a full text or at least a table of contents can be chosen opposite other items.

2. Popularity

Popularity ranking can also be applied to library materials. Popularity could be ranked either on the basis of individual items or on the basis of a group of items. For instance, a group can be formed from all items by the same author, all items from the same publisher, or all items within a book series.

All this popularity data is query-independent. Therefore, the values of an item do not have to be calculated at the time of the query but can be added to the item in advance. These values have to be refreshed only at certain intervals. Even if user ratings are taken into account, popularity measurements only need to be updated periodically even if they have changed over time.

3. Freshness

Although freshness (measured by the year of publication) is the most-used ranking criterion in catalogs today, there is more to freshness than simply ordering results by date. It is hard to know when fresh items are a particular priority, as the need for freshness may differ from one discipline to another. For example, fresh items may be crucial to a computer science researcher, but it may be a good idea to rely more heavily on authority than on freshness for ranking items related to philosophy.

It is therefore important to determine the need for fresh items and relate them to user needs. The need for fresh items can be determined from the circulation rate for items from a certain group. Such groups can be a broad discipline or even a specific subject heading. Again, the "need-for-freshness" factor can be calculated in advance and therefore does not take up calculation time when generating a results list according to a query.

4. Locality

Locality is a ranking factor that can take into account the physical location of the user as well as the availability of items in the results list. An item available at a local branch of the library could be ranked higher than items that are available only at another branch. One can also use lending data to rank items. For some users, items not currently available for lending may be of little or no use and could therefore be ranked lower.

The physical location of the user can also be used in ranking. When a user is at home, we can assume that they will prefer to find electronic items that can be downloaded (Mercun and Zumer, 2008). When they are at the library, this restriction will not apply, and items available in print form can be ranked alongside electronic results. The location of the user can be determined through the IP address of his or her computer.

5. Other Relevant Ranking Factors

Although the abovementioned ranking factors are adaptations of factors used by Web search engines, there are still some ranking factors that do not have a counterpart in one of the above named areas and only play a minor role. For instance, the size or type of the item may be considered. Monographs may be favored over edited books, books over journal articles (or vice versa), and physical materials over online materials. Moreover, the different needs of the individual subjects have to be taken into account. The exemplary comparison of informatics and philosophy shows that while informatics searches may rather be based on fresh literature from conference papers, philosophy may prefer monographs. Freshness data can be derived from lending data for certain subjects.

User groups may also determine ranking. For example, the needs of professors may differ greatly from the needs of undergraduate students. Professors may need exhaustive searches for their research, whereas textbooks might be preferred in student searches, for instance.

Dividing library users into groups leads us to the question of personalization of result rankings. This requires individual usage data as well as clickstream data from navigation. However, collecting individual user data is always problematic and should be restricted to scenarios where the user knows what data is collected and has chosen this option. There are many possibilities for improving ranking when anonymous statistical data can be gathered from general or specific group behavior. As this can be used, there is no real need to use individual user data.

The listed ranking factors are suitable to greatly improve ranking in library catalogs and indeed to implement any elaborate ranking at all. A compilation of ranking factors suitable for library materials is one thing, but only a good combination of ranking factors can lead to good results. Decisions concerning a combination depend heavily on individual collection and use cases.

E. Arrangement of Results Lists

However, every ranking system raises certain problems that need to be solved. One of these problems is the bias toward the same results due to ranking algorithms. Due to the fact that the same formula is applied to every item, items with the same or a very similar ranking value will be found in neighboring positions on the list. If we assume an item that does not differ from a counterpart by any factor (e.g., circulation rate and locality), then these two items will have equal ranking. This could be counteracted by detecting and clustering very similar items. *Google Scholar*, for instance, clusters different versions of an article (e.g. publisher's versions and preprints) in its results lists. Of course, it is still possible to gain access to the different versions, if needed. Such clustering of related items might seem simple at first sight, but it turns out to be difficult to implement. Ranking, however, requires clustering to secure satisfactory results.

Furthermore, ranking has to be supported by a deliberate rearrangement of the results list. The problem of similar items may be solved, but it is nevertheless possible that certain documents are rated higher than others. It is essential to think about this problem in advance. Not only should a user's intention be taken into consideration for the query, but it should also matter for results, to wit, which result does the user expect according to the query.

It is crucial for the ranking system to detect whether the user asks a general or a specific question. For a universal query, it would be helpful to present a dictionary, a textbook, a relevant database, a corresponding journal, and a fresh subject matter-related work. Thus, a small selection would be made, containing most likely at least one helpful item for the user. This example shows that it is necessary to think not only about suitable ranking factors but also about a suitable mixture of the results lists. None of these factors can be successful without the others.

IV. Conclusion

The main assumption of this chapter is that current OPACs, and also those known as "Next-generation OPACs," provide support for research but still lack user orientation. This is found particularly in the processing of queries and the expedient generation of results lists. Appropriate ranking factors for the library context have therefore been identified and discussed.

I would like to conclude with some recommendations on how far library and information scientists, developers in business companies, as well as responsible librarians and libraries can help to advance OPACS and library search engines.

1. To improve the OPACs, it is essential to know exactly what the user's intention is. Here, systematic analysis of mass data from the OPAC log files. Knowledge of the user's desire of information is necessary to enable improvement of the system. The log files alone can give information on the actual search frequency. These considerations could be the basis for library teams to think about how queries could ideally be responded to.

2. It is necessary to draw unsuccessful queries from the log file. In addition, the click paths of users having posted such queries should be followed. This should help to develop strategies to avoid zero results and how to deal with those.

3. It could be helpful to analyze the clickthrough data of the log files to identify different types of queries. The click frequency can give information on the type of query (Joachims, 2002; von Mach, and Otte, 2009).

4. Development and implementation of suitable ranking systems is needed. A clear idea of the assembly of "ideal results lists" should be developed before ranking systems are implemented. However, the traditional approach, based on the text- or field-based factors and that aims at a suitable ranking due to its weighting, does not seem promising.

When looking at OPACs today, we can see that they have fallen behind modern developments as represented by the most-advanced search systems, namely Web search engines. These are in continuous development and will continue to be the role model for other information systems. Libraries as well as library catalog vendors are well advised to monitor search engine developments closely and to analyze which of these developments could be adapted to improve the library catalogs.

References

Acharya, A., Cutts, M., Dean, J., Haahr, P., Henzinger, M., Hoelzle, U., Lawrence, S., Pfleger, K., Sercinoglu, O., and Tong, S. (2005). *Information Retrieval Based on Historical Data*. Fairfax,VA. Retrieved from http://www.seocertifiedservers.com/google.pdf

Bar-Ilan, J., Keenoy, K., Levene, M., and Yaari, E. (2009). Presentation bias is significant in determining user preference for search results: A user study. *Journal of the American Society for Information Science and Technology* 60(1), 135–149.

Beall, J. (2008). The weaknesses of full-text searching. *The Journal of Academic Librarianship* 34(5), 438–444.

Broder, A. (2002). A taxonomy of Web search. *SIGIR Forum* 36(2), 3–10.

Buckland, M. K., Norgard, B. A., and Plaunt, C. (1993). Filing, filtering, and the first few found. *Information Technology and Libraries* 12(3), 311–319.

Community Walk (forthcoming. *Next Generation Catalogs in Europe*. Retrieved from http://www.communitywalk.com/map/list/363838?order=0

Culliss, G. A. (2003). *Personalized Search Methods*. Ask Jeeves, Emeryville, CA.

Dean, J. A., Gomes, B., Bharat, K., Harik, G., and Henzinger, M. H. (2002). *Methods and Apparatus for Employing Usage Statistics in Document Retrieval*. Google, Mountain View, CA.

Dellit, A., and Boston, T. (2007). *Relevance Ranking of Results from Marc-Based Catalogues: From Guidelines to Implementation Exploiting Structured Metadata*. National Library of Australia, Canberra, AustraliaRetrieved from http://sawjet winfar.59.to/openpublish/index.php/nlasp/article/viewFile/1052/1321

Flimm, O. (2007). Die Open-Source-Software OpenBib an der USB Köln-Überblick und Entwicklungen in Richtung OPAC 2.0". *Bibliothek Forschung und Praxis* 31(2), 2–20.

Frants, V. I., Shapiro, J., and Voiskunskii, V. G. (1997). *Automated Information Retrieval: Theory and Methods*. Academic Press, San Diego, CA.

Granka, L. A., Joachims, T., and Gay, G. (2004, July). Eye-tracking analysis of user behavior in WWW search. In *Proceedings of Sheffield SIGIR-Twenty-Seventh Annual International ACM SIGIR Conference on Research and Development in Information Retrieval* (pp. 478–479). Association of Computing Machinery, New York, NY. Retrieved from http://portal.acm.org/citation.cfm?id=1008992.1009079&jmp= cit&coll=Portal&dl=ACM&CFID=89725774&CFTOKEN=53387369#CIT

Hennies, M., and Dressler, J. (2006, September). *Clients Information Seeking Behaviour: An Opac Transaction Log Analysis*. Paper presented at CLICK06, *ALIA 2006 Biennial Conference*. Perth, Australia. Retrieved from http://conferences. alia.org.au/alia2006/Papers/Markus_Hennies.pdf

Höchstötter, N., and Koch, M. (2008). Standard parameters for searching behaviour in search engines and their empirical evaluation. *Journal of Information Science* 34, 45–65.

Joachims, T. (2002, July). Optimizing search engines using click through data. In *Proceedings of the Eight ACM SIGKDD International Conference on Knowledge Discovery and Data Mining, Edmonton, Canada* (pp. 133–142). Association of Computing Machinery, New York.

Joachims, T., Granka, L., Pan, B., Hembrooke, H., and Gay, G. (2005, August). Accurately interpreting clickthrough data as implicit feedback. In *Proceedings of the 28th Annual International ACM SIGIR Conference on Research and Development in Information Retrieval* (pp. 154–161). Association of Computing Machinery, Salvador, Brazil; New York.

Kantor, P. B. (1976). Availability analysis. *Journal of the American Society for Information Science* 27(5–6), 311–319.

Keane, M. T., O'Brien, M., and Smyth, B. (2008). Are people biased in their use of search engines? *Communications of the ACM* 51(2), 49–52.

Kleinberg, J. M. (1999). Authoritative sources in a hyperlinked environment. *Journal of the ACM* 46(5), 604–632.

Lewandowski, D. (2004). Date-restricted queries in Web search engines. *Online Information Review* 28(6), 420–427.

Lewandowski, D. (2006). Suchmaschinen als Konkurrenten der Bibliothekskataloge: Wie Bibliotheken ihre Angebote durch Suchmaschinentechnologie attraktiver und durch öffnung für die allgemeinen Suchmaschinen populärer machen können. *Zeitschrift für Bibliothekswesen und Bibliographie* 53(2), 71–78.

Lewandowski, D. (2008a). Problems with the use of Web search engines to find results in foreign languages. *Online Information Review* 32(5), 668–672.

Lewandowski, D. (2008b). The retrieval effectiveness of Web search engines: Considering results descriptions. *Journal of Documentation* 64(6), 915–937.

Lewandowski, D. (2009). Ranking library materials. *Library Hi Tech* 27(4), 584–593.

Lewandowski, D. (2010). The retrieval effectiveness of search engines on navigational queries. *ASLIB Proceedings*. Retrieved from http://www.bui.haw-hamburg.de/fileadmin/user_upload/lewandowski/doc/ASLIB2009_preprint.pdf.

Lewandowski, D., and Höchstötter, N. (2007). Qualitätsmessung bei Suchmaschinen: System- und nutzerbezogene Evaluationsmaße. *Informatik Spektrum* 30(3), 159–169.

Lorigo, L., Haridasan, M., Brynjarsdóttir, H., Xia, L., Joachims, T., Gay, G., Granka, L., Pellacini, F., and Pan, B. (2008). Eye tracking and online search: Lessons learned and challenges ahead. *Journal of the American Society for Information Science and Technology* 59(7), 1041–1052.

Lown, C., and Hemminger, B. (2009). Extracting user interaction information from the transaction logs of a faceted navigation opac. *code4lib Journal* 7, 1633. Retrieved from http://journal.code4lib.org/articles/1633.

Mercun, T., and Zumer, M. (2008). New generation of catalogues for the new generation of users: A comparison of six library catalogues. *Program: Electronic Library and Information Systems* 43(3), 243–261.

Obermeier, F. (1999). Schlagwortsuche in einem lokalen OPAC am Beispiel der Universitätsbibliothek Eichstätt: Benutzerforschung anhand von OPAC—Protokolldaten. *Bibliotheksforum Bayern* 27(3), 296–319.

Page, L., Brin S., Motwani, R., and Winograd, T. (1999). *The Pagerank Citation Ranking: Bringing Order to the Web*. Retrieved from http://dbpubs.stanford.edu:8090/pub/1999-66

Remus, I. (2002). *Benutzerverhalten in Online-Systemen*. Fachhochschule Potsdam, Potsdam, Germany. Retrieved from http://freenet-homepage.de/Remus/TLA.htm

Sadeh, T. (2007). Time for a change: New approaches for a new generation of library users. *New Library World* 108(7/8), 307–316.

Stock, W. (2007). *Information retrieval: Informationen suchen und finden*. Oldenbourg, München, Germany.

von Mach, S., and Otte, J. (2009). Identifikation von navigationsorientierten und kommerziellen Suchanfragen anhand einer Klickdatenanalyse. *HAW Abstracts in Information Science and Services* 1(1), 39–52. Retrieved from http://www.bui.haw-hamburg.de/fileadmin/haiss/2009MachOtte.pdf.

Information Representation in Mainstream Videogames

Terrance S. Newell

School of Information Studies, University of Wisconsin-Milwaukee, Milwaukee, WI, USA

Abstract

Learning-via-gaming is an emerging area of interest and research within kindergarten to grade 12 (k-12), in US schools. As a vital part of the k-12 instructional mission, school libraries are exploring the potential role of videogames in mediating information-oriented skills development. Although the general concept of learning-via-gaming is not new to school libraries (e.g., library review card games), empirical knowledge of videogames' representational landscapes is needed to assist school librarians in developing instructional programming. This study examined representations of information across three distinct genres of mainstream videogames (shooters, action-adventure, and role-playing). Specifically, qualitative content analysis was used to examine the types of inscribed, information resources that players could use to generate solutions during problem-solving events. Across the three video gaming genres studied, there were seven strata of information: socially constructed, interpersonal, environmental, process, resource, task, and symbolic stratums. The results of this study could assist school librarians in (1) designing instructional lessons around videogames and/or (2) guiding students through the process of transporting meanings from the domain of gaming to other domains (e.g., academic, community, and everyday information problem-solving).

I. Introduction

Gaming and learning is a rich area of research within the larger kindergarten through grade 12 (k-12) educational landscape in the United States. There are a number of peer-reviewed journals and associations devoted to the topic (e.g., *Game Studies Journal* and Digital Games Research Association). Examples of studies in this area include Squire's (2004) case study that examined the use of *Civilization III* within a social studies classroom setting, and a year-long project, supported by Electronic Arts, Microsoft, Take-Two and the Interactive Software Federation of Europe's (ISFE), which examined the use

EXPLORING THE DIGITAL FRONTIER
ADVANCES IN LIBRARIANSHIP, VOL. 32
© 2010 by Emerald Group Publishing Limited
ISSN: 0065-2830
DOI: 10.1108/S0065-2830(2010)0000032006

of mainstream commercial games in the classroom. Researchers within the larger educational landscape have also used design research to develop and implement video games that allow students to learn historical content and problem-solving practices (e.g., Dede *et al.*, 2003; Jenkins and Squire, 2004).

Gaming and learning within libraries is an emerging area of interest and practice. A recent survey found that 77% of US public libraries support gaming activities, with 43% of them hosting formal gaming programs in the library (Nicholson, 2007). There are also a number of gaming-in-libraries conference streams (e.g., gaming, learning and libraries symposium), professional blogs (e.g., Game on: Games in libraries), web resources [e.g., American Library Association's (ALA) professional tips wiki on videogames], professional talking points (e.g., ALA gaming advocacy resources), and model programs (e.g., gaming the way to literacy). School libraries are exploring the potential role of videogames in mediating information-oriented skills development (Nicholson, 2008). However, a review of empirical research in the area of gaming and learning in school libraries reveals a dearth of knowledge. Although the general concept of learning-via-gaming is not new to school libraries (e.g., library review card games),[1] empirical knowledge of videogames' representational landscapes is needed to assist school librarians in developing instructional programming. This study examined representations of information across three distinct genres of mainstream videogames (shooters, action-adventure, and role-playing). Specifically, qualitative content analysis was used to examine the types of inscribed information resources that players could use to generate solutions during problem-solving events.

A. Background

School libraries in the United States have distinct educational roles within school settings. Since 1960, each set of school library guidelines has made significant contributions to the educational role of the profession. For instance, the fourth set of professional standards (American Association of School Librarians [AASL], 1960) began the "instructional turn," which shifted the school librarian to a more active educational role (e.g., participating in the material selection phase of instructional design and working to integrate library skills into class activities). The fifth set of standards (AASL and Department of Audiovisual Instruction [DAVI], 1969)

---

[1] 1980s games designed to reinforce the skills that students need to locate information on a catalog card.

highlighted an educational technology role for professionals. The sixth set of standards (AASL and Association of Educational Communication and Technology [AECT], 1975) provided a firmer understanding of fundamental instructional practices and clarified the implementation of those practices (Cleaver and Taylor, 1989). The seventh set of standards (AASL and AECT, 1988) added the role of instructional consultant to the established roles of information specialist and library skills integrator. The eighth set of standards (AASL and AECT, 1998) positioned school librarianship as a distinct domain of study and began the process of illuminating the *disciplinary content/skills* of the domain—core categories, standards, indicators of mastery and levels of mastery—that could be used by school librarians, teachers and curriculum designers as they developed programs of instruction and assessment (AASL and AECT, 1998). The current ninth set of standards (current standards) is firmly tied to the larger educational environment, which reflects a shift toward authentic disciplinary education. Authentic disciplinary education is an approach to student learning that requires them to engage the authentic problems, practices and resource contexts of specialists (e.g., historians, scientists, mathematicians, and information specialists), instead of simply learning the facts associated with their disciplines (Ford and Forman, 2006). In other words, students should have the opportunity to learn distinct ways of (1) meaning-making within disciplinary communities and (2) interacting with disciplinary objects, resources, and technologies.

The following statement, "videogames are good for learning," is an emerging academic position and area of research (Aldrich, 2005; Gee, 2007; Shaffer *et al.*, 2005; Shaffer, 2007), that is in concert with the authentic disciplinary education approach of teaching/learning. As an academic position, the view of videogames within the instructional landscape is theoretically persuasive. Within this position, videogames are viewed as potentially powerful learning spaces that could be integrated into the teaching/learning context. In other words, videogames are viewed as powerful learning environments (simulated worlds) that afford students the opportunity to develop various skills through the process of solving complex problems and participating in simulated practices (Shaffer *et al.*, 2005). These simulated learning environments allow students to potentially learn new practices (e.g., information literacy practices) and develop new identities (e.g. information literate identities) through the process of solving complex problems within authentic resource contexts (Shaffer *et al.*, 2005).

As an area of research empirical studies give insight into the affordances of gaming within the education landscape (Dempsey *et al.*, 1994; Emes, 1997; Gorriz and Medina, 2000; Harris, 2001; Laffey *et al.*, 2003; Prensky, 2001; Randel *et al.*, 1992; Rieber, 1996; Rosas *et al.*, 2003).

Randel *et al.*, (1992) examined empirical research studies in the area of gaming and education that were published between 1963 and 1991. This review of research focused strictly on studies comparing the instructional effectiveness of games to traditional classroom instruction. The researchers found that 38 of the 67 studies concluded that teaching via gaming was just as effective as teaching using traditional practices. The researchers also found that 27 of the 67 studies concluded instruction-as-gaming to be more effective than instruction within traditional practices. Other studies have found that videogame approaches to teaching can improve students' understanding of particular skills/concepts such as probability and statistic concepts (Pange, 2003), physics principles (White, 1984), health education knowledge (Serrano and Anderson, 2004), reading comprehension skills (e.g., Laffey *et al.*, 2003; Rosas *et al.*, 2003), mathematical problem-solving skills (Van Eck and Dempsey, 2002), basic logic (Costabile, *et al.*, 2003), geographical content knowledge (Virvou *et al.*, 2005; Wiebe and Martin, 1994), and vocabulary skills (Malouf, 1988). Researchers have concluded that disciplines with specific content could benefit from gaming approaches to teaching because the objectives, standards and resource landscapes of the disciplines can be readily identified—or not—within the games' manifest content.

II. Content in School Librarianship

School librarianship has three domains of content that could potentially benefit from gaming approaches to teaching/learning: information literacy, information problem-solving, and 21st century skills.

A. Information Literacy

The AASL information literacy standards (AASL/AECT, 1998), "describe the content and processes related to information that students must master to be considered information literate" (p. v). Within the AASL standards document, 3 broad information literacy content areas (i.e., access, evaluation, and use) and 13 indicators of information literacy are advanced. For each indicator, the standards articulate activity that represents basic, proficient, and exemplary levels of proficiency.

B. Standards for the 21st Century Learner

Standards for the 21st Century Learner (AASL, 2007) unfold four distinct areas of information-oriented content and social practices: (1) critical inquiry,

(2) situated connections, (3) communicative events, and (4) personal growth. The area of critical inquiry can be seen as a starting point, or orienting area, upon which the others expand, react to, and/or develop upon. This area is engaged within the context of *inquiry events*, activities in which inquiry plays a primary role. The critical inquiry area articulates the knowledge/skills needed to identify, seek, and evaluate multimodal information resources (i.e., resources that exist in the form of multimodal texts and those that exist aside from material realizations). This sets the stage for the reshaping (reorganizing) of information resources into a framework (blueprint) to be used during the creation of distinctive meanings/solutions. The situated connections area articulates knowledge/skills needed to mediate the material articulation of conclusions, solutions, and decisions. The area of communicative events articulates the knowledge/skills needed to use technologies, communicative modalities, and ethical standards to socially construct and share knowledge. The personal growth area focuses on the student's ability to form bridges between their everyday (personal) identity and their disciplinary (21st century) identity.

C. Information Problem-Solving

Information problem-solving is a disciplinary practice that has been positioned as a central focus of information literacy instruction on the k-12 level (Eisenberg and Berkowitz, 1990; Moore, 2003; Wisconsin Education Media Association and the American Association of School Librarians [WEMA] and AASL, 1993), and it refers to the teaching/learning of practices related to the creation of information-solutions to problems. The framework that underpins the concept is a process-oriented one, and a dominant theme that runs through the concept is the coupling of practices needed to access and use information with those needed to apply and solve information problems (Wolf *et al.*, 2003). The constitutive practices of information problem-solving are identifying tasks, employing search strategies, locating resources, accessing information physically/intellectually, interpreting information, communicating information, and evaluating the problem-solving product and process.

The practice of *task identification* is central to the information problem-solving process, and it refers to a practice of recognizing the existence of an information-based problem and defining the need(s) associated with that problem (WEMA and AASL, 1993). Various activities are embedded within the practice such as identifying the context and frame of reference, defining the information requirements of the task, articulating the task in the form of critical questions, situating the task within explicit expectations and relating the task to prior knowledge (Eisenberg and Berkowitz, 1990; Eisenberg and

Berkowitz, 2003; Irving, 1985; Marland, 1981; WEMA and AASL, 1993; Yucht, 1997).

The practice of *search strategy* initiation develops from task definition, and it refers to the development of a plan that will be employed to find information. Key activities within this practice are (1) clearly articulating needed information, (2) identifying salient terms and phrase tied to the task, (3) acknowledging the multimodal nature of resources, developing evaluation procedures, and setting source priorities (Eisenberg and Berkowitz, 1990; Irving, 1985; WEMA and AASL, 1993; Yucht, 1997).

The practice of *information location* refers to an ability to find resources within information landscapes and information within particular resources. Activities within the practice include (1) physically locating multimodal resources, (2) physically accessing information within sources using internal organizers, and (3) intellectually accessing ideas and concepts within sources (Eisenberg and Berkowitz, 1990; Irving, 1985; Mancall *et al.*, 1986; WEMA and AASL, 1993).

The practice of *information evaluation* refers to the determination of information accuracy, comprehensiveness, relevance and usefulness. Activities within this practice include (1) determining type of source, (2) comparing and contrasting sources, (3) determining the usefulness of format, (4) identifying facts and opinions, determining authority, judging significance, and (5) judging the completeness of information (Stripling and Pitts, 1988; WEMA and AASL, 1993).

The practice of *information use* refers to the integration and synthesis of information to solve a defined problem. Activities within this practice include (1) organizing information from multiple sources, (2) integrating ideas and concepts across sources, and (3) using information to create solutions to problems (Eisenberg and Berkowitz, 1990; Stripling and Pitts, 1988; WEMA and AASL, 1993).

The practice of *information communication* refers to the effective presentation of problem-solving resolutions. Activities within this practice include (1) illuminating the salient conclusions and resolutions, (2) determining appropriate modes of communication, and (3) generating original presentations within ethical practices (WEMA and AASL, 1993). The practice of problem-solving *product/process evaluation* refers to a critical assessment of the final resolution and the processes employed in generating it (WEMA and AASL, 1993).

The three domains of content that could potentially benefit from gaming approaches to teaching and learning (i.e., information literacy, information problem-solving, and 21st century skills) would all require that gaming-spaces are inscribed with (1) an expanded range of information resources and

(2) representations of information literacy, information problem-solving, and 21st century standards. This study examined representations of information across three distinct genres of mainstream videogames (shooters, action-adventure, and role-playing). Specifically, qualitative content analysis was used to examine the types of inscribed, information resources that players could use to generate solutions during problem-solving events.

III. Research Design

A qualitative content analysis (Patton, 2002), an inductive approach to generate themes and classifying representations within a body of material, was used to examine the types of inscribed resources.

A. Scope and Scale of Content

Shooter, action-adventure, and role-playing videogames constituted the body of materials analyzed by means of qualitative content analysis. The researcher generated a list of all seventh-generation, console-based, and PC titles published between 2007 and 2009. Over 2,686 titles were published in that period. For purposes of this study the list was further refined to include (1) titles classified as shooters, action-adventure and role-playing and (2) titles rated *Teen* or *Everyone*. From the resulting list, 30 videogames were randomly selected for the study with 10 games from each genre.

B. Unit of Analysis

Qualitative content analysis allows researchers to generate themes within/ across isolable parts of a medium. Within most videogames, game-levels (also called campaigns and episodes) represent the clear frames/boundaries within which players generate solutions to problem-solving events. Therefore, game-levels represented the isolable parts of the medium—like paragraphs and photographs within other mediums—within which themes were generated.

C. Data Preparation

Five levels of each game were played twice. During the first round of game-play, the researcher utilized video recording technology to capture in-screen actions and activities. During the second round of game-play, the researcher captured detailed notes using an observational protocol. The two rounds of game-play allowed the researcher to see and experience how game elements functioned and situated in context. Then, the video and observational notes were used to create a detailed written narrative of game-play objectives, actions, activities, and resources.

D. Coding

Inductive coding and pattern coding were used to analyze the written narratives. Inductive coding was used as a first-level coding method to analyze data by game. The inductive analytic approach reflected the grounded (or constant comparative) approach advocated by Strauss and Corbin (1990). In other words, the researcher examined the written narratives for salient categories and subcategories of information representation. The categories and subcategories were then saturated using the constant comparative approach. The term *saturation* refers to the researcher learning as much as possible about the categories, including disconfirming evidence and interrelationships. Pattern coding was used as a second-level coding method to analyze the patterns and recurrences across games and genres. In other words, it served as a cross-case analysis of the level-1 coding (i.e., the inductive level coding). This cross-case analysis (or pattern coding) focused on the common threads across the level-1 coding.

IV. Results

Across the three video gaming genres (shooter, action-adventure, and role-playing), there are seven strata (themes) of information that players can utilize to create meanings/solutions during in-game inquiry events. The seven strata are socially constructed, interpersonal, environmental, process, resource, task, and symbolic.

A. Stratum 1: External, Socially Constructed

This stratum exists outside of game-play, and it provides information that constructs a specific social context (e.g., aspects of reality within the simulated world). The player realizes the social context within/across three primary types of resources (Fig. 1). The game manual constitutes the first type of information resource within the socially-constructed stratum. Game manuals are usually 14–35 pages in length, and they provide players with information related to in-game realities (e.g., introduces plot, start character development, identifies game controls, etc.). Cut-scenes, in-game cinematic scenes, and audio emerging from black backgrounds represent the second

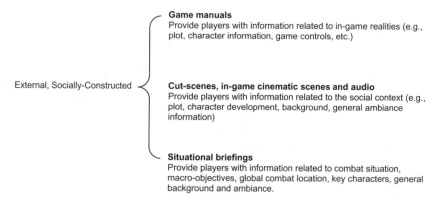

Game manuals
Provide players with information related to in-game realities (e.g., plot, character information, game controls, etc.)

External, Socially-Constructed

Cut-scenes, in-game cinematic scenes and audio
Provide players with information related to the social context (e.g., plot, character development, background, general ambiance information)

Situational briefings
Provide players with information related to combat situation, macro-objectives, global combat location, key characters, general background and ambiance.

Fig. 1   The three primary information resources situated within the external, socially constructed stratum.

type of information resource within the socially constructed stratum. Such resources usually appear before a game-level and/or significant event, and they provide players with information related to the social context (e.g., plot, character development, background, and general ambiance information). Situational briefings constitute the third type of information resource within the socially constructed stratum. Briefings usually appear before a game-level and/or significant event, and they provide players with information related to the combat situation, macro-objective(s), global combat location, characters, general background, and ambiance. This type of resource is less frequent outside of the shooter genre. Situational briefings usually present information using three modes of communication: text, audio, and 2D image of the combat environment.

B. Stratum 2: Interpersonal

This stratum refers to information embedded within patterns of communication (verbal and nonverbal) between the player and preprogrammed virtual characters (Fig. 2). There are two primary types of resources within this stratum: formal and informal interpersonal information. Formal interpersonal information (e.g., information emerging from an operations control officer, intelligence officer, real-time briefings, or information specialists) refers to information that (1) is tied to an office, institution, and/or person of authority and (2) has presumably gone through a process of validation or sanctioning. Informal interpersonal information is communicated by virtual characters, and it has not gone through an official process

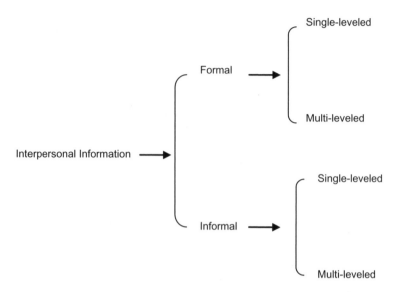

Fig. 2 The two primary types of information resources within the interpersonal stratum.

of validation, negotiation, or sanctioning. Both forms of interpersonal information could be either single-layered or multilayered. Single-layered, interpersonal information refers to one-way, two- to three-word communications from virtual teammates such as move-up, come-on and checks your gear. Single-layered information usually relates to forward movement, combat preparation, and visually locating enemies. Multilayered information refers to extended dialogues between the player and virtual characters, which are inscribed with information.

C. Stratum 3: Environmental

This stratum refers to resources within the built environment (3D space) that could be used during the meaning-making/problem-solving process. There are three distinct types of resources within this stratum: salience, activity paths, and data. Salience refers to elements within the environment that are made prominent through various design techniques (e.g., contrasting color, lighting, and size). Activity paths are pathways that players can take during the problem-solving process, and these pathways are realized through design elements creating degrees of separation (continuation of building style). Data refer to objects, artifacts, sounds, and events within the environment.

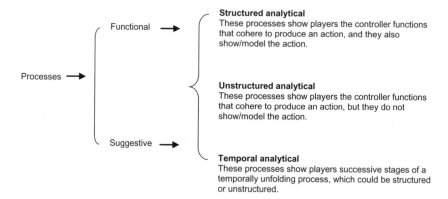

Fig. 3 The two primary types of information resources within the process stratum.

D. Stratum 4: Process

This stratum refers to information that communicates processes to the player (Fig. 3). There are two distinct types of processes within this stratum: functional and suggestive processes. Functional processes inform the player of how to perform a particular action, and suggestive processes are delivered to suggest tips and best practices. Functional and suggestive processes could be structured, unstructured, or temporal. Structured processes show players the controller functions that cohere to produce an action, and they also model the action (i.e., visually show the action and its end results). Unstructured processes show players the controller functions that cohere to produce an action, but they do not model the action. Temporal processes show players successive stages of a temporally unfolding process, which could be structured or unstructured.

E. Stratum 5: Knowledge Representation

This stratum refers to informative objects, artifacts, data, and documents that players could use to create meanings/solutions during in-game problem-solving events (Fig. 4). There are various representations across games and genres such as: 2D maps, 3D maps, interactive maps, compasses, journals, books, newspaper articles, posters, binoculars, weapon displays, squad displays, cameras, databases, and blueprints. However, there are three distinct types of knowledge representations: heads-up display (HUD), personal repository and in-space representations. HUD is a transparent display that visually presents information on the game's user interface. A repository is a

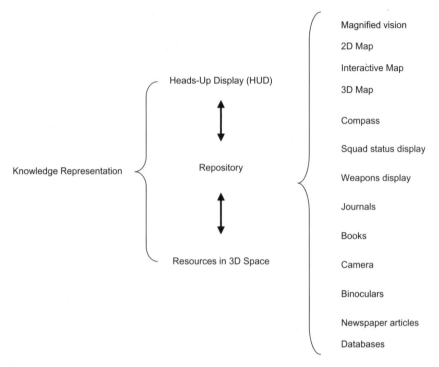

Fig. 4 The three primary types of information resources within knowledge representation.

mobile/virtual facility that players can use to retrieve specific information. In-space representations refer to objects, artifacts, data and documents in the 3D, gaming space.

F. Stratum 6: Task

This stratum refers to information communicated about the authentic, problems within the game-space. There are two primary types of task-oriented information: fixed-external and flexible-external. Fixed-external refers to specific task-oriented information supplied by the game-space that includes direct expectations, guided strategies and particular resources that the player must use. Flexible-external refers to supplied task-oriented information that features indirect expectations and allow players to manipulate the task, problem-solving resources and/or ways to address the problem.

G. Stratum 7: Symbolic

This stratum refers to semiotic information resources that players could use as they make meaning/solutions during problem-solving events. There are three primary types of symbolic resources: colors, icons, and soundscapes. Color is used as information within games, and it is often used to identify pathways (e.g., color of doorways), distinguish between different areas (e.g., parts of a building), draw player's attention to objects and text within documents, signify a mood and create textual cohesion. Icon-based information also exists within games. Icons are signs within the gaming-space that communicates information to the player, and soundscapes signify information using sounds and music.

V. Discussion

This study examined the types of inscribed, information resources that video gamers could use to generate solutions during problem-solving events. Across the three video gaming genres (shooter, action-adventure, and role-playing) studied, there were seven strata of information (i.e., socially constructed, interpersonal, environmental, process, resource, task, and symbolic) inscribed within the games. The results of this study show that shooter, action-adventure, and role-playing videogames require players to use various information resources during problem-solving events, and these results could assist school librarians as they help students transport meanings from the domain of gaming to other domains (e.g., academic, community, and everyday information problem-solving). In other words, the seven strata could serve a metaphorical meta-function (Halliday, 1978), which means that the landscape of information resources, within videogames, is able to represent ideas beyond game-play due to guided associations. For instance, videogames are socially constructed realities. The phrase *socially constructed*, refers to the fact that the in-game, social context is (partly) constructed during the game design process. In other words, aspects of reality such as broad contexts (e.g., East Asia), local contexts (e.g., particular family), institutional context (U.S. Army), events (e.g., Russian Revolution) and everyday practices (how and where the player lives) are constructed by the designers of the simulated worlds. Gamers use and enrich those realities using resources such as game manuals, cut-scenes, in-game cinematic scenes, situational briefings, and audio emerging from a black background. School librarians could use the same strata (i.e., in-game, socially constructed resources) to guide students through an understanding of abstract information literacy and 21st-century concepts such as topic exploration during the research process or the use of background knowledge as a context for inquiry.

Video games are also dynamic communication spaces. Information is embedded within patterns of communication (verbal and nonverbal) between the player and virtual characters within the game-space. This embedded information could be formal (e.g., tied to a person of authority) or informal (e.g., hasn't gone through a process of validation). Information could also be embedded within a very basic three-word structure, or it could exist within extended dialogues. School librarians could use the interpersonal strata to guide students through an understanding of abstract information literacy and 21st-century concepts such as: (1) acquiring information through formal and informal sources, (2) differences between objective and subjective information, (3) using the logics and affordances of distinct communicative modes to intellectually access information, and (4) evaluating/selecting appropriate sources based on criteria such as authority and task alignment.

Videogames have constructed 3D environments that could be used during the meaning-making/problem-solving process. During problem-solving events, players must examine information resources such as salience (making things prominent through design techniques), activity paths (routes that could be taken during problem-solving), and data (environmental objects, artifacts, and events). For example, players will often understand their focal point within a 3D environment due to the relative size and distinctive architecture of buildings/landmarks, and the use of physical barriers will present them with clear activity pathways that could be taken as they move toward the focal point. School librarians could use the environmental strata to guide students through an understanding of abstract concepts such as: (1) navigating a physical library context, (2) information seeking in physical and electronic environments, (3) activity pathways within web sites with varying site designs (e.g., hierarchical designs), (4) salient items of information, and (5) the use of environmental data, stimuli, messages, and cues (Ruben, 1992).

Videogames are activity spaces, and the term *activity* refers to the conscious performance of a chain of actions (a process) used to accomplish tasks. There are two primary types of processes within games: functional and suggestive processes. Functional processes inform the player of how to perform a particular action, and suggestive processes are delivered to suggest tips and best practices. Gamers attempt to collapse information processes into operations, which occurs overtime with experience and internalization of conscious processes. School librarians could use the process strata to guide students through an understanding of abstract concepts such as (1) Michael

Buckland's (1991) concept of information-as-process or (2) identifying best-practice searching processes for particular databases.

Videogames are inscribed with informative objects, artifacts, data, and documents that players could use to create meanings/solutions during in-game problem-solving events. This is the strata of information that librarians naturally think about when questioning representations within games. There are various knowledge representations across games (e.g., 2D maps, 3D maps, interactive maps, compasses, journals, books, newspaper articles, posters, binoculars, weapon displays, squad displays, cameras, databases, and blueprints), which vary greatly and seems to depend on the genre, plot, and tasks within the game. However, there are three distinct types of knowledge representations: HUD, personal repository and in-space representations. School librarians could use the knowledge representation strata to guide students through an understanding of abstract concepts such as: (1) Michael Buckland's (1991) concept of information-as-thing, (2) McCreadie and Rice's (1999) concept of knowledge representation or (3) using appropriate information resources during the academic, community, and everyday information problem-solving process.

Videogames are problem-solving spaces with varying task contexts. The task stratum provides the player with information regarding the problems within the game-space. There are two types of task-oriented information: fixed-external and flexible-external. Fixed-external refers to specific task-oriented information supplied by the game-space that includes direct expectations, guided strategies and particular resources that the player must use. Flexible-external refers to supplied task-oriented information that features indirect expectations and allow players to manipulate the task, problem-solving resources and/or ways to address the problem. School librarians could use the knowledge task stratum to guide students through an understanding of abstract concepts such as: (1) defining the information requirements of a task, (2) articulating the task in the form of critical questions, and (3) situating the task within explicit expectations.

Videogames are also semiotic resources that use colors, icon, and sound-scapes to signify meanings. School librarians could use the symbolic stratum to guide students through an understanding of abstract concepts such as the use of color, icons and soundscapes in electronic information seeking contexts. For instance, there are parallels between the use of color within games and the use of color in supporting user's information seeking experiences. There are six primary ways to support information seeking using color, which overlaps with its use in games: (1) identify subsystems, (2) add coding dimensions, (3) emphasize important information, (4) increase comprehensibility, (5) reduce interpretation errors, and

(6) engender emotional responses. There are also parallels between the (1) dual nature of icons (i.e., icons as representation of objects and icons as the objects themselves) and (2) search affordances of icons within games and electronic environments.

VI. Conclusion

Although the general concept of learning-via-gaming is not new to school libraries (e.g., library review card games), empirical knowledge of videogames' representational landscapes is needed to assist school librarians in developing instructional programming. Across the three video gaming genres studied here, there were seven strata of information: socially constructed, interpersonal, environmental, process, resource, task, and symbolic stratums. The results of this study could assist school librarians in (1) designing instructional lessons around videogames and/or (2) guiding students through the process of transporting meanings from the domain of gaming into other domains (e.g., academic, community and everyday information problem-solving). For example, librarians could help students transport meanings after gaming activities by guiding them through a critical reflection of how identifying tasks, employing search strategies, locating resources, accessing information, interpreting information, evaluating information, using information and communicating information are similar/different in real-world contexts.

References

American Association of School Librarians (AASL). (2007). Standards for the 21st-century learner. Retrieved January 1, 2009, from http://www.ala.org/aasl/standards.

American Association of School Librarians (1960). *Standards for School Library Programs*. American Library Association, Chicago, IL.

American Association of School Librarians and Association for Educational Communications and Technology (1975). *Media Programs: Districts and School*. American Library Association, Chicago. IL.

American Association of School Librarians and Association for Educational Communications and Technology (1988). *Information Power: Guidelines for School Library Media Programs*. American Library Association, Chicago, IL.

American Association of School Librarians and Association for Educational Communications and Technology (1998). *Information Power: Building Partnerships for Learning*. American Library Association, Chicago, IL.

American Association of School Librarians & Department of Audiovisual Instruction (1969). *Standards for School Media Programs*. American Library Association, Chicago, IL.

Aldrich, C. (2005). *Learning by doing: A comprehensive guide to simulations, computer games, and pedagogy in e-learning and other educational experiences*. Wiley, New York.

Buckland, M. (1991). Information as thing. *Journal of the American Society for Information Science* 42, 351–360.

Cleaver, B., and Taylor, W. (1989). *The Instructional Consultant Role of the School Library Media Specialist*. American Library Association, Chicago, IL.

Costabile, M., De Angeli, A., Roselli, T., Lanzilotti, R., and Plantamura, P. (2003). Evaluating the educational impact of a tutoring hypermedia for children. *Information Technology in Childhood Education Annual* 5, 289–308.

Dede, C., Ketelhut, D., and Ruess, K. (2003). *Designing for Motivation and Usability in a Museum-Based Multi-User Virtual Environment*. Retrieved from http://muve.gse.harvard.edu/muvees2003/documents/AELppr.pdf

Dempsey, J., Lucassen, B., Gilley, W., and Rasmussen, K. (1994). What's the score in the gaming literature? *Journal of Educational Technology Systems* 22, 173–183.

Eisenberg, M., and Berkowitz, R. (1990). *Information Problem-Solving: The Big Six Skills Approach to Library and Information Skills Instruction*. Ablex, Norwood, NJ.

Eisenberg, M., and Berkowitz, R. (2003). *The Definitive Big6 Workshop Handbook*. Linworth, Worthington, OH.

Emes, C. (1997). Is Mr. Pac Man eating our children? A review of the impact of video games on children. *Canadian Journal of Psychiatry* 42, 409–414.

Ford, M., and Forman, E. (2006). Redefining disciplinary learning in classroom contexts. *Review of Research in Education* 30, 1–32.

Gee, J. (2007). *What video games have to teach us about learning and literacy*. Palgrave, Macmillan, New York, NY.

Gorriz, C., and Medina, C. (2000). Engaging girls with computers through software games. *Communications of the ACM* 43, 42–49.

Halliday, M. (1978). *Language as Social Semiotic: The Social Interpretation of Language and Meaning*. University Park Press, Baltimore.

Harris, J. (2001). *The Effects of Computer Games on Young Children – A Review of the Research*. (RDS Occasional Paper No. 72). Research, Development and Statistics Directorate, Communications Development Unit, Home Office, London, England.

Irving, A. (1985). *Study and Information Skills across the Curriculum*. Heinemann, London, England.

Jenkins, H., and Squire, K. (2004). Harnessing the power of games in education. *Insight* 3, 5–33.

Laffey, J., Espinosa, L., Moore, L., and Lodree, A. (2003). Supporting learning and behavior of at-risk young children: Computers in urban education. *Journal of Research Technology in Education* 35, 423–440.

Malouf, D. (1988). The effect of instructional computer games on continuing student motivation. *The Journal of Special Education* 21, 27–38.

Mancall, J., Aaron, S., and Walker, S. (1986). Educating students to think: The role of the library media program. *School Library Media Quarterly* 15, 18–27.

Marland, M. (1981). *Information Skill in the Secondary Curriculum: The Recommendations of a Working Group Sponsored by the British Library and the Schools Council*. The British Library, London, England.

McCreadie, M., and Rice, R. (1999). Trends in analyzing access to information. *Information Processing and Management* 35, 45–76.

Moore, P. (2003). Information problem solving: A wider view of library skills. *Contemporary Educational Psychology* 20, 1–31.

Nicholson, S. (2007). *The Role of Gaming in Libraries: Taking the Pulse* [white paper]. Retrieved from http://boardgameswithscott.com/pulse2007.pdf.

Nicholson, S. (2008). Finish your games so you can start your schoolwork: A look at gaming in school libraries. *Library Media Connection* 26, 52–55.

Pange, J. (2003). Teaching probabilities and statistics to preschool children. *Information Technology in Childhood Education Annual*, 163–172.

Patton, M. (2002). *Qualitative Research and Evaluation Methods*. Sage, Thousand Oaks, CA.

Prensky, M. (2001). *Digital Game-based Learning*. McGraw-Hill, New York, NY.

Randel, J., Morris, B., Wetzel, C., and Whitehill, B. (1992). The effectiveness of games for educational purposes: A review of recent research. *Simulation & Gaming* 23, 261–276.

Rieber, L. (1996). Seriously considering play: Designing interactive learning environments based on the blending of microworlds, simulations, and games. *Educational Technology Research and Development* 44, 43–58.

Rosas, R., Nussbaum, M., Cumsille, P., Marianov, V., Correa, M., Flores, P., Grau, V., Lagos, F., López, X., López, V., Rodriguez, P., and Salinas, M. (2003). Beyond Nintendo: Design and assessment of educational video games for first and second grade students. *Computers & Education* 40, 71–94.

Ruben, B. (1992). The communication-information relationship in system-theoretic perspective. *Journal of the American Society for Information Science* 43, 15–27.

Serrano, E. L., and Anderson, J. E. (2004). The evaluation of food pyramid games, a bilingual computer nutrition education program for Latino youth. *Journal of Family and Consumer Sciences Education* 22(1), 1–16.

Shaffer, D. (2007). *How Computer Games Help Children Learn*. Palgrave, Macmillan, New York, NY.

Shaffer, D., Squire, H., and Gee, J. (2005). Video games and the future of learning. *Phi Delta Kappan* 87, 104–111.

Squire, K. D. (2004). Sid Meier's civilization III. *Simulations and Gaming* 35, 135–140.

Strauss, A., and Corbin, J. (1990). *Basics of qualitative research: Grounded theory procedures and techniques*. Sage Publications, Newbury Park, CA.

Stripling, B., and Pitts, J. (1988). *Brainstorms and Blueprints: Teaching Library Research as a Thinking Process*. Libraries Unlimited, Englewood, CO.

Van Eck, R., and Dempsey, J. (2002). The effect of competition and contextualized advisement on the transfer of mathematics skills in a computer-based instructional simulation game. *Educational Technology Research and Development* 50(3), 23–41.

Virvou, M., Katsionis, G., and Manos, K. (2005). Combining software games with education: Evaluation of its educational effectiveness. *Educational Technology & Society* 8, 54–65.

White, B. Y. (1984). Designing computer games to help physics students understand Newton's laws of motion. *Cognition and Instruction* 1(1), 69–108.

Wiebe, J., and Martin, N. (1994). The impact of a computer-based adventure game on achievement and attitudes in geography. *Journal of Computing in Childhood Education* 5, 61–71.

Wisconsin Education Media Association and the American Association of School Librarians. (1993). *Information Literacy: A Position Paper on Information Problem Solving*. ERIC Document ED 376817.

Wolf, S., Brush, T., and Saye, J. (2003). Using an information problem-solving model as a metacognitive scaffold for multimedia supported information-based problems. *Journal of Research on Technology in Education* 35, 321–341.

Yucht, A. (1997). *FLIP It! An Information Skills Strategy for Students Researchers*. Linworth, Worthington, OH.

Education and Training in the Digital World

Library and Information Science Education in the Digital Age

Heting Chu

Palmer School of Library and Information Science, Long Island University, Brookville, NY, USA

Abstract

Education in library and information science (LIS) in the first decade of the 21st century is reviewed and discussed in terms of changes, developments, and associated issues. Specifically, courses and concentrations newly added to the LIS curriculum are described along with a summary of what has been revised, including the core. Distance education in LIS is presented as a result of technology application while reposition, relocation, and closures of LIS schools are also examined. Of the organizational changes among LIS schools, the emergence of iSchools and related topics received particular coverage with data gathered recently. Issues persistent in LIS education (i.e., accreditation of LIS programs, library education crisis, and chasm between LIS education and practices) are revisited with analysis. The author believes on the basis of this review that the digital age has brought us in LIS education with opportunities greater than ever. LIS education will move forward and even thrive in this digital age when the field not only makes intelligent use of the technology but also changes in other dimensions as the society advances.

I. Introduction

The first decade in the 21st century has brought about great changes to the field of library and information science (LIS) in part because of the deep penetration of the Internet and rapid development of digital technologies. Such changes naturally have shaped and influenced how LIS professionals are educated. As a result, new subjects such as digital libraries (DL), knowledge management (KM), and information architecture (IA) have been added to LIS curricula while the core has been redefined. Delivering courses or even the entire LIS program digitally (e.g., through the Web) becomes a widely adopted mode of education. As information schools, or iSchools, emerge differently from traditional LIS schools, the wave of reorganizing LIS schools

EXPLORING THE DIGITAL FRONTIER
ADVANCES IN LIBRARIANSHIP, VOL. 32
© 2010 by Emerald Group Publishing Limited
ISSN: 0065-2830
DOI: 10.1108/S0065-2830(2010)0000032007

(including closures) has not subsided even though there seemed to be a brief quiet moment at the turn of the centuries (Hildreth and Koenig, 2002). In addition, cross-border and interdisciplinary collaboration in LIS education is increasingly being seen, thanks to globalization, networking technologies, as well as the good intentions of involved parties.

This chapter is intended to review what happened in LIS education based principally on literature published between 2000 and 2010. Unrelenting issues in LIS education (e.g., library education crisis and chasm between library education and practices) are briefly visited after new developments in the domain are presented. There is also discussion of what can be learned from the past to better prepare for the future in LIS education. Publications on LIS education before 2000 are generally not included here because they had already been reviewed extensively in Barlow and Aversa (2006), Durrance (2004), Logan and Hsieh-Yee (2001), and Mezick and Koenig (2008). Programs housed in LIS schools other than the American Library Association (ALA)-accredited master's program (e.g., doctoral and undergraduate programs) will not be examined in depth in this chapter. Also not covered are topics relating to professional development and lifelong learning of librarians.

II. The Changing LIS Curriculum

In any educational program, the curriculum perhaps is the best barometer of its nature and content. The same holds true for LIS education. In the past decade, new courses and concentrations were introduced into LIS curricula, whereas existing ones were reviewed to remove outdated matter and to modify some to cover better the more current topics. The core in the LIS curriculum was also regularly redefined to meet the challenges we face today. These curricular changes are reviewed in three subsections below.

A. Newly Added Courses and Concentrations

The past decade has witnessed the emergence of new courses and concentrations in LIS education. DL, KM, and IA represent the major ones, in addition to a considerable number of others, newly added as individual courses or a concentration/program.

1. Digital Libraries (DL)

The advent of the Internet and, especially, Web technologies boosted the building of digital libraries around the world. The Digital Library Initiatives

(DLI), funded by a consortium of government agencies under the leadership of the National Science Foundation (NSF), have further stimulated not only research in the area but also DL education. Even though there may not be full agreement about what constitutes a digital library, a digital collection with associated services, or just a collection of digital works, more and more courses in various formats and varying coverage are being designed and taught in LIS programs.

Saracevic and Dalbello's (2001) survey provided an overview of DL education in the 56 LIS programs accredited by the ALA. The authors found that, of the 56 LIS programs, 47 (84%) included DL in some form or to some degree in their curricula, whereas four programs (7%) showed no presence of DL education. For the remaining five programs (9%), the authors could not determine if DL was included in their curricula.

As part of a larger study, Chu (2006) did a content analysis of the curricula of 45 ALA-accredited LIS programs in the United States[1] and observed that 27 (60%) of the programs had a course titled Digital Libraries in their offerings. Although the percentage of LIS programs offering DL courses decreased from 84 in Saracevic and Dalbello (2001) to 60 in Chu (2006), it is probably a result of different definitions of what constitutes a DL course. Saracevic and Dalbello (2001) regarded courses as on DL if the course title, description, or syllabus carried wording synonymous with or related to DL, whereas the 27 courses covered in Chu (2006) all had the exact title of Digital Libraries.

In examining DL education in the United Kingdom and Slovenia, Bawden *et al.* (2005) reported that there were eight graduate courses with some DL content in the only LIS education institution of Slovenia and multiple courses with particular references to DL at two UK institutions (i.e., City University London and Sheffield University). A course bearing the specific title of DL is, without doubt, included in more LIS curricula nowadays than at the onset of the 21st century although hard data remain to be gathered.

In addition, DL has also been designated as a concentration in many LIS programs. For example, out of the 10 LIS programs Chu (2009) considered in her comparison of iSchools and LIS schools, four institutions (i.e., Catholic University of America, Drexel University, Kent State University, and University of South Carolina) had a concentration in DL at the time of data collection.

---

[1]Four ALA-accredited LIS programs in the United States were not included in that study for various reasons.

Parallel to the increased offerings of DL in LIS programs, large variances exist in how DL courses are taught. Saracevic and Dalbello (2001) categorized the content of DL offerings into four types, in addition to a detailed description of individual programs' coverage and approaches in course instruction:

1. Tools—technologies and technology-based processes.
2. Environments—the context in which digital libraries operate.
3. Objects—representation, structure, and life cycle of documents in various formats.
4. Combined—several areas of applications presented without any one being distinctive.

What Saracevic and Dalbello (2001) summarized 10 years ago remains a fitting depiction of the content variation in DL education. However, DL, as a course or a concentration, have seamlessly integrated into LIS education in this increasingly digital age.

2. Knowledge Management (KM)

KM, from the perspective of LIS, can be viewed as an extension or continuation of special libraries or librarianship. On the contrary, more fields such as business administration, computer science, information systems, management, and public policies also contribute to the development of KM. Chaudhry and Higgins (2003) therefore suggested a multidisciplinary approach to teaching KM after analyzing 37 KM courses offered in academic disciplines of business, computing, and information in Australia, Canada, Singapore, the United Kingdom, and the United States. The focus of the present discussion, nevertheless, is on KM in LIS education.

According to McKean (2005), knowledge is defined as,

1. Facts, information, and skills acquired by a person through experience or education; the theoretical or practical understanding of a subject;
2. What is known in a particular field or in total; facts and information; or
3. Awareness or familiarity gained by experience of a fact or situation.

The word "knowledge" in KM refers to point 1 in the above definition, whereas point 2 should be the choice in interpreting what "knowledge" means in the context of knowledge organization (KO). The linkage between KM and LIS, as observed by Koenig (2003), lies in the design, implementation, and operation of information systems, which include the creation of classifications and taxonomies. Hall (2010), based on decades of corporate work experience, also challenges LIS programs to produce more graduates whose subject competencies match the core competencies needed by corporate employers to help corporations manage their mission-critical information resources better. In other words, KM must be covered and must be taught well in the LIS curriculum.

KM as a distinct course title came about after the 21st century began. In retrospect, courses of similar nature but with different titles (e.g., special libraries) have long been included in the LIS curriculum. Even though a current, comprehensive survey of specific KM course offering is unavailable, Chu (2006) noted that 10 out of the 45 LIS programs offered a course titled Knowledge Management. In addition, among the 10 LIS schools Chu (2009) studied, Drexel University had a concentration in competitive intelligence and KM, whereas Kent State University provided an option for students to earn, on top of the MLIS degree, another master in information architecture and knowledge management (IAKM). Ur Rehman and Chaudhry (2005) surveyed the heads of 12 LIS schools (i.e., 8 in North America, 1 in Europe, and 3 in the Pacific region) about their perception of KM education and found there was strong interest in offering KM courses, cultivating collaborations with business and computing schools, and developing strategic partnerships with industry.

Two points become evident in having KM in LIS education. First, LIS schools are the right institutions for teaching KM and for training knowledge managers (Abell, 2000; Breen et al., 2002). Second, KM is interdisciplinary in nature, and thus, LIS schools should collaborate with academic units in business and computing to bring KM into their curricula (Al-Hawamdeh, 2005; Chaudhry and Higgins, 2003; Hyldegaard et al., 2002).

3. Information Architecture (IA)

IA emerged as a domain since the late 1990s when the Web became a dominating Internet application. IA involves the design of organization and navigation systems within web sites and intranets to help people find and manage information more successfully (Morville and Rosenfeld, 2007, pp. 4–5). The American Society for Information Science and Technology (ASIS&T) initiated annual international IA Summits in 2000 and EuroIA in 2005 (http://2010.iasummit.org). Also in 2000, a column on IA was created in ASIS&T's newsletter, *Bulletin of the ASIS&T* (Dillon, 2006), which still appears 10 years later.

IA, strictly speaking, originates from LIS in that it is concerned primarily with how information is organized and accessed in the Web architecture. This fact is at least reflected in part by how Morville and Rosenfeld (2007) titled their book, already in its third edition, *Information Architecture for the World Wide Web*. That is also why ASIS&T, the leading professional organization of the field, has been so active in the domain of IA. Over time, IA became a course in 11 LIS programs (Chu, 2006), a concentration at Catholic University of America, and even a degree program at Kent State University (Chu, 2009).

Despite having incomplete statistics on IA education, work has been done about how IA could be incorporated into the LIS curriculum. Latham (2002) described different approaches to IA education (i.e., craft tradition, romantic tradition, and rhetorical tradition). The author believed that key content to be covered in IA included information organization, graphic design, computer science, usability, and communication. This was echoed by Robbins (2002) but in more detail. Weinberg (2002), a veteran in thesaurus construction which is closely related to IA, wrote specifically about how a new IA course could be designed and provided sample units of instruction and assignments.

In contrast to DL and KM, IA has never reached a momentum the other two enjoy. Development of the Semantic Web, conceived and advocated by Berners-Lee and his colleagues (e.g., Berners-Lee *et al.*, 2001), certainly has a significant impact on the welfare of IA because the former is a much larger effort than the latter. In that sense, we may expect to see the future of IA in Semantic Web, which is at present under construction.

4. Other New Courses

Table 1, adapted from Chu (2006), shows other courses recently added to the LIS curriculum besides DL, KM, and IA. Courses with similar names (e.g., Web site Design and Web Applications) were grouped as clusters for clarity purposes in the presentation.

There were 292 courses that were labeled as new courses in Table 1 in the 45 LIS curricula Chu (2006) examined. As some LIS programs did not enumerate their special topic courses, the actual number should be larger, if not significantly so. This number was just one-third of what Callison and Tilley (2001) reported in their study because they obtained new course titles differently. Close scrutiny of the new courses reveals that among the top three listed in Table 1, DL apparently leads the rest as it was taught in 27 out of the 45 LIS programs (Chu, 2006). The other two new course clusters, derived from around half of the 45 LIS programs, are both related to the Internet. One cluster focuses on Web Design, Web Applications, and the like with 24 offerings, whereas the other cluster, consisting of 22 courses, is variously titled Computer Networks, Information Networks, or Internet Technology and Applications.

Table 1
New LIS Course Clusters

Frequency	New course
27	Digital libraries
24	Web site design; Web applications
22	Computer/information/Internet networks
12	Digitization; digital preservation/design
11	Information architecture
11	Cyberspace law & policy
10	Knowledge management
10	Competitive/business/strategic intelligence
10	Human–computer interaction (HCI); user–system interaction
9	Interface; user interface
9	Metadata
8	Computer/network security
8	Internet reference/applications
7	Information seeking behavior
6	Multimedia/moving images
6	XML; JAVA/C/script languages
5	Digital publishing
4	Natural language processing (NLP)
3	Electronic commerce
3	Visualization
3	Usability
3	Distributed systems
2	Computer supported cooperative work (CSCW)
79	Other single courses (e.g., Beyond Google; Data mining; Gender & computerization; Matching mechanism)

Other course clusters listed in Table 1 are created to cover additional emerging subject areas of the LIS profession. For instance, the cluster with course names such as Digitization or Digital Preservation/Design, to a large extent, symbolizes our efforts in making information more accessible digitally and for a long time to come. Further elaboration on Table 1 is made when related topics (e.g., interdisciplinarity) are discussed later in this chapter.

B. Revised Courses and Concentrations

Individual courses as well as concentrations need to be revised regularly to educate LIS professionals so that they can readily meet challenges of a changing society. Of all the revisions made to the LIS curriculum, most of them relate to technological evolution and development. Cataloging and Reference, two of the core courses in most LIS programs, can for example no longer be taught the way it was in the past. Many electives have been going through modifications as well. The same also holds true for concentrations in LIS programs.

1. The Cataloging Course

Cataloging, also variously named as Bibliographic Control, Cataloging and Classification, Knowledge Organization, and more, has been a fundamental course in LIS curricula since the very beginning. Changes brought upon this course stem not only from the technology but also from cooperative cataloging projects such as OCLC's WorldCat (http://www.worldcat.org). The latter literally makes it unnecessary to perform original cataloging in every individual library. Rather, each library can organize a large part, if not all, of their collection through copy cataloging while needing original cataloging only for relatively unique items (e.g., a noted person's manuscripts and publications for a unique educational program). Yet, cataloging remains essential to the foundation of LIS and hence should be part of the LIS curriculum (Gorman, 2002). According to the survey results of core courses offered in the 45 ALA-accredited LIS programs (Chu, 2006), all but one required a course on this subject, which also topped the list of required courses in terms of frequency (see Table 4).

Subsequent to the creation of metadata standards like Dublin Core, connotation of the word "metadata" was extended to include bibliographic data produced in cataloging of printed and other non-Web-based materials (Chu, 2010, p. 41). Topics such as taxonomies, folksonomies, and ontologies gradually appeared in cataloging courses to cover new developments above and beyond the established controlled vocabularies like classification schemes, subject headings, and thesauri (e.g., Weinberg, 2002).

The cataloging course cluster usually consists of courses such as Abstracting & Indexing, Advanced Cataloging, and Music Cataloging. In the digital age, existing courses are either expanded (e.g., adding tagging to Abstracting & Indexing) or revised (e.g., renaming Bibliographic Control as Metadata) so that all information and knowledge in a physical library as well as in the virtual world can be organized for access and retrieval.

2. The Reference Course

Information Sources and Services, or Reference in brief, is a course required in most, if not all, LIS programs (Chu, 2006). This course, along with other ones for specific domains (e.g., health, law, business, and economics), deals with how to provide reference services to users with appropriate sources. As more and more reference sources become available digitally besides the adoption of numerous technology applications (e.g., Web 1.0 and Web 2.0), both course coverage and instructional approaches move from traditional paradigms toward one that matches with reality today.

Syllabi for reference courses are modified content-wise because few sources are published in print nowadays. Yet, a similar set of topics, from developing a reference collection to evaluating reference tools, still need to be addressed but with an orientation toward the digital environment. Furthermore, shortly after the Web became a de facto platform for users and information professionals alike, Web 2.0 applications (e.g., blogs, wikis, and tagging) began to mushroom and are increasingly utilized for references purposes (e.g., Stephen, 2007; Xu *et al.*, 2009). For example, instant messaging (IM) can easily be implemented in reference services to replace or be used in parallel to conventional methods like e-mail or telephone. With IM, both parties in the reference process would not only communicate with each other but also keep a script of their exchanges if they so wish. In addition, IM offers synchronous communication whereas e-mail does not.

Reference services using digital means are often labeled digital reference services. Out of five education activities Smith (2003) listed for digital references, the first is a formal sequence of courses taken as part of an LIS master's degree. No matter what it is called, a reference course is taught differently now.

3. The Technology Course

As technology plays an important role in LIS, many courses in the LIS curriculum contain technological components or are simply about information technology. Naturally, such courses need to change as technology evolves. For example, Computer Programming is a course offered in quite a few LIS programs. The programming languages being taught, however, have been changed from COBOL or FORTRAIN to BASIC to C to XML, JAVA, and so on. Updates are constantly needed as well for courses like Information Retrieval (IR) because of the rapidly evolving digital, network environment, and other factors. For instance, IR systems such as search engines are altered frequently, if not daily (Schwartz, 2010). IR courses covering those search engines should therefore be changed likewise.

Courses of this nature may also be removed from curricula after they fulfilled their function. Library Automation, Introduction to Internet Applications, and the like all belong to this category. It is expected that the number of deleted courses in this group will grow over time. Similarly, it is not surprising that any technology course needs revision. Indeed, we should be shocked if such courses are taught over an extended period with little modification.

4. Concentrations in LIS Education

Concentrations, also known as tracks or specializations, are often created in LIS programs to guide students in planning their course work. Each concentration commonly has several or more designated courses to prepare students to become well versed in an area.

In the past, concentrations were typically created for public librarianship, academic librarianship, school media specialists, law librarianship, archives and records management, and so on. Different concentrations have been appearing in the digital age, which include DL, Web design and technology, and more. Table 2 compares the two sets of concentrations based on data collected from 10 LIS programs (Chu, 2009).

As indicated in Table 2, 8 of the 10 LIS programs have instituted new concentrations. Although some of the new concentrations actually contain the word "digital" in their names (e.g., digital preservation and digital image management), a good number of them originate from the digital world. Examples include e-government, IA, and social computing. In other words, most concentrations created in the past decade are stamped with the digital mark even if the "D" word is not explicit in the name.

It should be pointed out that data about the actual composition of each concentration listed in Table 2 were not collected in that study (Chu, 2009). Therefore, it is not feasible to examine in this chapter any changes at the course level in each traditional concentration. Given all the curricular changes discussed so far, however, it seems certain that the course content as well as composition of each traditional concentration must have been altered in some way.

C. Redefining the Core

What should constitute the core in the LIS curriculum has always been at the center of attention in the field (e.g., American Library Association, 2009; International Federation of Library Associations and Institutions, 2000; Markey, 2004; Raju, 2003). The core normally is translated as required courses in an LIS curriculum.

Table 2
Concentrations in 10 LIS Programs

Institution name	Traditional concentration	New concentration
Catholic University of America	Generalist, law librarianship, organization of information, school library media, user services	Cultural heritage information management, digital libraries, information architecture
Drexel University	Archival studies, library & information services, school library media, youth services	Competitive intelligence & knowledge management, digital libraries
Kent State University	Academic librarianship, catalogers – metadata, children's librarianship, K-12 school librarianship, library managers, public librarianship, reference librarianship, special librarianship, young adult librarianship	Digital libraries, digital preservation, information technology
Long Island University[a]	Archives & records management, school media, rare books & special collection, public librarianship	
University of Maryland	Archives, records & information management, history & library science, school library media, lifelong access	E-government
University of Michigan	Archival & records management, library & information services (including school library media)	Community informatics, human–computer interaction (HCI), incentive-centered design, information analysis & retrieval, information policy, preservation of information, social computing

Table 2. (*Continued*)

Institution name	Traditional concentration	New concentration
University of North Texas	General studies, health informatics, information organization, law & legal informatics, school librarianship, youth librarianship	Digital image management, Distributed learning, information systems
San Jose State University	Academic libraries, archival studies, information organization & description, management, public libraries, reference services & instruction, special libraries, teacher librarianship, youth librarianship	Web design & technology
University of South Carolina	Technical services, preservation, archives, school media center, specialty courses	Digital libraries, systems, Web design & implementation
University of Washington	Law librarianship, school library media	

[a]Long Island University stopped having concentrations in the early 1990s. What is listed in Table 2 are the certificates programs it offers.

International Federation of Library Associations and Institutions (2000) specified the following core elements that should be included in the LIS curriculum:

1. The Information Environment, Information Policy and Ethics, and the History of the Field
2. Information Generation, Communication, and Use
3. Assessing Information Needs and Designing Responsive Services
4. The Information Transfer Process
5. Organization, Retrieval, Preservation, and Conservation of Information
6. Research, Analysis, and Interpretation of Information
7. Applications of Information and Communication Technologies to Library and Information Products and Services
8. Information Resource Management and Knowledge Management
9. Management of Information Agencies
10. Quantitative and Qualitative Evaluation of Outcomes of Information and Library Use

The American Library Association (2009), on the contrary, put out its version of core competencies, which are terser, fewer in quantity, and target only ALA-accredited LIS programs:

1. Foundations of the Profession
2. Information Resources
3. Organization of Recorded Knowledge and Information
4. Technological Knowledge and Skills
5. Reference and User Services
6. Research
7. Continuing Education and Lifelong Learning
8. Administration and Management

As indicated earlier, core courses of LIS programs have often been the subject of research over the years. Markey (2004), for example, presented 11 required courses and their corresponding frequencies through analysis and comparison of relevant information gathered in 2000 and 2002 from the 54 ALA-accredited LIS programs' web sites. The results for the 2000 data set are recapitulated, in descending order of offering frequency, in Table 3, but without specific number because the frequencies were not explicitly given in the Markey's original figure.

Chu (2006) performed, among other tasks, a similar content analysis of required courses offered by the 45 ALA-accredited LIS programs in the United States. The results are summarized in Table 4.

The agreement in both ranking order and course name between Markey (2004) and Chu (2006), shown correspondingly in Table 3 and Table 4, is amazingly high even though there is one additional group of required course in the latter (i.e., no. 12), and course titles from that study appear more

Table 3
Required Courses based on the 2000 Data Set

Rank	Required course
1	Organization of information resources
2	Reference services & sources
3	Foundations of the field
4	Library management
5	Research methods & evaluation
6	Information technology
7	Collection development
8	Information retrieval
9	Information & society
10	User needs & behavior
11	Practicum

Source: Adapted from Markey (2004).

Table 4
Required Courses based on the 2005 Data Set

Frequency	Rank	Required course
44	1	Organization of information/knowledge/materials
39	2	Reference/Information resources & services
38	3	Introduction to LIS/information environment
30	4	Management
22	5	Research in LIS
14	6	Information technology
11	7	Collection development
9	8	Information use & users related courses (e.g., information use & users; human information behavior; information needs; understanding & serving users)
7	9	Internship/practicum
5	10	Information related courses (e.g., information & society/in social context; understanding/lifecycle of information)
5	11	Ethics & information policy related courses (e.g., ethics for LIS professionals; information policy; issues in LIS)
9	12	All other single topics (e.g., choice of learning; conceptual knowledge processing; evaluation of information systems; information systems, architectures & retrieval; libraries in American society; social systems & collections)

Source: Adapted from Chu (2006).

specific and enumerative. Yet, Chu was not aware of Markey's (2004) study until 2010 when she was preparing the manuscript of the current chapter. Specifically, the first seven required courses listed in both tables seem a mirror image of each other, whereas the differences displayed between the remaining courses in the two sets are essentially a matter of ordering. For instance, Practicum was no. 11 in Markey (2004) but ranked no. 9 in Chu (2006). This unexpected identicalness between the findings from the two separate studies, while data sets in 5 years apart, reflects the significant consensus reached among ALA-accredited LIS programs in redefining the core of their curricula. Nevertheless, further verification of what has been reported earlier is needed because no statistical sampling was involved in either study. In addition, as mentioned earlier, Chu (2006) was not intended as a replica of Markey (2004) at all.

Efforts to redefine the core of LIS programs are also evident in other parts of the world. Raju (2003), for example, described survey results on LIS core requirements as perceived by graduates, employers, and educators in South Africa. Taking a different stance, Roggema-van Heusden (2004) discussed the challenges in developing a competence-oriented curriculum in The Netherlands. Ur Rehman *et al.* (2002), going well beyond a single nation or two, explored the collective judgments of a group of academics from North America, Southeast Asia, and the Arabian Gulf region about the coverage of competencies in the LIS curriculum. Although it is unrealistic to expect complete global consensus on how the core in LIS education should be redefined among all the constituencies, their practices and views on this topic are indeed converging (e.g., Chu, 2006; Markey, 2004; Ur Rehman *et al.*, 2002).

III. Distance Education in Library and Information Science

In LIS education, technology can be either part of the course content or a means for pedagogy. Whereas the former leads to the many changes in the LIS curriculum discussed previously, the latter enables us to provide education through distance delivery. This, also known as online education and an assortment of other names, is rapidly gaining momentum in LIS as successful stories are relayed by pioneers (e.g., Library Education Experiment Project (LEEP) of University of Illinois at Urbana-Champaign and online programs at Drexel University). Meanwhile, other LIS institutions are also gradually going online when seeing its great potential or feeling pressured if remaining offline.

Publications and literature reviews (e.g., Barlow and Aversa, 2006; Mezick and Koenig, 2008) on distance education in LIS are abundant and many are descriptions of a single program's experience. For example, Frey *et al.* (2004) measured students' satisfaction with online MLIS program at University of Pittsburgh. Similar accounts were done for the University of Wisconsin-Milwaukee (Bruchanan, 2004) and by Marcella and Baxter (2001) for a distance learning program in Aberdeen, United Kingdom, including implications for interacting with students in this mode of education. On the basis of her own experience, Tedd (2003) reported three case studies of distance education in Wales, Slovakia, and the Asia-Pacific region.

As an approach different from the face-to-face teaching and learning, distance education can be traced to the days when correspondence was employed for that purpose. As the Web technology matures, it is increasingly used as the platform for today's distance education (e.g., Tyler, 2001). This tendency appears strong and growing stronger in the years to come.

The pros and cons of distance education have been deliberated in the LIS field and beyond (Mezick and Koenig, 2008; Robinson and Bawden, 2002). One issue to be explored is the impact of distance education on smaller and weaker LIS programs. The news about Louisiana State University (LSU)'s intention to close its LIS program apparently shocked the education community and other associated organizations (Blumenstein, 2010). The School of LIS at LSU even cited, as an argument opposing the proposed closure, its efforts to reach students beyond the Baton Rouge campus through distance education in the past 15 years. But could the same reason be used by certain university administration for eliminating an LIS program? In that sense, distance education becomes a double-edged sword because larger and stronger LIS programs indisputably have more resources for providing distance education than smaller and weaker ones.

Size matters, and so does reputation, in both face-to-face and distance education in LIS. That is why concerns are expressed by smaller LIS programs over distance learning programs operated by larger counterparts in their virtual backyards. This also explains why smaller LIS programs are inevitably pressured to deliver courses through distance education even if they are not ready or equipped to do so.

IV. Reposition, Relocation, and Closures of LIS Schools

The previous section ended on a pessimistic note for smaller LIS programs with regard to distance education. On the other hand, organizational changes in LIS education have not stopped since the 1980s although there were quiet periods from time to time. Organizational changes in LIS education typically take the forms of repositioning (e.g., school name change), relocation (e.g., merger with another academic unit), and closures.

A. Reposition and iSchools

Repositioning is not a new topic because, like any other disciplines, LIS has to stay current by adjusting its curriculum and educational approaches. Because these two kinds of repositioning were already discussed earlier, this subsection will look at repositioning through name change in general and the emergence of iSchools in particular.

Name changes of LIS schools in recent decades can generally be categorized in two kinds: (1) the removal of the L word or the adding of the I word, and (2) the establishment of iSchools. The peak time for heated discussion of the first type of name changes occurred before 2000 while the few articles that did touch upon the naming of LIS schools in the current decade were usually written from a different perspective (e.g., Markey, 2004; Wallace, 2009). By comparison, the iSchool movement is well underway and attracts a lot of attention from the LIS community near and far (e.g. Nolin and Åström, 2010; Wallace, 2009).

1. Emergence of iSchools

Burnett and Bonnici (2006) provided, through the accreditation history of library schools and computer science departments, an elaborate account of how these two major groups in the iSchool movement met and forged alliance. Larsen (2008), as the dean of the iSchool at Pittsburgh, depicted in detail the origins, motivation, positioning, empowerment, organization, vision, and recognition of iSchools. By June 2010, there were 27 iSchools according to its web site at www.ischools.org (Table 5).

Among the 27 iSchools, 15 (55.6%) of them have an ALA-accredited LIS program shown in bold face in Table 5. From a disciplinary perspective, iSchools come mainly from three fields (in descending order of membership): LIS, computer science, and management. From an institutional perspective, iSchools have arisen in three principal ways (King, 2006):

1. from the repositioning of pre-existing LIS schools (e.g., University of Pittsburgh, Drexel University),
2. from the merging of pre-existing but disparate academic programs (e.g., University of Michigan), and
3. from the creation of completely new programs by hiring faculty primarily from outside the institution (e.g., Pennsylvania State University).

Table 5
List of iSchools

University of California, Berkeley, School of Information
University of California, Irvine, The Donald Bren School of Information &
    Computer Science
University of California, Los Angeles, Graduate School of Education &
    Information Studies
Carnegie Mellon University, School of Information Systems & Management,
    Hein College
Drexel University, College of Information Science & Technology
Florida State University, College of Communication & Information
Georgia Institute of Technology, College of Computing
Humboldt-Universität zu Berlin, Berlin School of Library & Information Science
University of Illinois, Urbana-Champaign, Graduate School of Library &
    Information Science
Indiana University, School of Informatics & Computing
Indiana University, School of Library & Information Science
University of Maryland, College of Information Studies
University of Maryland, Baltimore County, Department of Information Systems
University of Michigan, The School of Information
University of North Carolina, Chapel Hill, School of Information & Library
    Science
University of North Texas, College of Information
The Pennsylvania State University, College of Information Sciences & Technology
University of Pittsburgh, School of Information Sciences
Royal School of Library & Information Science, Denmark
Rutgers, the State University of New Jersey, School of Communication
    & Information
University of Sheffield, England, Information Studies
Singapore Management University, School of Information Systems
Syracuse University, School of Information Studies
University of Texas, Austin, School of Information
University of Toronto, Faculty of Information
University of Washington, Information School
Wuhan University, China, School of Information Management

The evolution of iSchools, illustrated in Table 6, exhibits its deep origin in LIS because its members before the founding of the iSchool Caucus, or iCaucus in brief, in 2005 were all traditional LIS schools with one exception, namely the School of Informatics and Computing at Indiana University.

According to Larsen (2008), the collective efforts of the iSchools (e.g., the iConference, the web site, and special projects) are managed by the

Table 6
Evolution of iSchools

Year	Membership
1988	Gang of Three: Pittsburgh, Syracuse, & Drexel
1990	Gang of Four: Pittsburgh, Syracuse, Drexel, & Rutgers
2001	Gang of Five: Pittsburgh, Syracuse, Drexel, Washington, & Michigan
2003	Gang of Ten: Pittsburgh, Syracuse, Drexel, Washington, Michigan, Illinois, North Carolina, Florida State, Indiana (Informatics), & Texas at Austin
2005	iCaucus: Gang of Ten plus Berkeley, Irvine, UCLA, Georgia Tech, Indiana (LIS), Maryland, & Toronto
2009	27 members: See Table 5

iCaucus. Members of the iCaucus pay an annual fee and have one vote on iCaucus decisions. The iCaucus charter specifies its membership criteria that currently consist of three (iSchools, 2010):

1. substantial sponsored research activity (an average of $1 million in research expenditures per year over 3 years),
2. engagement in the training of future researchers (usually through an active, research-oriented doctoral program), and
3. a commitment to progress in the information field.

Apparently, the first criterion prevents many LIS schools from becoming an iSchool. The other two criteria appear much less restrictive in comparison.

2. LIS schools vs. iSchools

The LIS community's reaction to the emergence of iSchools is anything but quiet. A partition between LIS schools and iSchools is gradually built up although it might be invisible physically and unintentional on both sides. Discussions surrounding LIS schools vs. iSchools sometimes went as far as which schools were or were not members of the iSchool group. The issue of exclusiveness, however, was not an initial intention of the iSchool movement. As noted by Toni Carbo (2009), founder of iSchools, the original intent of setting up iSchools was to create an environment for LIS schools to communicate and collaborate in research and other areas. She also commented that iSchools were not meant to be exclusive in the beginning. Rather, they should be interactive.

Enthusiasm about the formation of iSchools is manifestly high. Cox and Larsen (2008), for example, believed that the iSchool movement would help the evolution of archival studies as the former can tackle the increasingly complex issues confronting a digital society. Seadle and Greifeneder (2007) also suggested an iSchool ought to be more than a library school with a name that implies modern times and thus it needs a unique curriculum. In doing so, iSchools are not preparing students for today's libraries but for leadership positions in tomorrow's information infrastructure, which they fully intend to help create.

Many in the LIS education community, nevertheless, do not share the same views as Seadle and Greifeneder (2007). Rather, some (e.g., Nolin and Åström, 2010) argue that iSchool movement is only a labeling problem. Similarly, Wallace (2009) posits that a major motivation for the iSchools has to do with branding. After articulating concerns over some other issues in LIS education, Leonhardt (2007) indicates that, despite all the talk and emphasis on iSchools, they are still all library schools for all intents and purposes because the large majority of their MLIS students want to be a librarian or work in a closely allied field.

Bonnici *et al.* (2009), through the theoretical lens of *the Chaos of Disciplines* (Abbott, 2001), conclude that the iField is not only at the heart of everything but also has ingested the L into its heart. Instead of describing LIS as a fragmented field in crisis, Nolin and Åström (2010) propose an epistemological convergent "info turn" to turn LIS' weakness into strength. Wallace (2009) states that, according to the enrollment data in past decades for ALA-accredited MLIS and all other programs at LIS schools, excessive concerns over the potential negative impact of the iSchools are not supported because enrollment has stayed healthy over the past years even after the emergence of iSchools.

Further comparisons between iSchools and LIS schools were made by Chu (2009) on the basis of the ALA-accredited master's program they all have. Five schools were selected from both categories before their web sites were visited for data collection. Specific aspects examined in that study included program requirements, core courses, concentrations, total course offerings, online education, and degree programs other than the ALA-accredited MLIS. Except the outcome on concentrations presented in Table 2, all other results will be reported in a separate publication. Chu's (2009) general finding is that there were few essential differences between the selected iSchools and LIS schools. In a study on LIS doctoral education, Sugimoto *et al.* (2009) showed that, among the 11 top PhD producers, eight were iSchools. This finding is to be expected because one of the three requirements for becoming an iSchool is to have a PhD program.

The discussion on iSchools vs. LIS schools is likely to continue. Whether iSchools can prove the significance and necessity of their emergence remains to be seen. Perhaps, it is the process rather than the result, which is of interest these days in the community of LIS education.

B. Relocation

Unlike disciplines in hard sciences, relocation seems a commonplace in LIS. Hildreth and Koenig (2002) prepared a comprehensive report about the organizational realignment of LIS programs in academia, reporting five types of mergers they identified by 2001:

1. LIS school is the junior partner in merger with a pre-existing, usually larger, dominant unit.
2. LIS school is a junior partner in a newly established unit.
3. LIS school is an equal partner in old or new unit.
4. LIS school is the senior partner in a newly established unit.
5. Repositioning, but no merger, within the academy.

In the study by Hildreth and Koenig (2002), 17 LIS schools were involved in relocation between 1982 and 2001. This number had risen to 30 by June 2010 based on data gathered from the web sites of 57 ALA-accredited LIS programs. This accounts for close to 53% of the total. These 30 LIS schools, now all part of a larger unit within a university, are listed in Table 7 with the names of their parent units and their academic siblings (i.e., non-LIS disciplines) in the same organization.

Fig. 1 presents the distribution of non-LIS disciplines by counting the first one within each parent unit. As shown, Communication (including Mass Communication) and Education share an academic home with 10 (33.3%) and 9 (30%) LIS schools, respectively, whereas Learning Technology, Management, Media Studies, and Social Sciences each become co-inhabitant of one LIS school. In other words, Communication or Education seems increasingly the common choice to subsume or partner with LIS schools when academic relocation is considered.

The rationale behind all the relocations or organizational realignments is usually triggered by financial factors along with institutional politics, all of which are beyond the scope of this chapter. Moreover, the list of relocated LIS schools in Table 7, although almost doubled in size, definitely does not signal an end to the latest wave of mergers because University of Illinois at Urbana-Champaign, one of the top LIS schools, is surprisingly becoming a target of reorganization (Easter and Wheeler, 2010; Unsworth, 2010). Other issues (e.g., staying strong within the university) aside, relocating LIS

Table 7
Parent Units and Academic Siblings of 30 LIS Schools

LIS school	Parent unit	Non-LIS discipline
Alabama	College of Communication & Information Sciences	Communication
SUNY at Albany	College of Computing & Information	Computer Science, Informatics
SUNY at Buffalo	Graduate School of Education	Education
UCLA	Graduate School of Education & Information Studies	Education
Clarion	College of Education & Human Services	Communication, Education
Dalhousie	Faculty of Management	Management
Denver	College of Education	Education
Florida State	College of Communication & Information	Communication
Hawaii	Information & Computer Sciences Department	Computer Science
Kent	College of Communication & Information	Communication
Kentucky	College of Communication & Information Studies	Communication
Long Island	College of Education & Information Sciences	Education, Computer Science
McGill	Faculty of Education	Education
Missouri	College of Education	Education
Montreal	Faculty of Arts & Sciences	Arts & Sciences
North Carolina at Greensboro	College of Education	Education
North Texas	College of Information	Learning Technologies
Oklahoma	College of Arts & Sciences	Arts & Sciences
Queens	Division of Social Sciences	Social Sciences

Table 7. (Continued)

LIS school	Parent unit	Non-LIS discipline
Rhode Island	College of Arts & Sciences	Arts & Sciences
Rutgers	School of Communication & Information	Communication
St. John's	College of Liberal Arts & Sciences	Arts & Sciences
San José	College of Applied Sciences & Arts	Applied Sciences & Arts
South Carolina	College of Mass Communications & Information Studies	Mass Communications
Southern Connecticut	School of Communication, Information, & Library Science	Communication, Computer Science, Journalism
Southern Mississippi	College of Education & Psychology	Education, Psychology
Tennessee	College of Communication & Information	Communication
Texas Woman's	College of Professional Education	Education
Valdosta	Graduate School	Communication, Education
Western Ontario	Faculty of Information & Media Studies	Media Studies

schools from a stand-alone academic unit to one subordinate of another remains a challenge we in LIS education ought to meet.

C. Closures

LIS school closures set off alarms again not so long ago. Several years after talks of library school closures were thought to have faded (Cronin, 2002) or replaced by relocation (Hildreth and Koenig, 2002), the alarms have returned. As briefly mentioned earlier, LSU has proposed to close the only LIS school in the state (Blumenstein, 2010).

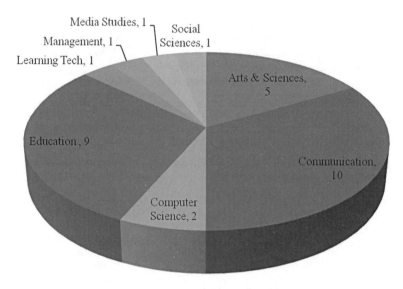

Fig. 1   Distribution of non-LIS disciplines.

Although it is hard to predict if LSU's proposal will prompt another round of LIS school closures, this news does make us to stay vigilant and, as always, to try our best in providing LIS education. Nothing can be taken for granted, particularly in the digital age. The only panacea we have to prevent further LIS school closures is to advance as the society does. On the other hand, what we perhaps can use to console ourselves a little is that organizational changes imposed upon us (e.g., relocation and closures) do not result from our incompetency in LIS education. Rather, it is to a great extent determined by the nature of our profession: service-oriented and practice-based.

V. Growth in LIS Education

On the positive side, LIS education is growing through establishing programs at all levels and collaborating with other disciplines or across borders. The next three subsections will be devoted to specific topics on the theme of growth in LIS education.

A. Establishing Programs at All Levels

LIS schools have traditionally been the home of the ALA-accredited master's programs. Many schools, nevertheless, have begun hosting undergraduate, doctoral, as well as additional master's programs in recent years. According to Association for Library & Information Science Education (ALISE) statistics (Wallace, 2009), there were 4143 undergraduate students enrolled in schools with an ALA-accredited master's programs and 998 doctoral students in 31 programs (Sugimoto *et al.*, 2009) in Fall, 2008. According to Saye (2005), 15 LIS schools had an undergraduate program in 2004 (pp. 78–79). In general, the undergraduate program tends to lean toward technology. Doctoral program focused, as expected, on research in LIS and might be interdisciplinary because of joint efforts with other disciplines (e.g., Long Island University, McGill University, and University of Tennessee).

As Cronin (2002) aptly put, LIS schools hold the center while prospecting at the periphery. These schools also launch other master's programs in addition to one accredited by the ALA and degree programs at the undergraduate and doctoral levels. For example, University of Washington offers Master of Science in Information Management and at Kent State University, as described earlier, the LIS school cohosts Master of Science in Information Architecture and Knowledge Management.

B. Interdisciplinarity in LIS education

Information, people, and technology can be regarded as the three axes around which LIS education is centered. Meanwhile, knowledge and experience from other disciplines are needed for us to provide quality LIS education. For example, sociology and psychology would help us become more knowledgeable about the kinds of information and services our users desire to have. Computer science would enable us to take full advantage of technologies in educating LIS professionals. Indeed, LIS education is becoming more interdisciplinary as demonstrated not only in LIS courses but also through other dimensions.

Åström (2008) looked at the academic affiliations of five LIS programs in Nordic countries as well as their research orientation, finding a close connection between the two. That is, LIS programs affiliated with, for example, the humanities tend to conduct research in the same domain. Through a citation analysis of the literature published between 1977 and 2006 in information studies that include LIS, Cronin and Meho (2008) point out that over the past decade, information studies have become a successful exporter of ideas by contributing significantly to the literatures of disciplines such as computer science and engineering on the one hand and business and management on the other. Both research projects cited previously indicate that intellectual relationship between LIS and other disciplines is getting stronger and more reciprocal, thus making LIS more interdisciplinary.

Interdisciplinarity is also featured within the LIS curriculum. Table 1 lists new course clusters Chu (2006) extracted from the ALA-accredited LIS programs' curricula. In addition to the courses on DL, KM, or IA, there are many others that substantiate the interdisciplinary nature of the LIS education. For example, the 11-member cluster on Cyberspace Law and Policy shows its connection with the field of law. Courses related to Competitive/Business Intelligence (10 courses) or Electronic Commerce (3 offerings) bear a clear relationship with business information management. Furthermore, correlations between LIS and the following fields can be unmistakably observed:

- Psychology/Computer science in course clusters such as Human Computer Interaction (10 offerings), Interface (9 courses), and Computer Supported Cooperative Work (2);
- Computer science in course clusters such as Computer/Network Security (8 courses) and XML/JAVA/C/Script languages (6 courses); and
- Sociology/Psychology in the Information Seeking Behavior (7 offerings) cluster as well as in other individual courses such as Information Needs Analysis and Understanding the Information User.

Another form of interdisciplinarity, namely, sponsoring a program jointly with a non-LIS school, is often seen today. For example, University of Amsterdam combines LIS and business education in its executive master's program (Maes, 2003). Programs in information management, a synonym of LIS, are offered in LIS schools in the Baltic States, Nordic countries, and the United Kingdom often with an orientation toward management, business, and economics (Maceviciute, 2002).

As for what promotes interdisciplinarity in LIS education, technology alone does not appear fully responsible although it does play an important role in the digital age. Other factors such as cultural changes (Stoker, 2000) and societal changes (Curry, 2000) also have an impact on making LIS education more interdisciplinary.

C. LIS Education across Borders

Digital technologies certainly have shortened physical distances among LIS schools all over the world through distance education. Collaboration between different parties further facilitates LIS education across borders. In general, LIS schools in Europe have made more effort and progress in collaboration than their counterparts in other parts of the globe. This is illustrated through projects such as the Bologna declaration (Kajberg, 2002) and SOCRATES (Kajberg, 2003). Another example was an international master's program in information studies, which was delivered between two universities, one in Italy and the other in the United Kingdom (Dixon and Tammaro, 2003).

Juznic and Badovinac (2005) found homogeneity among the LIS programs in the European Union based on their comparison, which could become the foundation for future collaboration in the field.

Across the ocean, European Association for Library & Information Education & Research (EUCLID) and ALISE held a joint conference at Potsdam, Germany, in 2003 (Juznic and Badovinac, 2005). Many LIS schools in Canada and the United States arrange for students to take a summer course or seminar overseas. One example is the Summer Seminar to London, organized jointly by University of North Carolina (UNC) at Chapel Hill and University College London (University of North Carolina, 2010).

Collaboration between other continents (e.g., between Asia and North America) also exists despite of great cultural and language barriers. Townley *et al.* (2003), for instance, described a distance course on KM taught in China and the United States. The authors believe that using distance education technology is a feasible means to internationalizing LIS education. The course titled "Introduction to Chinese Information Services," offered by the Graduate School of Library & Information Studies at University of Rhode Island, in China in Summer, 2010, is another example of collaboration in LIS education across the border (University of Rhode Island, 2010).

Abdullahi and Kajberg (2004) conducted a survey, specifically inquiring LIS schools in Europe, the United States, and Canada about their practice in international collaboration. Their findings indicate that most LIS schools participated in the survey are equally interested in international exchanges such as hosting visiting scholars and supporting study abroad programs. All the above signify that LIS education is no longer bounded by a country's border in the digital age.

VI. Issues and Concerns in LIS Education

Researchers and practitioners in the field have voiced their views and suggested remedies about issues and concerns in LIS education. At the dawn of the 21st century, Stoker (2000) added two more issues (i.e., nature and extent of the information disciplines; the changing pattern of higher education in the United Kingdom and character of the student body) to those viewed as persistent:

1. library school or not?
2. control by the profession,
3. theory vs. practice,
4. fieldwork, and
5. the core curriculum.

Whereas the second issue Stoker (2000) newly added focuses particularly on the United Kingdom, the rest still populate list discussions (e.g., http://JESSE@listserv.utk.edu), conference talks (e.g., ALA and ALISE), and publications (e.g., Burger, 2007; Koenig, 2007). Among all the issues raised, three appear to be recurring even a full decade after the Stoker's (2000) publication appeared. Therefore, these issues are revisited in the following sections.

A. Library Education Crisis

Gorman (2004), a noted figure in the domain, advanced his statement of library education crisis after voicing his views on this issue. Dillon and Norris (2005) subsequently refuted Gorman's arguments from the following three perspectives by collapsing some of the over a dozen he presented:

1. Librarianship vs. information science,
2. A gender divide between librarianship-oriented female faculty and information science-oriented male faculty, and
3. A curriculum failing to adequately address the education of librarians.

In addition to Dillon and Norris (2005), Durrance (2004) provided her view on the first point by questioning on purpose whether the relationship between librarianship and information science is competition or convergence. The other critical point of the debate on LIS education crisis is the curriculum, which was extensively addressed earlier in this chapter.

In retrospect, the Panda Syndrome coined by Van House and Sutton (1996) and based on the ecological theory painted a gloomier picture than the perceived crisis about the state of LIS education. Wilson (2002), on the other hand, proposed that strategies including collaboration and diversification should be undertaken to prevent the alleged crisis in LIS education from turning into a catastrophe. Indeed, appropriate measures must be adopted and in a timely fashion to ensure the vigorous development of LIS education.

B. Chasm between LIS Education and Practices

The debate about the chasm between LIS education and practices, despite its prolonged existence, still lingers and reappeared on JESSE (a discussion list on LIS education) as recently as the early months of 2010. Typically, LIS practitioners initiate the debate (e.g., Stoffle and Leader, 2005) because of their dissatisfaction with LIS graduates in the workplace, which naturally leads to the conclusion that practices in the profession are not covered in LIS programs. LIS educators, on the other hand, would argue that the core competencies needed for LIS professionals to function properly are all included in the LIS curriculum (e.g., Dillon and Norris, 2005; Koenig, 2007).

Moran (2001) attributed the chasm to problems such as too few students to offer all the courses desired by practitioners and having to serve two masters, namely the profession and the university. In addition, both practitioners and LIS educators had different views on how the master's program should be operated. Yet, the nature of LIS education, like that in any other disciplines, should focus on education, not on training for the workplace.

C. Accreditation of LIS Programs

Another issue of magnitude in LIS education is accreditation of LIS master's programs. Cronin (2000) listed the following five options, with tongue in cheek, when pondering over the controversial accreditation under the auspices of ALA's Committee on Accreditation (COA):

1. Stick with the status quo and progressively dumb-down the profession;
2. Transfer responsibility for accreditation from the COA to some other body;
3. Lay LIS accreditation firmly to rest;
4. Reengineer the overall process; and
5. Move away from accrediting academic programs to accrediting libraries.

The debate on ALA accreditation centers mainly on three elements: what, who, and how. Unlike their thoughts on the issue of the perceived chasm between LIS education and practices, even members within their own cohort of practitioners or educators cannot seem reach consensus among themselves about accreditation. Meanwhile, ASIS&T, a major association for information science, started exploring if it should commence a similar effort in the field (Prentince et al., 2007).

Accreditation in other countries (e.g., the United Kingdom) appears less contested (Enser, 2002). International Federation of Library Associations and Institutions (2000) on the other hand has actively been investigating the necessity and feasibility of such endeavors worldwide. Khoo et al. (2003), for example, suggested a framework for developing standards and procedures for regional accreditation in Southeast Asia. Dalton and Levinson (2000) described, among other things, an approach for creating a global database of LIS education standards and accreditation criteria for measuring LIS qualifications. Efforts headed by International Federation of Library Associations and Institutions (IFLA) and other international organizations for quality assurance in LIS education were also detailed by Tammaro (2006).

Returning to the five options Cronin (2000) enumerated in the beginning of this subsection, which one appears more likely to become the reality? The author gave his answer to the question a decade ago, in the order of unacceptable, feasible, wishful thinking, commonsensical, and no specification to the last option. What will happen in the long run, however, might not be among the five: that is, revising the standards and procedures for future accreditations.

VII. Conclusion

Education in LIS has developed notably in the past decade through curricular revision, distance education, educational reposition, and other actions. Furthermore, the field is able to take proactive measures in dealing with the challenges in the digital age. LIS programs, for example, introduced new courses and concentrations while revising existing ones in the curricula. Besides initiating new programs at different levels and beyond the ALA-accredited master's programs, LIS schools also collaborated with others across disciplines and across borders in their educational endeavors.

LIS education in the digital age will move forward and even thrive when the field not only makes intelligent use of the technology but also changes in other dimensions as the society advances. Discussion of the issues, old and new, should continue because debates and exchanges, if carried out properly, would keep the field attentive and clear about what is the best for LIS education.

The digital age, without exaggeration, has brought LIS education opportunities greater than ever with its domain of activities being expanded both spatially and temporally. LIS educators are no longer limited in a digital age by having physical resources in proximity when fulfilling their teaching responsibilities. Students can be reached in the classroom and beyond, and receive the same, if not a better, quality education through the use of digital technologies.

References

Abbott, A. (2001). *The Chaos of Disciplines*. University of Chicago Press, Chicago, IL.

Abdullahi, I., and Kajberg, L. (2004). A study of international issues in library and information science education: Survey of LIS schools in Europe, the USA and Canada. *New Library World* 105(9/10), 345–356.

Abell, A. (2000). Skills for knowledge environments. *Information Management Journal* 34(3), 33–40.

Al-Hawamdeh, S. (2005). Designing an interdisciplinary graduate program in knowledge management. *Journal of the American Society for Information Science and Technology* 56(11), 1200–1206.

American Library Association (2009). *Core Competencies of Librariaship.* Approved and adopted as policy by the ALA Council. Retrieved from http://www.ala.org/ala/educationcareers/careers/corecomp/corecompetences/finalcorecompstat09.pdf

Åström, F. (2008). Formalizing a discipline: The institutionalization of library and information science research in the Nordic countries. *Journal of Documentation* 64(5), 721–737.

Barlow, D. L., and Aversa, E. (2006). Library professionals for the 21 century academy. In *Advances in Librarianship* (D. A. Nitecki and E. G. Abels, eds.), vol. 30, pp. 327–364, Academic Press, New York.

Bawden, D., Vilar, P., and Zabukovec, V. (2005). Education and training for digital librarians: A Slovenia/UK comparison. *Aslib Proceedings* 57(1), 85–98.

Berners-Lee, T., Hendler, J., and Lassila, O. (2001). The semantic Web. *Scientific American* 284(5), 35–43.

Blumenstein, L. (2010, May 27). *LIS school at LSU threatened with closure.* Retrieved from Library Journal web site: http://www.libraryjournal.com/article/CA6729330.html

Bonnici, L. J., Subramaniam, M. M., and Burnett, K. (2009). Everything old is new again: The evolution of library and information science education from LIS to iField. *Journal of Education for Library and Information Science* 50(4), 263–274.

Breen, C., Farragher, A., McQuaid, M., Callanan, M., and Burke, M. A. (2002). New information management opportunities in a changing world. *Library Review* 51(3/4), 127–138.

Bruchanan, E. A. (2004). Institutional challenges in Web-based programs: Student challenges and institutional responses. *Journal of Library Administration* 41(1/2), 65–74.

Burger, L. (2007). Changing library education. *American Libraries* 38(4), 5.

Burnett, K., and Bonnici, L. J. (2006). Contested terrain: Accreditation and the future of the profession of librarianship. *The Library Quarterly* 76(2), 193–219.

Callison, D., and Tilley, C. L. (2001). Descriptive impressions of the library and information education evolution in 1988–1998 as reflected in job announcements, ALISE descriptors, and new course titles. *Journal of Education for Library & Information Science* 42(3), 181–199.

Carbo, T. (2009). Comments made on November 19, 2009 in the session titled "Diversity & Commonality of Information Science Education in a Pluralistic World" at the 2009 Annual Meeting of the American Society for Information Science and Technology.

Chaudhry, A. S., and Higgins, S. (2003). On the need for a multidisciplinary approach to education for knowledge management. *Library Review* 52(2), 65–69.

Chu, H. (2006). Curricula of LIS programs in the USA: A content analysis. In *Proceedings of the Asia-Pacific Conference on Library & Information Education & Practice (A-LIEP 2006)* (C. Khoo, D. Singh and A. S. Chaudhry, eds.), pp. 328–337, School of Communication & Information, Nanyang Technological University, Singapore. Also available at http://citeseerx.ist.psu.edu/viewdoc/download?doi=10.1.1.89.1470&rep=rep1&type=pdf

Chu, H. (2009). *Comparison of LIS programs at 10 LIS schools* [PowerPoint slides]. Presentation in the session titled "Diversity & Commonality of Information Science Education in a Pluralistic World" at the 2009 Annual Meeting of the American Society for Information Science and Technology. Retrieved from http://myweb.cwpost.liu.edu/hchu/LISProgramComparison-ASIST2009.pdf

Chu, H. (2010). *Information Representation and Retrieval in the Digital Age*, 2nd ed. Information Today, Medford, NJ.

Cox, R. J., and Larsen, R. L. (2008). iSchools and archival studies. *Archival Science* 8(4), 307–326.

Cronin, B. (2000). Accreditation: Retool it or kill it. *Library Journal* 125(11), 54.

Cronin, B. (2002). Holding the center while prospecting at the periphery: Domain identity and coherence in North American information studies education. *Education for Information* 20(1), 3–10.

Cronin, B., and Meho, L. I. (2008). The shifting balance of intellectual trade in information Studies. *Journal of the American Society for Information Science and Technology* 59(4), 551–564.

Curry, A. (2000). Canadian LIS education: Trends and issues. *Education for Information* 18(4), 325–337.

Dalton, P., and Levinson, K. (2000). An investigation of LIS qualifications throughout the world. In *Proceedings of the 66th IFLA Council and General Conference*. International Federation of Library Associations and Institutions, The Hague, Netherlands. Retrieved from http://archive.ifla.org/IV/ifla66/papers/061-161e.htm

Dillon, A. (). The end is nigh. *Bulletin of the American Society for Information Science and Technology* 32(2), 26–27.

Dillon, A., and Norris, A. (2005). Crying wolf: An examination and reconsideration of the perception of crisis in LIS education. *Journal of Education for Library and Information Science* 46(4), 280–298.

Dixon, P., and Tammaro, A. M. (2003). Strengths and issues in implementing a collaborative inter-university course: The international masters in information studies by distance. *Education for Information* 21(2/3), 85–96.

Durrance, J. C. (2004). Competition or convergence? Library and information science education at a critical crossroad. In *Advances in Librarianship* (D. A. Nitecki, ed.), vol. 28, pp. 171–198, Academic Press, New York.

Easter, R. A., and Wheeler, R. P. (2010, March 5). *Letter to the project team of academic unit reviews*. Office of the Chancellor, University of Illinois at Urbana-Champaign. Retrieved from http://oc.illinois.edu/budget/unit_reviews_charge.pdf

Enser, P. (2002). The role of professional body accreditation in library & information science education in the UK. *Libri* 52(4), 214–219.

Frey, B. A., Alman, S. W., Barron, D., and Steffens, A. (2004). Student satisfaction with the online MLIS program at the University of Pittsburgh. *Journal of Education for Library and Information Science* 45(2), 82–97.

Gorman, M. (2002). Why teach cataloguing and classification? *Cataloging & Classification Quarterly* 34(1/2), 1–13.

Gorman, M. (2004). Whither library education? *New Library World* 105 (1204/1205), 376–380.

Hall, D. M. (2010). The corporation as a stakeholder in information education. *Bulletin of the American Society for Information Science and Technology* 36(5), 43–50.

Hildreth, C. R., and Koenig, M. E. D. (2002). Organizational realignment of LIS programs in academia: From independent standalone units to incorporated programs. *Journal of Education for Library and Information Science* 43(2), 126–133.

Hyldegaard, J., Lund, H., and Seiden, P. (2002). LIS meets the EIP. *Library Review* 51(3/4), 149–156.

International Federation of Library Associations and Institutions, Education and Training Section (2000). *Guidelines for professional library/information educational programs.* Retrieved from http://archive.ifla.org/VII/s23/bulletin/guidelines.htm

iSchools (2010). *Joining the iSchools.* Retrieved from http://www.ischools.org/site/join/

Juznic, P., and Badovinac, B. (2005). Toward library and information science education in the European Union. *New Library World* 106(3/4), 173–186.

Kajberg, L. (2002). Cross-country partnerships in European library and information science education: Education at the crossroads. *Library Review* 15(3/4), 164–170.

Kajberg, L. (2003). Cross-country partnerships in international library and information science education. *New Library World* 104(1189), 218–226.

Khoo, C., Majid, S., and Chaudhry, A. S. (2003). Developing an accreditation system for LIS professional education programmes in Southeast Asia: Issues and perspectives. *Malaysian Journal of Library & Information Science* 8(2), 131–149.

King, J. L. (2006). Identity in the I-school movement. *Bulletin of the American Society for Information Science and Technology* 32(4). Retrieved from http://www.asis.org/Bulletin/Apr-06/king.html

Koenig, M. E. D. (2003). Knowledge management, user education, and librarianship. *Library Review* 52(2), 10–17.

Koenig, M. E. D. (2007). Looking back: A review for four key articles from volume one. *Education for Information* 25(1), 57–61.

Larsen, R. L. (2008). *History of the iSchools.* Retrieved from http://www.ischools.org/site/history/

Latham, D. (2002). Information architecture: Notes toward a new curriculum. *Journal of the American Society for Information Science and Technology* 53(10), 824–830.

Leonhardt, T. W. (2007). Library and information science education. *Technicalities* 27(2), 3–6.

Logan, E., and Hsieh-Yee, I. (2001). Library and information science education in the nineties. In *Annual Review of Information Science and Technology* (M. E. Williams, ed.), vol. 35, pp. 425–477, Information Today, Medford, NJ.

Maceviciute, E. (2002). Information management in the Baltic, Nordic, and UK LIS schools. *Library Review* 51(3/4), 190–199.

Maes, R. (2003). On the alliance of executive education and research information management at the University of Amsterdam. *International Journal of Information Management* 23(3), 249–257.

Marcella, R., and Baxter, G. (2001). Information and library studies on a virtual campus. *New Library World* 102(1169), 362–371.

Markey, K. (2004). Current educational trends in the information and library science curriculum. *Journal of Education for Library and Information Science* 45(4), 317–399.

McKean, E. (Prep.) (2005). *The New Oxford American Dictionary.* 2nd edn, Oxford University Press, New York.

Mezick, E. M., and Koenig, M. E. D. (2008). Education for information science. In *Annual Review of Information Science and Technology* (B. Cronin, ed.), vol. 42, pp. 593–624, Information Today, Medford, NJ.

Moran, B. (2001). Practitioners vs. LIS educators: Time to reconnect. *Library Journal* 126(18), 52–55.

Morville, P., and Rosenfeld, L. (2007). *Information Architecture for the World Wide Web*, 3rd ed. O'Reilly, Sebastopol, CA.

Nolin, J., and Åström, F. (2010). Turning weakness into strength: Strategies for future LIS. *Journal of Documentation* 66(1), 7–27.

Prentice, A., Barlow, D., Dalrymple, P., Griffiths, J. M., McCain, K., & Roderer, N. (2007, October 20). ASIS&T white paper: Accreditation of programs for the education of information professionals. American Society for Information Science and Technology. MD: Silver Spring. Retrieved from http://www.asis.org/white_paper.htmlwww.asis.org/white_paper.html

Raju, J. (2003). The 'core' in the library and/or information science education and training. *Education for Information* 21(4), 229–242.

Robbins, D. (2002). Information architecture in library and information science curricula. *Bulletin of the American Society for Information Science and Technology* 28(2), 20–22.

Robinson, L., and Bawden, D. (2002). Distance learning and LIS professional development. *Aslib Proceedings* 54(1), 48–55.

Roggema-van Heusden, M. (2004). The challenge of developing a competence oriented curriculum: An integrative framework. *Library Review* 53(2), 98–103.

Saracevic, T., & Dalbello, M. (2001). A survey of digital library education. In *Proceedings of the 2001 Annual Meeting of the American Society for Information Science and Technology* (pp. 209–223), Information Today, Medford, NJ.

Saye, J. D. (ed.) (2005). *Library and Information Science Education 2005 Statistical Report*. Association for Library and Information Science Education, Chicago, IL.

Schwartz, B. (2010, April 22). Google makes one change per day to search engine algorithm. *SearchCap, Search Engine Land*. Retrieved from http://searchengine-land.com/google-makes-one-change-per-day-to-search-algorithm-40508

Seadle, M., and Greifeneder, E. (2007). Envisioning an iSchool curriculum. *Information Research* 12(4). paper colise02. Retrieved from http://InformationR.net/ir/12-4/colis/colise02

Smith, L. C. (2003). Chapter 8. Education for digital reference services. In *The Digital Reference Research Agenda* (R. D. Lankes, S. Nicholson and A. Goodrum, eds.), pp. 148–176, Association of College and Research Libraries, Chicago, IL.

Stephen, M. (2007). Web 2.0 & libraries, Part 2: Trends and technologies. *Library Technology Reports* 43(5), 41–43.

Stoffle, C. J., and Leader, K. (2005). Practitioners and library education: A crisis of understanding. *Journal of Education for Library and Information Science* 46(4), 313–319.

Stoker, D. (2000). Persistence and change: Issues for LIS educators in the first decade of the twenty first century. *Education for Information* 18(2), 115–122.

Sugimoto, C. R., Russell, T. G., and Grant, S. (2009). Library and information science doctoral education: The landscape from 1930–2007. *Journal of Education for Library and Information Science* 50(3), 190–202.

Tammaro, A. M. (2006). Quality assurance in library and information science (LIS) schools: Major trends and issues. In *Advances in Librarianship* (D. A. Nitecki and E. G. Abels, eds.), vol. 30, pp. 389–423, Academic Press, New York.

Tedd, L. A. (2003). The what? And how? Of education and training for information professionals in a changing world: Some experience from Wales, Slovakia and the Asia-Pacific region. *Journal of Information Science* 29(1), 79–86.

Townley, C. T., Geng, Q., and Zhang, J. (2003). Using distance education to internationalize library and information science scholarship. *Libri* 53(2), 82–93.

Tyler, A. (2001). A survey of distance learning library and information science courses delivered via the Internet. *Education for Information* 19(1), 47–59.

University of North Carolina, School of Information & Library Science (2010). *London seminar overview*. Retrieved from http://sils.unc.edu/programs/international/london.htm

University of Rhode Island, Graduate School of Library & Information Studies (2010). *Seminar in Chinese librarianship*. Retrieved from http://www.uri.edu/artsci/lsc/Academics/GELIP/LSC597_china.html

Unsworth, J. (2010, April 11). *Draft responses to questions from the letter to the project team of academic unit reviews by Dean of Graduate School of Library & Information Science*. University of Illinois at Urbana-Champaign. Retrieved from http://webdocs.lis.illinois.edu/comm/gslis.se.response.pdf

Ur Rehman, S., Al-Ansari, H., and Yousef, N. (2002). Coverage of competencies in the curriculum of information studies: An international perspective. *Education for Information* 20(3/4), 199–215.

Ur Rehman, S., and Chaudhry, A. S. (2005). KM education in LIS programs. *Education for Information* 23(4), 245–258.

Van House, N., and Sutton, S. A. (1996). The Panda Syndrome: An ecology of LIS education. *Journal of Education for Library and Information Science* 37(2), 131–147.

Wallace, D. P. (2009). The iSchools, education for librarianship, and the voice of doom and gloom. *The Journal of Academic Librarianship* 35(5), 405–409.

Weinberg, B. H. (2002). New course design: Classification schemes and information architecture. *Bulletin of the American Society for Information Science and Technology* 28(5), 14–17.

Wilson, T. D. (2002). Curriculum and catastrophe: change in professional education. *Journal of Education for Library and Information Science* 43(4), 296–304.

Xu, C., Ouyang, F., and Chu, H. (2009). The academic library meets Web 2.0: Applications and implications. *The Journal of Academic Librarianship* 35(4), 324–331.

E-Government and Public Access Computers in Public Libraries

Diane L. Velasquez

Graduate School of Library & Information Science, Dominican University, River Forest, IL, USA

Abstract

This chapter presents results of a survey conducted over the summer of 2009 to 1485 libraries that serve populations of 25,000–100,000 in the United States about Internet connected public access computers and e-government. The methodology used was a mixed-methods questionnaire using 33 closed ended and three qualitative questions. The main finding was that public library staff do not have enough training in e-government and government documents to help patrons with their questions on these topics. Another aspect of the survey was to find out whether public libraries plan, fund, and allocate monies for computer hardware and software in their budgets.

The limitation of the research was the size of the libraries and the results can only be generalized to this group of libraries. There could be a bias by size of library and the way the questions were worded. The practical implications of the research indicate that future librarians in library and information science programs are unaware of the need to take either government information or e-government courses. Recent emerging roles for the public library includes being the freely available place to access e-government information in lieu of the actual federal, state, or local agencies.

I. Introduction

This chapter presents the results of a research project with a mixed-methods questionnaire designed to discover how e-government has influenced the usage of Internet connected public access computers (PACs) in 1485 U.S. public libraries that serve populations of 25,000–100,000 (Chute, *et al.*, 2006; Hennen, 2008; U.S. Census Bureau, 2009b). This particular population, according to previous research, has approximately an average of 12 PACs and has been affected by the e-government movement (Bertot *et al.*, 2009). Libraries of this size tend to have approximately 8–10 full-time employees and 10–20 part-time employees (Velasquez, 2007). In the United

EXPLORING THE DIGITAL FRONTIER
ADVANCES IN LIBRARIANSHIP, VOL. 32
© 2010 by Emerald Group Publishing Limited
ISSN: 0065-2830
DOI: 10.1108/S0065-2830(2010)0000032008

States, there are approximately 1485 main libraries (with no branches) that serve the identified population. The entire group received a survey designed to discover whether there are any marked differences between libraries in different geographic locations (by being in either a rural, suburban, or urban area).

A. Definitions

E-government is defined as "technology, particularly the Internet, to enhance the access to and delivery of government information and services to citizens, business, government employees, and other agencies" (Hernon *et al.*, 2002; Jaeger, 2003; Roy, 2003). Another way e-government is described is as a communication between the government and its citizens via computers and a web-enabled telecommunication Internet device (Evans and Yen, 2006; Jaeger, 2003; Roy, 2003).

PACs, for this chapter, are defined as Internet-connected PCs that serve the public. These can be PCs or Apple Macintoshes, but in public libraries, the tendency is for the computers to be PCs with a Microsoft Windows or Linux operating system. On the basis of the research reported in this chapter, the majority of libraries had either some combination of Microsoft Office Suite (Word, Excel, etc.) or Open Office software.

The digital divide has been defined as "patterns of unequal access to information technology based on income, race, ethnicity, gender, age, and geography that surfaced during the mid-1990s" (Mossberger *et al.*, 2003, p. 1). Digital literacy for this chapter will be defined as those individuals with the basic skills necessary to traverse the Internet to conduct searches for information.

B. Literature Review

E-government in the United States has become a new standard for finding federal and state government information. The E-Government Act (P.L. 107-347) mandated the use of e-government for the dissemination of government information and changed the way federal departments and agencies interacted with citizens. One of the ways the agencies and departments changed was to send their clients to the local public library to access desired information because the civil servants knew that free Internet-connected PACs would be available there. The public libraries, however, were not being funded by the federal government for this new role. The literature supports that the public library has taken on this new role as an unfunded mandate by the state and federal governments (Jaeger and Fleischmann, 2007;

Jaeger *et al.*, 2006a). According to Gibson *et al.* (2008), this new model makes the state agencies, in this particular case, more cost effective in providing information to their customers.

Part of this new role that public libraries have begun to take on is training their patrons on how to access and use e-government information (Jaeger and Bertot, 2009). Many public librarians did not get instruction and training in their Library and Information Science (LIS) master's degree during course work (Jaeger, 2008). Many patrons do not have access to broadband services in their home. According to a report by the Pew Institute and American Life Project, only 63% of adults have broadband Internet connections at home (Horrigan, 2009a). Access to e-government forms and documents may be only on the government agency or department web site. For example, Federal Emergency Management Agency (FEMA) only accepts forms via their web site. FEMA's acceptance of their forms only by an e-government web portal became well-known after Hurricanes Katrina, Rita, and others in the gulf coast of the United States in 2004 (Jaeger *et al.*, 2006b). Those who were in the Gulf Coast at the time of the hurricanes in 2004 and 2005 related that some public libraries were open 24 hours a day to accommodate the public's need to use the Internet connected computers (E. Bodewes, 2009, personal communication). Some of the services provided by the public libraries in the hurricane-hit communities included:

1. Downloading and filing forms with FEMA and their personal home insurance companies;
2. Trying to find information about the condition of their homes and workplaces;
3. Contacting family members that were missing, evacuated or displaced; and
4. Checking for news and updates about evacuated communities in (Jaeger *et al.*, 2006a, b; E. Bodewes, 2009, personal communication).

The ability to use Internet access in the public library when no one else in the community had connectivity was a vital life-line during the hurricanes.

The recession of 2008–2010 has created an interesting dichotomy between funding and services. The funding agencies need to cut their budgets in light of the downward spiral of tax revenues. For instance, in Illinois there has been a decrease in property taxes. Many of the public libraries receive their tax payments from property tax payments. When the revenue goes down, their incoming revenue payments decrease (Miller, 2010; Oder, 2010; Bundy, 2009; Martell, 2009). This decrease in turn causes the city's or county's general fund to be reduced which in turn creates fewer dollars to be divided among the departments including libraries. The dichotomy comes from the fact that circulation, PAC usage, and programming are continuing to see record numbers of patrons. So service is up but revenues are down. How do you pay for increasing needs with decreasing funds? As can be seen in weekly American Library Association (ALA) newsletters, libraries are laying off staff, decreasing hours, or closing branches. None of this is what the patrons want but this is the classic definition of a catch-22 (Miller, 2010; Oder, 2010; Bundy, 2009; Martell, 2009).

When looking at e-government, government information and documents, all of which are available through Internet access, takes only a computer (laptop, net book, or desk top computer) and a telecommunications connection (dial up, DSL, cable modem, etc.). The next thing the patrons need to have to be able to access the information via a web browser is the information needed to connect to local, state, or federal agencies. What if the person who is attempting to find this information has a barrier? The digital divide is still alive and well in our society but according to the Pew Internet and American Family Life studies, the gap is closing. This digital divide gap is closing in an interesting way with cell phone users who can access the Internet. African-Americans and Latinos, in particular, are heavier cell phone users than whites according to Pew Internet and American Family Life studies (Fox and Livingston, 2007; Horrigan, 2009b).

In the report entitled "Latinos Online," when looking at the entire population of Latinos, both English language–dominant and Spanish-dominant, the summary of findings stated that "Latinos comprise 14% of the U.S. adult population and about half of this growing group (56%) goes online" (Fox and Livingston, 2007, p. 1). When the Latinos are Spanish-dominant, this number drops to 32% of adults (Fox & Livingston).

The 2009 Pew Internet reported entitled "Wireless Internet Use" looks at laptops and cell phone access to the Internet through wireless access. There has been an increase in wireless usage from 24% in December 2007 to 32% in April 2009 according to Horrigan (2009b):

> African Americans are the most active users of the mobile internet—and their use of it is also growing the fastest. This means the digital divide between African Americans and white Americans diminishes when mobile use is taken into account. (p. 4)

The report states the at least 48% of African Americans have used the Internet at least once using their mobile device (Horrigan, 2009b). The ability to use smart phones or cell phones to access the Internet narrows the gap in the digital divide. The use of mobile devices to access the Internet also has implications for broadband uses.

According to a report issued in April 2010 entitled "Government Online," the report states that "40% of Americans have gone online for data about the business of government" (Smith, 2010, p. 3). In the summary of the finding, Smith reports that "Fully 82% of internet users (representing

61% of all American adults) looked for information or completed a transaction on a government website in the twelve months preceding this survey" (p. 12).

This research examined Internet connectivity using only PACs in public libraries. The survey was sent out to library directors and asked very specific questions. Nothing in the survey asked about the digital divide or digital literacy but inadvertently those issues arose. In the comment section, survey respondents made remarks about the skill level of those looking for e-government sites or government information. The skill level tended to be beginners or less. That informed, in part, the previous literature review.

II. Methodology

The research used a mixed-methods questionnaire that contained a total of 35 questions sent to a purposive sample of public libraries determined to be single public libraries not affiliated with a larger system that served a population between 25,000 to less than 100,000. These libraries were chosen through the *American Library Directory* and Hennen's American Public Library Ratings, which show populations served (Hennen, 2008; American Library Directory, 2008). The population was verified through the U.S. Census Bureau for each city where there were variations in population between the *American Library Directory* and Hennen's data (U.S. Census Bureau, 2009b). Any public library where the population was either under 25,000 or over 100,000 was eliminated from the list.

Surveys were sent via U.S. mail to 1485 public library directors and 843 completed responses were received, for a 56.8% response rate. Of the 843 completed responses returned, 832 were useable. The useable surveys had answered the majority (more than 94%) of the questions. The 11 that were eliminated had blocks of questions that were not answered, and these were deemed inadequate for the resulting analysis. When the surveys were sent out the cover letter stated that respondents had the option to be removed from future mailings and 48 or 3.2% chose that option. As the mailing was sent out twice, there were 19 or 1.3% duplicate responses. There were a total of 912 or 61.4% responses of some kind from two mailings sent out six weeks apart.

The survey instrument included questions that requested information regarding Internet-connected PACs such as how the computers were acquired, how often the PACs were replaced, and how funding was allocated for both hardware and software. Information was asked about wireless fidelity (Wi-Fi) connectivity as well. General information was requested about the type of software installed on computers and one question asked about computers in the children's and/or young adult (YA) sections of the library.

Current research showed that many libraries are not ready for the onslaught of services that need to be provided for patrons with the transference of services from federal and state agencies to the local public library (Jaeger, 2008; Jaeger and Bertot, 2009). Likert-type scale questions were included about assumptions regarding e-government and government documents librarians and staff. The respondents chose a level of agreement with the statement "My library has adequate training on e-government and government documents in today's environment." Other questions asked for general information on government documents and e-government processes and procedures that occur in the library.

Another portion of the survey asked about whether there was a librarian position designated to deal specifically with government information. Several questions asked respondents whether they ever had to look for e-government information and, if so, they were asked to comment on the difficulty of the search. The respondents could indicate which "in their opinion" e-government agencies and department web sites were being used in their library. Some state and federal agencies and departments were listed in the questionnaire, and the respondents were asked to check the ones being used. Respondents were also given the opportunity to add any department sites that were not listed. Individuals answering the survey were asked to provide some general demographic information which included position title, gender, age, and educational level.

On the back of the survey form respondents had the opportunity to comment on concerns they have about e-government, PACs, and anything else they thought relevant. Many respondents took the time to make comments about e-government and PACs in their libraries. Quite a few made comments regarding the unfunded mandate and e-government in relationship to library layoffs and tight staffing and funding.

Survey response variables were categorical or ordinal with the exception of the questions asking about the number of PACs and the number of increased PACs (if there were any). Basic descriptive results are presented below for answers to most of the close-ended questions.

III. Results

Of the 843 surveys returned, there were 832 useable results. The beginning of the survey looked at how the public libraries acquired their PACs. The question asked whether libraries purchased or had their computers donated to the institution. A majority of 537 (64.5%) purchased new computers that are used in their libraries. The minority of 244 (29.3%) of the group used a combination of donations and purchasing to acquire their computers. Only 18 (2.2%) used donations alone. The remainder of 33 (4.4%) used a combination of ways to acquire computers such as lease, purchase, grant funding, and donations.

How often a computer is replaced is something each public library has to consider for itself. Many times purchase is contingent on available funds to replace the Internet access computers. In the survey a wide range of years for replacement were given by the respondents. Table 1 shows that the majority of the public libraries (494, 59.4%) in the sample replace their public computers every 4–5 years.

The survey also asked about computer conditions: Was it brand new, out of the box, or refurbished? Many times a library will purchase a refurbished machine because it is a little cheaper and have more options such as extra RAM or a larger hard drive. Despite expecting to see high numbers of refurbished purchases, it turned out that most public libraries in this group purchased their computers brand new as shown in Table 2.

Another aspect of providing Internet access to the public is Wi-Fi connectivity. Many public libraries find it easier to install Wi-Fi in their facility than to install more PACs because of space shortages in the building, lack of surfaces on which to put workstations, or an inadequate wiring infrastructure (Bertot *et al.*, 2009). Respondents in this study indicated that 93% (774) have Wi-Fi. The remaining 58 libraries that responded to the survey said that their library did not currently have Wi-Fi. Of those

Table 1
Replacement of Internet-Connected Public Access Computers

Time frame	Number ($n = 832$)	%
0–3 years	192	23.1
4–5 years	494	59.4
6–8 years	97	11.7
9–10 years	10	1.2
11+ years	3	0.4
As needed	11	1.3
Never	12	1.4
Didn't answer question	13	1.5
Total	*832*	*100.0*

Table 2
Type of Internet-Connected Public Access Computers Purchased

	Number ($n = 832$)	%
New	690	82.9
Refurbished	28	3.4
Donation	16	1.9
Other (combination of new, refurbished, and donation)	98	9.0
Didn't answer question	23	2.8
Total	*832*	*100.0*

58 libraries, 39 (67.2%) reported that they intend to move forward with plans to install Wi-Fi in the near future.

In response to the one question which asked about Internet connectivity of PACs in either the children's or YA section, a majority or 617 (74.2%) reported having Internet-connected computers in their children's or YA sections.

A. Allocation of Funds

When purchasing new computers or upgrading software, adequate funding is necessary. How do the libraries fund the purchase of computers or upgrading software? There are two ways public libraries typically fund these needs: grants or their normal budget lines. The ability to fund through the budget and to try to replace the computers every three or four years is something the directors have tried to do, but they have found it increasingly difficult to do with budgets being reduced. The libraries surveyed which have funded both replacement computers and upgraded software through their regular budgets as can be seen below in Tables 3 and 4.

B. Software on PACs

The software available on the computers in the public library determines the kind of productivity that patrons will have when they visit. One of the most interesting aspects of U.S. public libraries is that the majority have some kind of reservation system and time limit associated with their PACs to manage the peak user times (Bertot *et al.*, 2009). Libraries that do not have a software system to manage time limits and reservations, do it manually

Table 3
Budgeted Funds Allocated to Replace Computers

Funds allocated	Number (*n* = 832)	%
No	138	16.5
Yes	686	82.5
Didn't answer question	8	1.0
Total	*832*	*100.0*

Table 4
Budgeted Funds Allocated to Upgrade Software

Funds allocated	Number (*n* = 832)	%
No	103	12.4
Yes	721	86.7
Didn't answer question	8	0.9
Total	*832*	*100.0*

taking up scarce staff time (Bertot *et al.*, 2009; Velasquez, 2007). Sometimes a decision has to be made regarding the cost of the software system to manage the reservations and time limits versus staff productivity. This issue then becomes a management issue about the best use of staff productivity and taxpayers' money.

In the United Sates, the PC platform is prevalent in public libraries. The Apple Macintosh computer or "Mac" has a very small percentage of the public library market. The question regarding software on PACs was, therefore, focused on the PC platform and asked about common software that most businesses, schools, universities, and colleges tend to use. Microsoft Office products (MS Word, Excel, Power Point, etc.) are the standard for most businesses and other institutions. The same is true of the public libraries in this study with 782 (94%) of the respondents using some version of the Microsoft Office Suite.

The respondents were offered a list of software and asked to check off all software loaded on their PACs at the time of the survey. There were two well-known choices for web browsers at the time the survey was written—Internet Explorer and Mozilla Firefox. Microsoft's Internet Explorer was the browser of choice for 782 (94%) of the respondents. Firefox had 366 (44%)

of the respondents. The interesting aspect about browsers is that it is not an "either/or" choice but a library can choose both.

Questions about various Adobe products were asked, but only one product was used by a majority of the public libraries responding to the survey. That was Adobe Reader, which is a free product, and was loaded onto PACs by 714 (86%) of the respondents. Two other Adobe products asked about were Photoshop in use by 57 libraries (7%) and Adobe Professional used in 56 libraries (7%). In short, neither was widely used in the size of public libraries that responded to the survey.

The last type of software asked about was antivirus software. With a PC platform, antivirus software is critical. An assumption was made by the researcher that either MacAfee or Norton would be a default choice but only 482 (58%) used either of those brands for antivirus protection. If the respondents did not choose either MacAfee or Norton, many of them chose not to state their antivirus protection.

C. E-Government Impact in the Library

The E-Government Act of 2002 changed the role of the public library in U.S. society and libraries became the "go to" place for patrons to procure e-government information. One of the major barriers to access is that the E-Government Act, as mentioned previously, is an unfunded mandate by the federal government to public libraries. This unfunded mandate has created stress on public libraries because no attendant support, financial or other, has been forthcoming. Public libraries have had to absorb both a new financial burden as well as the additional load on an already overburdened staff. The financial burden shifted from the federal and state agencies and departments to the public libraries and this burden has not had a reciprocal increase in federal and state funding to public libraries (Gibson *et al.*, 2008).

This shift is challenging public libraries and the burden falls on the library's librarians and staff. However, e-government services may not be something all librarians have been trained to access. Some librarians may have taken a class in government documents or have a glancing acquaintance with an e-government web site through a policy or general reference class. The lightweight training that has been previously the norm for most future librarians in LIS programs will not be enough when they are on the job and being asked the hard questions. Government web sites are not intuitive and can often be difficult to traverse.

On the survey, Likert-type questions focused on patron service, librarian training, and navigating e-government sites. The kinds of questions that patrons ask are not something that can be ascertained through a survey.

That type of question can be better determined through one-on-one interviews or focus group sessions. The majority of respondents (706 or 85%) disagreed that patrons never used e-government. When 85% of the respondents reported that patrons use e-government sources, there should be finding aids available. Finding aids can be as simple as bookmarks on web pages. Only 299 (36%) had pathfinders or other finding aids available to assist their patrons on their library web pages.

Training librarians and staff in e-government, as mentioned earlier, is a gnawing concern. The lack of training is evident be it in LIS programs or on-the-job training. There were three different questions asked about training, and all respondents felt that more training of librarians and other staff is needed on e-government and government documents. Table 5 illustrates the answers to those questions. It is telling that most respondents felt that both formal and other training is considered highly inadequate. Too often, when staff members are pushed to do more with less, their in-house and informal training opportunities diminish.

If the library is a member of the Federal Depository Library Program (FDLP) that is administered by the Government Printing Program (GPO), it might possibly have someone who is a dedicated e-government librarian. The number of public libraries in the U.S. that participate in the FDLP was 216, which is only 17.5% of the 1237 total member libraries. (GPO, 2010).

The survey asked the respondents whether there was a dedicated position to deal with e-government and government e-information. The majority, or 700 (84%), of the respondents reported that they did not have any one employee whose sole position was to work with e-government information.

Another question asked was whether the respondents were concerned by their own personal need to find government information. More than 90% of the respondents reported that they have had to find a government document for their own use. A follow-up question asked about the difficulty in finding the e-government sources. Many librarians who do not normally work with e-government information sometimes find working with the different web sites challenging. The question had a range on a varying scale of difficulty from easy to impossible. The majority of the participants or 67% (559) felt there was a slight difficulty in looking for government information on web sites.

D. E-Government Sites Accessed

The survey asked the participants to mark which e-government sites "in their opinion" are typically used in their library. Table 6 sets out the responses to the question.

Table 5
E-Government in the Library

Statement (n = 832)	Strongly disagree		Disagree		No opinion		Agree		Strongly agree	
	#	%	#	%	#	%	#	%	#	%
Most MLIS holding librarians take a government documents course	94	11.3	456	54.8	54	6.5	217	26.1	11	1.3
My library has adequate training on e-government and government documents in today's environment	94	11.3	517	62.1	14	1.7	197	23.7	10	1.2
The librarians and staff need training on e-government and government documents to assist our patron	9	1.1	141	16.9	7	0.8	572	68.8	103	12.4
Patrons never use e-government	202	24.3	507	60.9	17	2.0	96	11.5	10	1.2
Librarians do not like government documents	165	19.8	489	58.9	20	2.4	146	17.5	11	1.3
Our library has a good pathfinder or other location features on federal and state government documents	87	10.5	424	51.0	21	2.5	279	33.5	21	2.5
Federal government forms like tax forms can be easily obtained from the government agencies	87	10.5	191	23.0	10	1.2	399	48.0	145	17.4
The library does not have enough public access computers to handle the demand of e-government along with the other uses the public makes at the library	133	16.0	408	49.0	11	1.3	218	26.2	62	7.5

Table 6
E-Government Sites Most Often Requested

Web site	Number ($n = 832$)	%[1]
Internal Revenue Service (IRS)	814	98
Unemployment	506	61
USA Jobs	472	57
Social Security Administration	460	55
Medicare	334	40
Election Information	224	27
Welfare	180	22
Congressional Bills	90	11
White House & the President	78	9
Congress	76	9
Library of Congress	67	8
Aid for Families	55	7
Smithsonian Institution	12	1

[1]Will not equal 100% as respondents could choose more than one answer.

The Internal Revenue Service's (IRS) web site was the number one e-government site accessed. There were general comments made by the some of the respondents that patrons are accessing e-government sites during the busy tax season from January 1 to April 15 of each calendar year.

The respondents were able to write in other e-government web sites that are often asked about in their libraries if the sites were not on the list. While not all the public libraries contributed to the list, Table 7 gives a list of the most common ones added. Each site listed here had to be mentioned a minimum of three times.

The final question in this section was whether or not the respondents had discussed e-government with their colleagues in the public library. The majority or 489 (59%) of those answering the survey reported that did not have conversations with the staff in the library about e-government.

E. Librarian and Patron Skill Sets for E-Government

In the open comment section of the survey, many of the libraries reported having concerns about e-government sites in general. Web site design and navigation of the sites were some of the main complaints. The ability to traverse a government site takes practice and skill. Some web sites seem to change with some regularity such as that of the Census Bureau. All the

Table 7
E-Government Sites Added

Web sites

Court documents
Free Application for Federal Student Aid (FAFSA)
Immigration
Local (City & County) Government Information
Medline & Pub Med
National Park Service
Passports
State Civil Codes
State Drivers License Information
State Government Information
State Tax Codes
U.S. Census Bureau
United States Code (USC)

---

open comments are reported here verbatim with no grammatical corrections or changes.

Most respondents mentioned that the IRS' site is one that most of them use. The site itself has changed over the past year and is reputedly less user friendly than it used to be. One suggestion was for the IRS was: "My vision of the "perfect" IRS service would be an "automatically delivered to all public libraries" COMPLETE set of publications and forms in "reproducible" format, accompanied by an equally complete web site." While this particular respondent appeared to be hoping for a utopian vision of the IRS web site, the changes at the site and the lack of delivery of the major U.S. tax forms to public libraries has caused problems for them. In the not so recent past, public libraries could order paper copies of federal tax forms but unless they are on a list maintained by the IRS, they can no longer order paper forms. Other respondents mentioned problems with state tax sites.

A number of respondents commented that there are "those who will always mistrust electronic sources." The naiveté of someone who mistrusts electronic sources are people who are not accustomed to working with them on a regular basis. Some of the respondents mentioned that "I don't think the public is aware of e-government websites." Another made a similar comment with the caveat that as time goes on, more and more patrons will need to access documents, forms, and information online.

Unsurprisingly, many respondents commented that patrons who need to access e-government forms and information have little or few computer skills. Here is a smattering of comments:

1. "Library staff almost always have to help patrons. They (the patron) usually are not equipped to do this themselves."
2. "Many e-govt. websites are next to impossible for library patrons to navigate—these sites appear to be created by tech savvy people, not for "normal" folks!"
3. "Many (patrons) have never used a computer before."
4. "We could use trained individuals to help patron's access e-documents."
5. "The public has about three clicks to any website when looking for information before they quit looking."
6. "Our experience is that it is typically difficult to locate gov. documents online, and that it requires considerable expertise."
7. "Our biggest concern is the constant expectation by govt. that they can cut direct interface w/public and the public can "do it" at the library—library staff is untrained in specifics of unemployment and emergency food stamp registration, but despite repeated attempt to work with LA Workforce Comm and other agencies, they leave us to serve the public untrained and with no contact for problems that develop."
8. "The patrons using public access computers to obtain govt. information, primarily forms, generally have limited or no computer skills, requiring a level of individualized assistance not feasible in a regular work day."
9. "That many people don't have the computer skills needed to manipulate the site/forms/info AND much of the information is personal or sensitive in nature, making it difficult for staff to act as a go-between."
10. "Most patrons require staff help to find what they need. They either cannot use the Internet or cannot find correct website or webpage. Many have no computer experience at all."
11. "Many of our users are not computer literate to the extent required to fill out forms, save, print, etc. Our staff spends much time assisting people—attempting to translate "gov language" for patrons, etc."

The digital divide is a hard reality in the United States. According to "Information Searches that Solve Problems" by the Pew Internet and American Life Project, those with limited or no access to the Internet are older, less affluent, and less well educated (Rainie *et al.*, 2007). Of the three indicators mentioned—age, income, and education in the Pew study—age is the strongest indicator to determine whether or not Internet connectivity is important (Rainie *et al.*). Income below $40,000 and education beyond high school are the remaining factors (Rainie *et al.*).

The need to train public library patrons was not an unexpected finding. Many of those needing to use government information besides tax forms may need a Medicare Part D Prescription form or may be looking for a job and, for the first time in their lives, using the Internet. The current economic recession of 2008–2010 has displaced many workers who have not had to look for a job since computers have become a reality in our society.

Table 8
Community of the Public Library

	Number ($n = 832$)	%
Rural	302	36.3
Suburban	366	44.0
Urban	157	18.9
Decline to State	7	0.8
Total	*832*	*100.0*

Searching for employment has changed dramatically in our current culture. Many employers only accept applications via the Internet. This entails preparing a resume on a word processing program, having an email account, and then sending it to employers via email. The online job search process can be brand new for someone who is looking for a job for the first time in 20 years.

F. Demographics of Participants

Respondents to the survey were asked to self characterize the library as rural, suburban, or urban. A small number chose to decline to identify their community type (Table 8).

To determine who was filling out the survey, each respondent was asked to voluntarily give their gender, an age range, and the highest educational degree they had obtained. The majority of the participants did this. There were some who declined to state some of this information. Information on the demographics of the individuals who filled out the survey is given in Table 9.

IV. Discussion

To broaden the view on e-government, the researcher focused on one section of the public library population in the United States and sent the survey to that entire population of single public libraries and not systems. As with any research project, some library systems inadvertently made it into the data set.

The findings agree with literature in the field that there needs to be more training of public library staff so that they can better assist the patrons coming into the public library. Jaeger has written on librarian e-government

Table 9
Demographic Information

	Number ($n = 832$)	%
Gender		
Female	563	67.7
Male	252	30.3
Declined to state	17	2.0
Total by Gender	*832*	*100.0*
Age		
20–29 years	19	2.3
30–39 years	82	9.9
40–49 years	153	18.4
50–59 years	377	45.3
60–69 years	173	20.8
70+ years	5	0.6
Declined to state	23	2.8
Total by Age	*832*	*100.0*
Education		
Some college	22	2.6
Graduated from college	26	3.1
Some graduate education	29	3.5
Master's degree in another field	15	1.8
MLIS/MLS	712	85.6
PhD/EdD	16	1.9
Other	6	0.7
Decline to State	6	0.7
Total by Education	*832*	*100.0*

education and the survey results agree with his findings as well (Jaeger and Bertot, 2009; Jaeger, 2008). When combining the strongly disagree and disagree results together, 66% of the respondents disagree with the statement that "Most MLIS holding librarians take a government documents course." There were two statements on the survey that are in Table 10 that combine the strongly disagree and disagree numbers and the strongly agree and agree numbers.

The comments that respondents made on the back of the survey forms also mentioned the need for librarian and staff training about e-government.

Table 10

Public Librarians Needing Training

Statement ($n = 832$)	Strongly disagree/disagree		No opinion		Strongly agree/agree	
	#	%	#	%	#	%
Most MLIS holding librarians take a government documents course	550	66.1	54	6.5	228	27.4
My library has adequate training on e-government and government documents in today's environment	611	73.4	14	1.7	207	24.9
The librarians and staff need training in e-government and government documents to assist our patrons	150	18.0	7	0.8	675	81.1

Some state libraries have e-government training but evidently some respondents did not feel that was enough. The other aspect of training that goes hand-in-hand with staff training is the need for training of the public.

Many of the respondents noted that the patrons who come in to use e-government had little or no computer skills. One of the participants mentioned that "Last month our suburban library hosted over 6500 user sessions on public access computers. This month the total will be higher." Teaching patrons how to use a computer is time consuming; learning how to access e-government sources on top of that can take even more time than a librarian may have available, particularly in a busy library. Increasing the level of patron computer literacy is something the LIS profession is concerned about in general, not just with e-government issues. E-government literacy must be increased for staff and librarians because as time goes by, more and more federal, state, local, and international information will be pushed out via the Internet and the world wide web.

It was also mentioned in the open comments that there had been layoffs by some of the libraries. Librarians are working with patrons who have little or no computer skills, who need to fill out government forms that can sometimes be complicated, and the library staff may not have the time, patience, or training to deal with the situation. Another difficulty is that the number of Internet-connected PACs may be limited and the time limit each patron has per day may be as little as 30 minutes with the maximum being only be an hour or two. Can someone walking in off the street who does not have an email address, little or no experience with a computer, and needs to find and fill out a complicated state or federal government form do so in an hour? Can everything this patron needs to be done happen in an hour or two? Perhaps not. I would say probably not!

V. Conclusion

This study on e-government and Internet-connected PAC was informative in that it answered questions about staff and patron training. The survey also provided insight into what type of e-government sites that are being accessed in public libraries. Clearly public libraries serving a population of 25,000–100,000 have challenges in providing e-government services to their patrons. The size of the community, staffing levels, and the number of computers available, all influence the type and depth of services and assistance a patron receives when working on a PAC.

The study of this size and type of public library, while providing answers to the questions in the survey, created more questions that need to be answered either by another survey or through face to face qualitative means. The desire to provide services to patrons that encompasses computer literacy and e-government (including government documents) is commendable but in these tight economic times but the question that emerges is how long can public libraries provide and sustain this service? As can be seen in the library literature as well as newspapers and magazines, cities, counties, and states are under severe budget constraints and in many ways, libraries are being seen as a luxury item (ALA, 2010). Curiously the movement of e-government provision to the public library from state and federal agencies as an unfunded mandate just exacerbates an already tenuous situation where there are staffing, technology, and funding issues (ALA, 2010). The resolution is obvious—increased funding—but from where?

Research is also needed to determine what patrons believe they need when it comes to Internet-connected PACs. What librarians believe they need and what patrons think may be very different. Patrons are given access to an Internet computer with no input into the type of software that is made available. Patrons also need more training but again, they need to be asked what they perceive to be needed. Again, what library staff offer is usually based on their own assumptions.

Future research into the connection between reading literacy, computer or digital literacy, and the digital divide is another aspect of PACs and public libraries that needs exploration. While there is contention that the United States has a highly literate population, is this really true? To use a computer and access web sites, one needs to be able to read at better than an eighth grade level. Government web sites can sometimes be unintelligible unless one understands government jargon and legalese. The language in which the web site is created can place another unintentional barrier into the digital divide stemming from the assumption that everyone is well educated. When looking at the American Community Survey (2009a), it shows that all adults over 25 years 6.4% have less than a 9th grade education and 9.1% have less than a 12th grade. Adults who have not graduated high school is one of the groups less likely to want to get online according to Horrigan's (2009b) research at Pew and the FCC's "Broadband Adoption and Use in America" (Horrigan, 2010). The other groups who tend not to go online are those who have just graduated high school and those over the age of 65 (Horrigan, 2009b, 2010; U.S. Census Bureau, 2009a).

The last aspect of looking at the digital divide is ethnicity, age, and income. In the past, those three indicators have made a difference in whether or not someone has a computer and Internet connection (broadband or dial-up) at home. However, current research from the Pew Internet is showing that some changes in thinking need to be made (Horrigan, 2009b). Smart phones and other mobile devices are able to access the wireless Internet as well as regular computers (Horrigan, 2009b). African Americans comprise the largest group that use mobile devices to access the Internet, with Latinos following closely behind (Horrigan, 2009b).

Another area for future research is in the education and training of librarians. The education of future librarians who are either considering programs at LIS schools or those in current programs need to be revised in light of e-government. Anyone thinking about becoming a public librarian needs to carefully consider their program of study. Continuing education needs for those who are public librarians or staff needs to be researched. The e-government phenomenon is relatively new and many current library staff members who have not been trained about it, need to be. The provision of e-government training is another question that needs to be asked and answered—including who will provide it and pay for it?

Acknowledgments

This research, done over the summer of 2009, was funded through a faculty development grant from Dominican University. This study would not have been possible if not for the assistance from my graduate assistant, Sheila Cody. The other person I have to thank is my colleague, Dr. Janice M. Del Negro, who edited the chapter prior to submission and assisted by making everything read better.

References

American Library Association. (2010). *State of America's Libraries—2010*. American Library Association, Chicago. Retrieved from http://www.ala.org/ala/newspresscenter/mediapresscenter/americaslibraries/ALA_Report_2010-ATI001-NEW1.pdf

American Library Directory. (2008). 61st ed., Information Today, Medford, NJ.

Bertot, J. C., McClure, C. R., Wright, C. B., Jensen, E., and Thomas, S. (2009). *Public Libraries and the Internet 2008: Study Results and Findings*. Florida State University, Information Institute, College of Information, Tallahassee, FL.

Bundy, A. (2009). The economic downturn—challenge and opportunity for public libraries? *APLIS* 22(1), 3–5.

Chute, A., Kroe, P. E., O'shea, P., Craig, T., Freeman, M., Hardesty, L., et al. (2006). *Public Libraries in the United States: Fiscal Year 2004*. National Center for Education Statistics, Institution of Education Sciences, Library Statistics Program, U.S. Department of Education, Washington, DC.

E-Government Act of 2002, P. L. 107-347.

Evans, D., and Yen, D. C. (2006). E-government: Evolving relationship of citizens, government, domestic, and international development. *Government Information Quarterly* 23(2), 207–235.

Fox, S., and Livingston, G. (2007). *Latinos Online: Hispanics with Lower Levels of Education and English Proficiency Remain Largely Disconnected from the Internet*. Pew Hispanic Center and Pew Internet Project, Washington, DC. Retrieved from www.pewhispanic.org

Gibson, A., McClure, C. R., Bertot, J. C., McGilvray, J., and Andrade, J. (2008). Community leadership through public library e-government services. *Florida Libraries* 51(1), 5–7.

Government Printing Office. (2010). *Federal Depository Library Directory*. Retrieved from http://www.gpo.gov

Hennen, T. J. (2008). *Hennen's American Public Library Ratings*. Retrieved from http://www.haplr-index.com/index.html

Hernon, P., Reylea, H. C., Dugan, R. E., and Cheverie, J. F. (2002). *United States Government Information: Policies and Sources*. Libraries Unlimited, Westport, CT.

Horrigan, J. (2009a). *Home Broadband Adoption 2009: Broadband Adoption Increases but Monthly Prices Go up too, June 2009*. Pew Internet & American Life Project, Washington, DC. Retrieved from http://pewinternet.org/Reports/2009/10-Home-Broadband-Adoption-2009.aspx

Horrigan, J. (2009b). *Wireless Internet Use: More than Half of Americans—56%—Have Accessed the Internet Wirelessly on Some Device, such as a Laptop, Cell Phone, MP3 Player, or Game Console*. Pew Internet & American Life Project, Washington, DC. Retrieved from http://pewinternet.org/Reports/2009/12-Wireless-Internet-Use.aspx

Horrigan, J. B. (2010). *Broadband Adoption and Use in America: OBI*. Working Paper Series No. 1. Federal Communications Commission, Washington, DC. Retrieved from www.fcc.gov

Jaeger, P. T. (2003). The endless wire: E-government as global phenomenon. *Government Information Quarterly* 20(4), 323–331.

Jaeger, P. T. (2008). Building e-government into the library and information science curriculum: The future of government information and services. *Journal of Education for Library and Information Science* 49(3), 167–179.

Jaeger, P. T., and Bertot, J. C. (2009). E-government education in public libraries: New service roles and expanding social responsibilities. *Journal of Education for Library and Information Science* 50(1), 39–49.

Jaeger, P. T., and Fleischmann, K. R. (2007). Public libraries, values, trust, and e-government. *Information Technology and Libraries* 26(4), 34–43.

Jaeger, P. T., Bertot, J. C., McClure, C. R., and Langa, L. A. (2006a). The policy implications of internet connectivity in public libraries. *Government Information Quarterly* 23, 123–141.

Jaeger, P. T., Langa, L. A., McClure, C. R., and Bertot, J. C. (2006b). The 2004 and 2005 Gulf Coast hurricanes: Evolving roles and lessons learned for public libraries in disaster preparedness and community services. *Public Library Quarterly* 25(3/4), 199–214.

Martell, C. (2009). Hanging tough at our neighborhood libraries. *Public Library Quarterly* 28, 336–343.

Miller, R. (2010). Fundraising in the downturn. *Library Journal* 135(1), 48–50.

Mossberger, K., Tolbert, C. J., and Stansbury, M. (2003). *Virtual Inequality: Beyond the Digital Divide*. Georgetown University Press, Washington, DC.

Oder, N. (2010). Permanent shift? As many libraries are hit by gloomy times, they're challenged to offer less and work differently. *Library Journal* 135(1), 44–46.

Rainie, L., Estabrook, L., and Witt, E. (2007). *Information Searches that Solve Problems*. Pew Internet & American Life Project, Washington, DC. Retrieved from www.pewinternet.org

Roy, J. (2003). Introduction: E-government. *Social Science Computer Review* 21(1), 3–5.

Smith, A. (2010). *Government Online: The Internet gives Citizens New Paths to Government Services and Information*. Pew Internet & American Life Project, Washington, DC. Retrieved on April 27, 2010, from http://pewinternet.org/Reports/2010/Government-Online.aspx

U.S. Census Bureau. (2009a). *American Community Survey 2006–2008, United States*. Retrieved from http://www.census.gov

U.S. Census Bureau. (2009b). *American Fact Finder*. Retrieved from http://www.census.gov

Velasquez, D. L. (2007). *The Impact of Technology on Organizational Change in Public Libraries: A Qualitative Study*. Ph.D. dissertation (Publication No. AAT 3349069), University of Missouri, Columbia, MO.

Knowledge Organization,
Management and Policy Issues

Social Semantic Corporate Digital Libraries: Joining Knowledge Representation and Knowledge Management

Wolfgang G. Stock, Isabella Peters and Katrin Weller
Department of Information Science, Heinrich-Heine-University,
Düsseldorf, Germany

Abstract

Through a theoretical review of the literature, this chapter assesses the potential of different knowledge organisation systems (KOS) to support corporate knowledge management systems (KMS), namely digital libraries (DL) in companies and other institutions. Questions are framed through which the chapter discusses how classical KOS, such as nomenclatures, classification systems, thesauri and ontologies, are able to reflect explicit knowledge in sense of the Semantic Web and also introduces persons as documents along with folksonomies as a means for externalising implicit knowledge in sense of the Web 2.0.

> Well, his position is unique . . . The conclusions of every department are passed to him, and he is the central exchange, the clearinghouse, which makes out the balance. All other men are specialists, but his specialism is omniscience. We will suppose that a minister needs information as to a point which involves the Navy, India, Canada and the bimetallic question; he could get his separate advices from various departments upon each, but only Mycroft can focus them all, and say offhand how each factor would affect the other. They began by using him as a short-cut, a convenience; now he has made himself an essential. In that great brain of his everything is pigeon-holed and can be handed out in an instant. Again and again his word has decided the national policy.
>
> Sherlock on his brother Mycroft Holmes.

EXPLORING THE DIGITAL FRONTIER
ADVANCES IN LIBRARIANSHIP, VOL. 32
© 2010 by Emerald Group Publishing Limited
ISSN: 0065-2830
DOI: 10.1108/S0065-2830(2010)0000032009

I. Introduction

Mycroft Holmes is one of the first knowledge managers mentioned in the literature (Conan Doyle, 1908). In the service of the British government, he managed the information dissemination of all kinds of the requested knowledge—Navy, foreign affairs, financial questions and so on. Obviously, he had had a perfect overview on

- all appropriate documents,
- all relevant access points to the documents and
- the information needs and the information behaviour of his clients and their organisations.

For today's librarians and knowledge managers, it is impressive to learn that Mycroft's position is "unique" and that his word has decided national policy.

What exactly is "knowledge management" and what role do digital libraries (DL) play in knowledge management? And what does "knowledge representation" mean? Knowledge management (KM) is the science and practice of the administration of internal and external information in institutions. It includes typical tasks such as knowledge sharing and information dissemination. As Yainik (2010) states,

> In the corporate world of today it is very important that knowledge is shared with employees as well as with the outside world. The improper transfer of knowledge can put a company in a position of disadvantage. Digital libraries are a very powerful tool to enable knowledge management in organizations. (p. 698)

According to Gust von Loh (2009), KM consists of social methods (e.g., communities of practice, storytelling and knowledge cafés) and technical tools and systems (e.g., records management, content management and intranets). An important subtask is the creation and maintenance of a corporate memory (Dieng et al., 1999; Stein, 1995). According to Prasad and Plaza (1996),

> Corporate memory consists of the sum total of the information and knowledge resources within an organization. Such resources are typically distributed and are characterized by multiplicity and diversity: company databases, machine-readable texts, documentation resources and reports, product requirements, design rationale etc. (p. 2)

It should be noted that KM also includes the knowledge of employees and other stakeholders of the institution. A corporate memory is the basis for reuse of knowledge in the company. Technically spoken, this means the construction and operation of an information retrieval system. Both the technical information retrieval system and the stored content form a corporate DL (Lytras et al., 2005). After Pejtersen et al. (2008), "most contemporary digital libraries are repositories of information wherein contents can be searched or browsed by the user" (p. 2). Corporate DL are the institutional manifestations of corporate memories with the purpose of enabling knowledge reuse in contrast to other DL (e.g., on the free Web) according to Pomerantz *et al.* (2008). Corporate DL (Matarazzo and Pearlstein, 2008) are funded by the company, but only if the firm's management and its other stakeholders are convinced that the DL is a key success factor for the company. In this way, corporate libraries act as KM centres in companies (Parker *et al.*, 2005).

To guarantee optimal access to DL, methods and tools of knowledge representation (KR) have to be applied. The main task of KR is the creation of metadata, which can be attached to documents to permit searching and browsing of their content. To represent the documents' content, KR compiles several tools for knowledge organisation (Knowledge Organisation Systems (KOS)), namely folksonomies, nomenclatures, classification systems, thesauri and ontologies (Stock and Stock, 2008). Users of corporate DL are all stakeholders of the company, namely employees, management, owners, suppliers and customers. This does not mean that all stakeholders have access to all information however. There are customised or even personalised information solutions for all user groups or single users.

II. Research Questions

This review paper describes a theoretical approach to combine KM and knowledge management systems (KMS) with KR in DL. It takes a multidisciplinary approach consisting of business administration (KM), information systems research (KMS) and library and information science (KR). These scientific fields form the foundations of DL research.

As knowledge has two dimensions—explicit and implicit (sometimes referred to as tacit) knowledge—we have to find KR methods for both dimensions. This fact leads us to two basic research questions:

- Research question *one*: Which KR methods are appropriate to map *explicit* knowledge?
- Research question *two*: Which KR methods are appropriate to map *implicit* knowledge? Furthermore, is it possible at all to capture implicit knowledge?

In corporate environments, KM is confronted with myriads of documents, which are more or less relevant for storing and being processed.

- Research question *three*: Are all documents equal in regard to KM? If not, how can we model the documents' space of a company?

KR consists of several methods, elaborated KOS such as thesauri or ontologies, and user-driven methods as folksonomic tagging as well. The corporate KOS should represent the corporate language. If there is an opportunity for employees to tag documents, they will probably use their corporate language to index these pieces of information.

- Research question *four*: What kinds of KOS (which can be applied in DL) exist and are there differences in the semantic richness of the various types of KOS?
- Research question *five*: Can we construct a corporate KOS by using the employees' tags? Is it possible to automate the process of emergent semantics or are we in need of intellectual endeavours?

Knowledge managers in contemporary institutions make heavy use of information technology, store digital documents in huge databases and advice users to work with powerful information retrieval systems. Brown and Duguid (2002) in their book, *The Social Life of Information*, call this IT-driven approach "information fetishism." Their monograph is "concerned with the superficially plausible idea ... that information and its technologies without problems can replace the nuanced relations between people" (p. XVI). If we measure progress of KM in organisations, it is measured in terms of amounts of digital information (in Gigabyte, Terabyte and so on), and this leads to the paradigm: the more information stored, the better is the KM system. "Consequently, knowledge bases can reach maximum capacity very quickly—and at exactly the same time maximum inutility" (Brown and Duguid, 2002, p. XIII). They say that,

> "At the root of the problem lie issues of meaning, judgment, sense making, context, and interpretation—issues far beyond a simple search and embedded in social life" (p. XIV). It looks like people and their social and cultural contexts have been forgotten. People in "networks of practice"—such as the famous Mycroft Holmes—have "practice and knowledge in common" according to Brown and Duguid. (p. 141)

People use—or do not use—KMS or corporate DL. The main indicators of the users' acceptance of systems are ease of use, perceived usefulness (Davis, 1989), trust (Kim and Han, 2009) and fun (Knautz *et al.*, 2010). DeLone and McLean (2003), in their information systems success model, add the dimensions of service quality and information quality besides the dimension of technical system's quality. Jennex and Olfman (2006) rename the information dimension by the term "knowledge quality" and split it into the KM strategy and process, richness and linkages. Jennex *et al.* (2007) put the knowledge itself into the focal point of KM and KMS. These authors assert that

> KM and KMS success are a multidimensional concept. Each includes capturing the right knowledge, getting the right knowledge to the right user, and using this knowledge to

improve organisational and/or individual performance. KM success is measured using the dimensions of impact on business processes, strategy, leadership, efficiency and effectiveness of KM processes, efficiency and effectiveness of the KM system, organisational culture, and knowledge content. (Jennex *et al.*, 2007, p. 5)

How is it possible to store knowledge content and the "right" knowledge in a KMS, such that the user will improve her or his institution's performance by using this KMS? There are two sub-tasks:

- to represent the "right" knowledge (and only the right one) in the KMS or DL and
- to search and find the "right" knowledge (and only this) by using the KMS or DL

From an information science point of view, the first task leads to theories, methods and tools of KR (Stock and Stock, 2008) and the second one to information retrieval (Stock, 2007a). But what does the word "right" mean?

III. Explicit and Implicit Knowledge in Digital Libraries

What is knowledge in KM, DL and KMS? In a first approximation, we can define "knowledge" philosophically as a true proposition (e.g., Chisholm, 1989). But there are more kinds of knowledge besides propositions, which are true. Ryle (1946) warns that "it is a ruinous but popular mistake to suppose that intelligence operates only in the production and manipulation of propositions, that is, that only in ratiocinating are we rational" (p. 8). Ryle distinguishes "knowing that" (propositions) from "knowing how" (when a person knows to do things of a certain sort). "Knowing how" has two subspecies—implicit knowledge, which can be reconstructed (e.g., know-how on cooking omelettes), and implicit knowledge, which is exhibited only by deeds and not by dicta and which cannot be fully reconstructed (e.g., making good jokes). Polanyi (1967) deepens Ryle's observations on knowing how. He states, "I shall consider human knowledge by starting from the fact that *we can know more than we can tell*" (p. 4). This so-called tacit knowledge is embedded in the body of the knowing person. The structure of tacit knowing "shows that all thought contains components of which we are subsidiary aware in the focal content of our thinking, and that all thought dwells in its subsidiaries, as if they were parts of our body" (Polanyi, 1967, p. X).

How can we pass on implicit knowledge? The first possibility is to communicate knowledge bodily. "The performer co-ordinates his moves by dwelling in them as parts of his body, while the watcher tries to correlate these moves by seeking to dwell in them from outside. He dwells in these moves by interiorizing them" (Polanyi, 1967, p. 30). The second way of passing on tacit knowledge is to try to understand the knower's thought. It is a kind of empathy. "Chess players enter into a master's spirit by rehearsing the games he played, to discover what he had in mind" (Polanyi, 1967, p. 30).

"Knowing that" and the subspecies of implicit knowledge that can be reconstructed are objects of externalisation, that is, such knowledge can be materialised in documents. The documents containing the knowledge are objects of KR techniques. If there exist "shared conceptualizations" (Gruber, 1993, p. 199), it will be possible to arrange the knowledge in so-called KOS. KOS are the basis for any applications of the Semantic Web. In the area of explicit knowledge we are able to work with (externalised) documents and Knowledge Organisation Systems to represent the right knowledge in answer to the first research question. Implicit knowledge, which cannot be reconstructed, will be expressed—if at all—by vague descriptions like analogies or metaphors (Nonaka and Takeuchi, 1995). In this case, computer-driven KMS will fail to be constructed. "Humans make excellent use of tacit knowledge. Anaphora, ellipses, unstated shared understanding are all used in the service of our collaborative relationships. But when human-human collaboration becomes human-computer-human collaboration, tacit knowl-edge becomes a problem" (Reeves and Shipman, 1996, p. 24). Nonaka and Takeuchi (1995) point out that such tacit knowledge has to be learnt by "socialisation". As Memmi (2004) states,

> In short, know-how and expertise are only accessible through contact with the appropriate individuals. Find the right people to talk or to work with, and you can start acquiring their knowledge. Otherwise there is simply very little you could do (watching videos of expert behaviour is a poor substitute indeed). (p. 876)

It is a task of KM to bring together people with similar interest and with the same or similar skills. For Schreyögg and Geiger (2003), KM will in this case be "skill management" as well. Implicit knowledge is inseparably connected with persons. Therefore, persons are "documents" for KM purposes. This unusual concept of a document, which includes persons and other material objects, is common in information science (Buckland, 1997). In Web 2.0 applications (such as wikis, blogs, social bookmarking services and file sharing services), all kinds of persons can (and do) participate. It would be a misinterpretation that people externalise their tacit knowledge in such applications, but for KM tasks, we obtain hints on the topics (not the knowledge itself) of some implicit knowledge.

With respect to Ryle's and Polanyi's analyses of implicit knowledge, it is not possible to externalise knowledge to the full extent, but what is possible is to arrange cooperation between people in order to exchange information through face-to-face communication. It is a big challenge for libraries to invest in digitisation projects but—for the management of implicit or tacit knowledge—it must not be forgotten that libraries are physical spaces as well (Ludwig and Starr, 2005; Vårheim, 2008). Social methods of KM ask for knowledge cafés (Gurteen, 2009), space for story telling (Brown *et al.*, 2005) and for corporate libraries as places.

Let's come back to DL! When persons index resources of Web 2.0 services, they use their own (maybe otherwise tacit) concepts and their own words to describe the content of the resource. Indexing within Web 2.0 services is called "tagging" and all tags of a service form a "folksonomy." In KM, we learn about the person's explicit and some aspects of tacit knowledge by monitoring his or her tagging behaviour. In the area of implicit knowledge, we are able to work with persons as documents and folksonomies to represent the right knowledge. Herein lies the answer to research question *two*.

The authors basic idea is a mash-up of Web 2.0 technologies (folksonomies) and Semantic Web technologies (KOS), or—in other words—of social KR methods and semantic KR methods for the application in DL. Our ambition is to construct social semantic KR methods, which are able to represent documents (normal documents and persons as well) and therefore explicit knowledge (to the full extent) and some aspects of implicit knowledge.

IV. The Shell Model of Corporate Documents

This chapter stresses the term "document" with even persons considered as documents along with normal documents, informally published documents, and internal documents. Normal documents are formally published documents (e.g., scientific works, patents and other documents of intellectual property rights, news articles, legal texts and grey literature). Informally published documents might include Web pages, blogs and posts in forums, wikis on the WWW, files like photos, videos, pieces of music on file sharing services, while internal documents could be reports, memos, mail, invoices or individual files. Optimally, documents in KMS are stored in a digital form and are specified by formal aspects (author, year, source and so on) and by content aspects (applying KOS or folksonomies). This specification of the document is called a surrogate and consists of metadata. As material

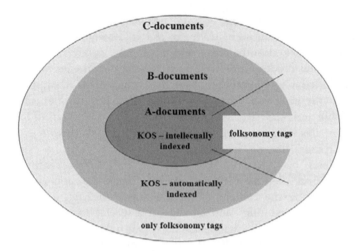

Fig. 1   Shell model of corporate documents and preferred methods of indexing.

documents (such as persons or companies) cannot become digitised, we have to work only with the surrogates (Stock, 2007b) (Fig. 1).

Internal documents of a company and relevant external documents are more or less important for the institution and so for KM. We will work with a layer, or shell model, of a document importance, which was introduced into the information science literature by Krause (2006). In a corporate environment (Peters, 2006), we have some A-documents or core documents, which are very important for the organisation, say, a strategy paper by the CEO or a fundamental patent describing the company's main invention. Every A-document (normal document or person) has to be found every time it is searched for—with a maximum degree of findability. B-documents are not as important as core documents, but have to be found in certain situations. Finally, C-documents consist of little important information, but they are worth being stored in a KMS on the assumption that some day there is need to find a given document. With the shell model and the A/B/C-documents, we are able to answer our research question *three*.

All users of the corporate KMS are allowed to tag all documents. Because everyone will tag a given document with his or her specific (even implicit) concepts, the corporate folksonomy will directly reflect the language of the institution. The less important C-documents are indexed only by tags, if at all. All other documents are represented in terms of the corporate KOS. Professional indexing is an elaborate, time-consuming and therefore costly task. So only A-documents are indexed intellectually by professional indexers, and B-documents are indexed automatically. If the full texts of the documents are stored as well, there are many additional (but uncontrolled) access points to the documents such as a full text search.

As the shell model needs KOS for indexing documents of high quality and a KOS which reflects the particular language of the company, the concept of emergent semantics within folksonomies is used to generate this specific KOS.

V. Knowledge Organisation Systems

KOS consist of (a) concepts and (b) relations between the concepts (Stock, 2009). A relation is called paradigmatic, when two concepts are rigidly coupled in the KOS. A relation is called syntagmatic, when two terms co-occur in documents (Peters and Weller, 2008a).

In information science and in practice, there are three classical KOS, differing in their semantic expressiveness: nomenclatures, classification systems, and thesauri (Table 1). Nomenclatures work with controlled terms, making mainly use of one semantic relation, namely the relation of equivalence (synonymy and quasi-synonymy). A typical example of a nomenclature is the Registry File of the Chemical Abstracts Service (Weisgerber, 1997). In classification systems, the concepts are denominated by artificial notations, which are connected by relations of equivalence and unspecific hierarchy (Batley, 2005). Examples are the Dewey Decimal Classification (DDC) and the International Patent Classification (IPC). In a thesaurus, the concepts are called descriptors. They are related by equivalence, hierarchical relations (hyponymic

Table 1
Main Semantic Relations in KOS

	Folksonomy	Nomen-clature	Classifi-cation	Thesaurus	Ontology
Equivalence	–	Yes	Yes	Yes	Yes
Hierarchy	–	–	Yes	Yes	Yes
Hyponymy	–	–	–	Yes	Yes
Meronymy	–	–	–	Yes	Yes
Association	–	–	–	Yes	–
Specific relations	–	–	–	–	Yes
Syntagmatic relations	Yes	Yes	Yes	Yes	–

(is-a) and meronymic (part-of) relations), and by association ("see also") (Aitchison *et al.*, 2000). Well-known thesauri are the Medical Subject Headings (MeSH) and the physics thesaurus of Inspec (Fig. 2).

Documents will be indexed through the controlled terms of the KOS, and documents will be retrieved by the same controlled terms thus reducing the vocabulary problem (Furnas *et al.*, 1987) in information retrieval.

Ontologies adopted from research on Artificial Intelligence are a new form of KOS. They make use of a standardised language (e.g., OWL, the Web Ontology Language), permit automatic reasoning (e.g., adopting description logics), make use of general and individual terms and do not apply unspecific associative relations, but many specific relations besides hierarchy (Stock and Stock, 2008). Normally, ontologies do not form syntagmatic relations, because they are not used for indexing documents, but for representing the knowledge itself. The youngest kind of KOS is the folksonomy (Peters, 2009; Weller *et al.*, 2010). Here, users tag documents with uncontrolled terms with no indexing rules at all. Folksonomies do not make use of paradigmatic relations, but only of syntagmatic relations, that is of tag co-occurrences.

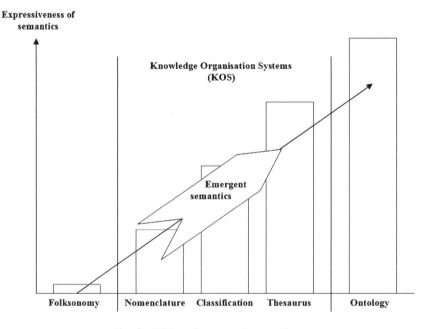

Fig. 2   KOS and emergent semantics.

In terms of semantic relations, folksonomies are the weakest form of KOS and ontologies are the most expressive one. The upgrading from one KOS to a richer one (in Fig. 2 on the way from left to right) is called by various names: "semantic enrichment" (Angeletou *et al.*, 2007), "ontology maturing" (Braun *et al.*, 2007) or "emergent semantics" (Zhang *et al.*, 2006). This provides the answer to research question *four*.

Indexing procedure with the aid of concepts taken from a KOS always consists of two elements, namely the document and the concepts (Fig. 3a). The concepts are linked to the document through the work of one single professional indexer. Ontologies are exceptions to this proposition because they only link concepts through different relations and, in the majority of cases, do not attach concepts to documents. Indexing with folksonomic tags forms a tri-partite graph between documents, tags, and—what is a new element—users (as in Fig. 3b) (Marlow *et al.*, 2006; Yeung *et al.*, 2006).

This structural change is important because we are now able to gain information about users and we are able to analyse the users' tagging

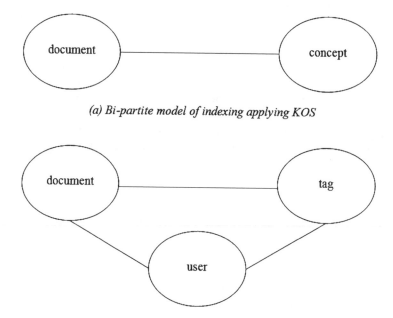

(a) Bi-partite model of indexing applying KOS

(b) Tri-partite model of indexing applying folksonomy tags

Fig. 3   Indexing models. (a) Bi-partite model of indexing applying KOS. (b) Tri-partite model of indexing applying folksonomy tags.

behaviour (which documents did the user tag? which tags did the user apply?). Because of the tri-partite structure of folksonomies, we can search and browse for users through tags (e.g., who used this tag at least once for indexing) and documents (e.g., who saved and indexed this document) and we are able to recommend users with specific knowledge on requested topics (e.g., who indexed a lot of documents with a specific tag). On the contrary, users are now able to link themselves to documents through tags and thus allocate documents in specific contexts (Boeije *et al.*, 2009). Of course, in a corporate setting, we can additionally create surrogate documents about employees (e.g., yellow pages), which can be indexed by means of KOS concepts and by folksonomy tags through the users of the yellow pages. It is also possible to add the tags (which the user indexed within the KMS) to his profile in the yellow pages to gain a personal description of his interests and activities. In this way, explicit information about a person is combined with implicit information about his or her daily work and interests. As such, it is easier for other users to find out from yellow pages what competencies a person has and if he or she matches information seekers needs.

Folksonomies show only little semantic structures, which has important implications for the development of KMS using tags as an organisation tool. The main problems result from the variability of natural language and the absence of a controlled vocabulary. In folksonomies can be found different word forms, nouns in singular, nouns in plural and abbreviations (Peters and Stock, 2007), all mixed up. Therefore, in professional environments and for A- and B-documents, it is advisable to work with folksonomies only in combination with other KOS-based indexing methods (Peters, 2006). The processes of manipulating and re-engineering folksonomy tags and combining them with KOS to make folksonomies more productive and effective are described in the literature as "tag gardening" (Peters and Weller, 2008b).

VI. From Tags to Controlled Terms of KOS: Or from the Social to the Semantic Web

Although folksonomies are uncontrolled collections of tags, they typically include syntagmatic relations between them. If these semantic relations can be made explicit during the procedures of tag gardening, we obtain gradually enriched semantics, that is, the more fine-grained the used relations, the richer the semantics.

Relations between tags can be found out with co-occurrence analyses that may work on two levels. On the one hand, it is possible to find co-occurrences on the document level, which means that two tags are somehow related when they are both indexed for the same document. On the other hand, tag co-occurrences appear on the folksonomy level, which means that several documents of a folksonomy may be indexed with the same tag, and therefore, tag co-occurrences of the document level can be cumulated across all documents of the folksonomy. It is not sufficient to calculate co-occurrences to obtain semantic relations. Co-occurrences can only work as indicators that some kind of relations may exist between two concepts.

Yet, to determine which kind of relation is at hand, we have to add intellectual analyses supported by partly automatic suggestions. Fig. 4 shows an example of how semantic interrelations may be hidden in folksonomy tags. A resource "What is Web 2.0. Design Patterns and Business Models for the Next Generation of Software" is saved in the social bookmarking system *BibSonomy* (http://www.bibsonomy.org) and was indexed with different tags, for example, "Web2.0," "SocialSoftware" and "tagging." On the level of this single document, we can detect specific relations such as the part-of relation between "Web2.0" and "social software." To establish semantics, we would now have to render this relation into a paradigmatic one, valid within the whole DL. This semantic enrichment of tags would enable the system's users to broaden a search for all documents about "Web2.0" in a way that also would include documents tagged with "social software."

However, intellectual detection of semantic relations is laborious. What is more, since tagging systems are dynamic and steadily increasing, activities

Fig. 4 Hidden semantic relations in *BibSonomy*.

for the detection of tag relations have to be executed on a regular basis to guarantee a current reflection of the tagging community's needs and changes. Thus, some frequency computations are needed leading to the most promising areas for deeper analysis. Candidate tags have to be extracted from the tagging system as starting points for which we propose power tags.

The determination of power tags depends on the distribution of tags regarding the frequency of their assignment to a digital resource. The basic assumption is that different distributions of tags may appear in folksonomies:

1. an inverse Power Law distribution, a Lotka-like curve (Huang, 2006; Munk and Mork, 2007);
2. an inverse logistic distribution (Stock, 2006; Stock, 2007b) and
3. other distributions.

These distributions can be detected on two levels, the document level (which tags are used for indexing and how often is a particular tag assigned to the document?) and the database level (the overall summarisation of tags per document for the whole information service). A Lotka-like power law (Egghe and Rousseau, 1990) has the the following form:

$$f(x) = \frac{C}{x^a}$$

where C is a constant, x is the rank of the tag relative to the resource and a is a value ranging normally from about 1 to about 2. If this assumption is true, we see a curve with only few tags at the top of the distribution, and a "long tail" of numerous tags on the lower ranks on the right-hand side of the curve. The discussions about "collective intelligence" are mainly based on this observation: the first n tags of the left hand side of the power law reflect the collective intelligence in giving meaning to the annotated documents (Weiss, 2005).

The inverse logistic distribution shows a lot of relevant tags at the beginning of the curve (the "long trunk") and the known "long tail." This distribution follows the formula,

$$f(x) = e^{-C'(x-1)^b}$$

where e is the Euler number, x is the rank of the tag, C' is a constant and the exponent b is approximately 3.

In comparison with the power law, the inverse logistic distribution reflects the collective intelligence differently. The curve shows a long trunk on the left and a long tail of tags on the right. As all tags in the long trunk have been applied with similar (high) frequency, all left-hand tags up to the turning point of the curve should be considered as a reflection of collective intelligence.

For the determination of power tags, we have to keep in mind both known tag distributions. If the document-specific distribution of tags follows the inverse power law, the first n tags are considered as "power tags." The value of n is dependent on the exponent a. If the tag distribution forms an inverse logistic distribution, all tags on the left-hand side of the curve (up to the turning point) are marked as "power tags" (Peters and Stock, 2010) (Fig. 5).

Activities that turn tags into controlled terms need some candidate tags as starting points, for which we propose power tags. As we prune both curves at a particular point and neglect the rest of the curve and the long tail tags, we call this approach for determining tag gardening candidates "exclusive." The concrete processing of power tags works as follows: the first step is to determine power tags on the resource level. This calculation is carried out for each and every resource of the collaborative information service. According to the preceding explanations, two different tag distributions may appear, which each identify different numbers of power tags (we call them power tags I). As these power tags I are important tags in giving meaning to the resource, they have to be processed in the next step. Now, the n numbers of power tags I should each be investigated regarding their relationships to other tags of the whole database—in other words, a calculation of co-occurrence is carried out for the power tags I. This calculation produces again specific tag distributions, where we can determine power tags as well (we call them power tags II). These new power tags II are now the candidate tags for the emergence of semantics because their connection to the power

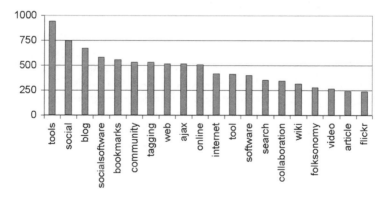

Fig. 5 Tag co-occurrences with tag "web2.0."

tags I seem to be very fruitful. In this connection, the existence of semantic relations between power tags I and power tags II will be most obvious. Let us explain the procedure with an example from the social bookmarking service *BibSonomy* (see Fig. 5):

The tags for the resource displayed in Fig. 4 form a power law distribution as the tag "web2.0" is indexed 13 times, "wismasys0809" (a course-specific tag of our institute) is indexed 4 times, "imported" and "web" are each indexed 3 times, "2.0," "basics," "folksonomy" and "technology" are each indexed two times and the rest is used only once (mouse over tags displays indexing frequency of each tag, not displayed in the figure). As "wismasys0809" is a course-specific tag, we exclude it from the further processing and just consider "web2.0" and "imported" as power tags I. For those two tags, we examine co-occurrences with all other tags of the database. An exemplary search in *BibSonomy* for the tag "web2.0" results in the co-occurring tags displayed in Fig. 5 and says that the tag "web2.0" appears together with the tag "tools" in 941 documents.

Those co-occurring tags follow an inverse-logistic distribution. The first n tags (say $n = 10$) are now considered as power tags II and are the basis for the intellectual tag gardening activities and the detection of tag relations. Fig. 5 shows that the tag "web2.0" is frequently combined with the tags "tools," "social," "blog" and "social software." Accordingly, the basic assumption for emergent semantics in folksonomies and tag interrelations, respectively, is that tags that often co-occur have to be of similar meaning or have to be linked in a meaningful relationship. Thus, to name an example of these power tags II, the tags "tagging" and "web2.0" form part-of relation where "tagging" is a part of "web2.0." To achieve richer semantics, we would thus establish these newly detected hierarchical connections as paradigmatic relations within the folksonomy (which in return grows to become a more formal KOS). The goal is to enhance precision and recall of search results and the expressiveness of the folksonomy by adding semantics, to enable query expansion during retrieval through semantic relations, to enhance indexing functionalities, to improve navigation within the folksonomy and to build a basis for semantic-oriented visualisations of the folksonomy.

The given assumptions result in a set of descriptors with which we are now able to build a thesaurus or other kinds of KOS. This thesaurus can then be used as a basis for the indexing of documents, for example, through recommendations of tags or descriptors during indexing, or the retrieval of documents, when it is used for query expansion. According to preceding example, a set of descriptors may look like Table 2. Here, we are able to answer research question *five* saying yes, it is possible to construct a corporate KOS by using the employees' tags. However, it is not possible to automate

Table 2
Descriptor Set Extracted from Tags

Descriptor set			Relation
	Web2.0		
UF	Social software	Used for	Synonymy
BT	Web	Broader term	Hierarchy
NTP	Blog	Narrower term partitive	Meronymy
NTP	Bookmarks		Meronymy
NTP	Tagging		Meronymy
NTP	Community		Meronymy
NTP	Ajax		Meronymy
RT	Online	Related term	Association

this process of emergent semantics to the full extent. There is always need of some intellectual endeavours.

VII. Conclusion

This review describes (based mainly on a theoretical background) the combination of KM (as an object of business administration), KMS (as objects of information systems research) and KR (as an object of library and information science) in corporate DL. So, what's new? We formulated five research questions and were able to give answers.

1. *Which KR methods are appropriate to map explicit knowledge?*
Concerning explicit knowledge, we are able to work with (externalised) documents and KOS. KM applies to DL as KMS.
2. *Which KR methods are appropriate to map implicit knowledge?*
As it is not possible to externalise all implicit knowledge as a matter of principle, we cannot apply a purely technological solution. Contrariwise, we have to arrange that people meet and collaborate. So we must insist on libraries as places, for example, as knowledge cafés. People need to be connected to exchange their implicit knowledge. But DL are able to help connect people. In this case, people have to be treated as documents and described by surrogates in DL. In Web 2.0 environments, people are placed in the centre of attention—a way of thinking which could be transferred to KMS. In Web 2.0, people turn implicit knowledge into explicit knowledge when they add comments to documents or index documents with tags. Comments or tags are each manifestations of the person's thoughts and knowledge. This is the social aspect of DL, or "social digital libraries."
3. *Are all documents equal in regard to KM? If not, how can we model the documents' space of a company?*

Documents are of different importance for the company. We distinguish between A-documents (core documents), B-documents (other important documents) and C-documents (only little importance). We are able to model those document types in the shell model (originated by Krause). In a DL, all documents are able to be tagged by users, but only A-documents become intellectually indexed with controlled terms of a KOS, B-documents are indexed automatically using a KOS and finally C-documents are indexed by user-specific tagging only. We have to recall that "documents" are classical documents (reports, patents, memos and so on) and surrogates of persons as well. Corporate DL have to distinguish between documents by their importance for the institution.

4. *What kinds of KOS (which can be applied in DL) do exist? Are there differences in the semantic richness of the types of KOS?*

In terms of semantic relations, folksonomies are a very weak form of KOS, and ontologies are the most expressive one. Between those two borderline cases, there are the "classical" KOS: nomenclatures, classification systems and thesauri. Indexing with classical KOS or ontologies can be mapped as a bi-partite model of documents and concepts; indexing with a folksonomy leads to a tri-partite model of documents, tags and users. With the appearance of the user, DL are able to gain information about users and their tagging behaviour. All kinds of KOS, not only ontologies, form the basis for the semantic aspect of DL or "semantic digital libraries."

5. *Can we construct a corporate KOS by using the employees' tags? Is it possible to automate the process of emergent semantics? Or are we in need of intellectual endeavours?*

To construct a corporate KOS, we proposed a mash-up of Web 2.0 and Semantic Web techniques to simultaneously represent explicit knowledge through KOS and implicit knowledge through folksonomies. A simple way of combining Web 2.0 and Semantic Web is the application of the shell model that allows different indexing methods and qualities for different sorts of documents. Because the shell model requires KOS for indexing documents of high quality and KOS, which reflect the particular language of the company, the approach of emergent semantics within folksonomies is used to generate this specific corporate KOS. We discussed how to enrich folksonomies with semantic relations to achieve semantically richer results in indexing and along with it more precise results in information retrieval. Thus, we proposed co-occurrence analyses based on power tags I and power tags II to gain candidate tag pairs that are fruitful for detection of semantic relations and for the creation of descriptor sets. In this way, we turned simple tags as manifestations of implicit knowledge into more formal descriptors that then change into explicit knowledge of the KMS. Simultaneously, these tags become part of the established corporate KOS and enhance its expressiveness. So, retrievability of all kinds of documents becomes better. For there is a feedback loop between folksonomy tags and controlled terms, KOS spirals up and leads to an ever-optimising DL.

It is possible to construct a corporate KOS by using the employees' tags. But it is not possible to automate this process of emergent semantics to the full extent. We are always in need of some intellectual endeavours.

Final Remarks

Only the combination of the social and the semantic aspects of DL leads to successful constructions and maintenances of DL as KMS in companies. The social aspect refers to people, namely to all stakeholders of the company. The semantic aspect refers to all approaches of KOS. Here, we speak about social semantic corporate DL, which are manifestations of the Social Semantic Web

(Weller, 2010) in the world of DL. Research and practice in corporate DL are interdisciplinary tasks. Involved are the following:

- KM (which is mainly a branch of business administration),
- information systems research (which is part of computer science) and
- KR and information retrieval (which are subjects of library and information science).

Acknowledgments

This chapter is a revised version of a paper presented at the *International Conference on Digital Libraries*, New Delhi, India, February 23–26, 2010. Isabella Peters' research on power tags is supported by a grant (no. STO 764/4-1) of the German Research Foundation (Deutsche Forschungsgemeinschaft).

References

Aitchison, J., Gilchrist, A., and Bawden, D. (2000). *Thesaurus Construction and Use*, 4th ed. Europa, London, England; New York.

Angeletou, S., Sabou, M., Specia, L., and Motta, E. (2007). Bridging the gap between folksonomies and the semantic web: An experience report. In *Bridging the Gap Between Semantic Web and Web 2.0* (pp. 30–32). European semantic web conference. Retrieved from http://people.kmi.open.ac.uk/marta/papers/semnet 2007.pdf

Batley, S. (2005). *Classification in Theory and Practice*. Chandos, Oxford, England.

Boeije, R., de Vries, P., Kolfschoten, G. L., and Veen, W. (2009). Knowledge workers and the realm of social tagging. In *Proceedings of the 42nd Hawaii International Conference on System Sciences (HICSS-42)*. IEEE Computer Society, Washington, DC, Retrieved from http://www.computer.org/portal/weg/csdl/doi/ 10.1109/HICSS.2009.801

Braun, S., Schmidt, A., Walter, A., and Zacharias, V. (2007). The ontology maturing approach for collaborative and work integrated ontology development: Evaluation results and future directions. In *Proceedings of the International Workshop on Emergent Semantics and Ontology Evolution (ESOE)* (pp. 5–18). Busan, Korea. Retrieved from http://ftp.informatik.rwth-aachen.de/Publications/CEUR-WS/vol-292/paper3.pdf

Brown, J. S., and Duguid, P. (2002). *The Social Life of Information*, 2nd ed. Harvard Business School Press, Boston, MA.

Brown, J. S., Denning, S., Groh, K., and Prusak, L. (2005). *Storytelling in Organizations*. Elsevier Butterworth-Heinemann, Oxford, England.

Buckland, M. K. (1997). What is a document. *Journal of the American Society for Information Science* 48, 804–809.

Chisholm, R. M. (1989). *Theory of Knowledge*, 3rd ed. Prentice-Hall International, Englewood Cliffs, NJ.

Conan Doyle, A. (1908). The Adventure of the Bruce-Partington Plans. *The Strand Magazine* 35, 215.

Davis, F. D. (1989). Perceived usefulness, perceived ease of use, and user acceptance of information technology. *MIS Quarterly* 13(3), 319–340.

DeLone, W. H., and McLean, E. R. (2003). The DeLone and McLean model of information systems success: A ten-year update. *Journal of Management Information Systems* 19(4), 9–30.

Dieng, R., Corby, O., Giboin, A., and Ribière, M. (1999). Methods and tools for corporate knowledge management. *International Journal for Human-Computer Studies* 51, 567–598.

Egghe, L., and Rousseau, R. (1990). *Introduction to Informetrics*. Elsevier, Amsterdam, Netherlands.

Furnas, G. W., Landauer, T. K., Gomez, L. M., and Dumais, S. T. (1987). The vocabulary problem in human-system communication. *Communications of the ACM* 30(11), 964–971.

Gruber, T. R. (1993). A translation approach to portable ontology specifications. *Knowledge Acquisition* 5(2), 99–220.

Gurteen, D. (2009). Knowledge cafe. *Inside Knowledge* 13(3), 8–13.

Gust von Loh, S. (2009). *Evidenzbasiertes Wissensmanagement* [*Evidence-based knowledge management*]. Gabler, Wiesbaden, Germany.

Huang, H. (2006). Tag distribution analysis using the power law to evaluate social tagging systems: A case study in the flickr database. In *Proceedings of the 17th ASIS&T SIG/CR Classification Research Workshop* (pp. 14–15). American Society for Information Science and Technology, Austin, TX.

Jennex, M. E., and Olfman, L. (2006). A model of knowledge management success. *International Journal of Knowledge Management* 2(3), 51–68.

Jennex, M. E., Smolnik, S., and Croasdell, D. (2007). Towards defining knowledge management success. In *Proceedings of the 40th Hawaii International Conference on Systems Sciences (HICSS-40)*. IEEE Computer Society Press, Washington, DC. Retrieved from http://www.computer.org/portal/web/csdl/doi/10.1109/HICSS. 2007.571.

Kim, B., and Han, I. (2009). The role of trust belief and its antecedents in a community-driven knowledge environment. *Journal of the American Society for Information Science and Technology* 60(5), 1012–1026.

Knautz, K., Soubusta, S., and Stock, W. G. (2010). Tag clusters as information retrieval interfaces. In *Proceedings of the 43rd Annual Hawaii International Conference on System Sciences (HICSS-43)*. IEEE Computer Society Press, Washington, DC. Retrieved from http://www.computer.org/portal/web/csdl/proceedings/h#5

Krause, J. (2006). Shell model, semantic web and web information retrieval. In *Information und Sprache* (I. Harms, H. D. Luckhardt and H. W. Giessen, eds.), pp. 95–106, Saur, Munich, Germany.

Ludwig, L., and Starr, S. (2005). Library as place: Results of a Delphi study. *Journal of the Medical Library Association* 93(3), 315–326.

Lytras, M., Sicilia, M. A., Davies, J., and Kashyap, V. (2005). Digital libraries in the knowledge era: Knowledge management and semantic web technologies. *Library Management* 26(4/5), 170–175.

Marlow, C., Naaman, M., Boyd, D., and Davis, M. (2006). HT06, tagging paper, taxonomy, flickr, academic article, to read. In *Proceedings of the 17th Conference on Hypertext and Hypermedia* (pp. 31–40). Association of Computing Machinery, New York. Retrieved from http://portal.acm.org/citation.cfm?id = 1149949

Matarazzo, J. M., and Pearlstein, T. (2008). A review of research related to management of corporate libraries. *Advances in Librarianship* 31, 93–114.

Memmi, D. (2004). Towards tacit information retrieval. In *RIAO 2004 Conference Proceedings* (pp. 874–884). Le Centre de Haute Études Internationales d'Informatique Documentaire, Paris, France. Retrieved from http://citeseerx.ist. psu.edu/virewdoc/summary?doi=10.1.1.59.4007

Munk, T., and Mork, K. (2007). Folksonomy: The power law and the significance of the least effort. *Knowledge Organisation* 34(1), 16–33.

Nonaka, I., and Takeuchi, H. (1995). *The Knowledge-Creating Company: How Japanese Companies Create the Dynamics of Innovation.* Oxford University Press, Oxford, England.

Parker, K. R., Nitse, P. S., and Flowers, K. A. (2005). Libraries as knowledge management centers. *Library Management* 26(4/5), 176–189.

Pejtersen, A. M., Hansen, P., and Albrechtsen, H. (2008). A work-centred approach to evaluation of a digital library: Annotation system for knowledge sharing in collaborative work. *World Digital Libraries* 1(1), 1–17.

Peters, I. (2006). Against folksonomies: Indexing blogs and podcasts for corporate knowledge management. In *Preparing for Information 2.0. Proceedings of Online Information Conference* (pp. 90–97). Learned Information Europe, London, England.

Peters, I. (2009). *Folksonomies: Indexing and Retrieval in Web 2.0.* De Gruyter Saur, Berlin, Germany.

Peters, I., and Stock, W. G. (2010). Power tags in information retrieval. *Library Hi Tech* 28(1), 81–93.

Peters, I., and Weller, K. (2008a). Paradigmatic and syntagmatic relations in knowledge organization systems. *Information—Wissenschaft und Praxis* 59(1), 100–107.

Peters, I., and Weller, K. (2008b). Tag gardening for folksonomy enrichment and maintenance. *Webology* 5(3). Retrieved from http://webology.ir/2008/v5n3/a58.html

Peters, I., and Stock, W. G. (2007). Folksonomies and information retrieval. In *Proceedings of the 70th ASIS&T Annual Meeting* (pp. 1510–1542). [CD-ROM].

Polanyi, M. (1967). *The Tacit Dimension.* Doubleday, Garden City, NY.

Pomerantz, J., Choemprayong, S., and Eakin, L. (2008). The development and impact of digital library funding in the United States. *Advances in Librarianship* 31, 37–92.

Prasad, M. V. N., and Plaza, E. (1996). Corporate memories as distributed case libraries. In *Proceedings of the 10th Knowledge Acquisition for Knowledge-Based Systems Workshop.* Banff, Alberta, Canada. Retrieved from http://ksi.cpsc.ucalgary.ca/KAW/KAW96/prasad/cm.html

Reeves, B. N., and Shipman, F. (1996). Tacit knowledge: Icebergs in collaborative design. *SIGOIS Bulletin* 17(3), 24–33.

Ryle, G. (1946). Knowing how and knowing that. *Proceedings of the Aristotelian Society* 46, 1–16.

Schreyögg, G., and Geiger, D. (2003). *Kann die Wissensspirale Grundlage des Wissensmanagement sein?* [*Can the knowledge spiral be a foundation of knowledge management?*]. Diskussionsbeiträge des Instituts für Management. Neue Folge 20/03. Freie Universität, Berlin, Germany.

Stein, E. (1995). Organizational memory: Review of concepts and recommendations for management. *International Journal of Information Management* 15(2), 17–32.

Stock, W. G. (2006). On relevance distributions. *Journal of the American Society for Information Science and Technology* 57(8), 1126–1129.

Stock, W. G. (2007a). *Information Retrieval*. Oldenbourg, Munich, Germany.

Stock, W. G. (2007b). Folksonomies and science communication: A mash-up of professional science databases and web 2.0 services. *Information Services & Use* 27, 97–103.

Stock, W. G. (2009). Begriffe und semantische Relationen in der Wissensrepräsentation. [Concepts and semantic relations in knowledge representation]. *Information—Wissenschaft und Praxis* 60(8), 403–420.

Stock, W. G., and Stock, M. (2008). *Wissensrepräsentation* [*Knowledge representation*]. Oldenbourg, Munich, Germany.

Vårheim, A. (2008, August 10–14). Theoretical approaches on public libraries as places creating social capital. *World Library and Information Congress: 74th IFLA General Conference and Council*, Québec, Quebec, Canada. Retrieved from http://archive.ifla.org/IV/ifla74/papers/091-varheim-en.pdf.

Weisgerber, D. W. (1997). Chemical Abstracts Service chemical registry system: History, scope, and impacts. *Journal of the American Society for Information Science* 48, 349–360.

Weiss, A. (2005). The power of collective intelligence. *netWorker* 9(3), 16–23.

Weller, K. (2010). *Knowledge Representation on the Social Semantic Web*. De Gruyter Saur, Berlin, Germany.

Weller, K., Peters, I., and Stock, W. G. (2010). Folksonomy: The collaborative knowledge organization system. In *Handbook of Research on Social Interaction Technologies and Collaborative Software: Concepts and Trends* (T. Dumova and R. Fiordo, eds.), pp. 132–146, Information Science Reference, Hershey, PA.

Yainik, N. M. (2010). Knowledge management and organizational digital libraries. *International Conference on Digital Libraries (ICDL): Shaping the Information Paradigm* (pp. 697–700), The Energy and Resources Institute, Indira Ghandi National Open University, New Delhi, India.

Yeung, C. M. A., Gibbins, N., and Shadbolt, N. (2006). Mutual contextualization in tripartite graphs of folksonomies. *Lecture Notes in Computer Science* 4825, 966–970.

Zhang, L., Wu, X., and Yu, Y. (2006). Emergent semantics from folksonomies: A quantitative study. *Lecture Notes in Computer Science* 4090, 168–186.

Planning Strategically, Designing Architecturally: A Framework for Digital Library Services

Steven Buchanan

Department of Computer and Information Sciences, University of Strathclyde, Glasgow, UK

Abstract

In an era of unprecedented technological innovation and evolving user expectations and information seeking behaviour, we are arguably now an online society, with digital services increasingly common and increasingly preferred. As a trusted information provider, libraries are in an advantageous position to respond, but this requires integrated strategic and enterprise architecture planning, for information technology (IT) has evolved from a support role to a strategic role, providing the core management systems, communication networks and delivery channels of the modern library. Furthermore, IT components do not function in isolation from one another but are interdependent elements of distributed and multi-dimensional systems encompassing people, processes and technologies, which must consider social, economic, legal, organisational and ergonomic requirements and relationships, as well as being logically sound from a technical perspective. Strategic planning provides direction, while enterprise architecture strategically aligns and holistically integrates business and information system architectures. While challenging, such integrated planning should be regarded as an opportunity for the library to evolve as an enterprise in the digital age, or at minimum, to simply keep pace with societal change and alternative service providers. Without strategy, a library risks being directed by outside forces with independent motivations and inadequate understanding of its broader societal role. Without enterprise architecture, it risks technological disparity, redundancy and obsolescence. Adopting an interdisciplinary approach, this conceptual chapter provides an integrated framework for strategic and architectural planning of digital library services. The concept of the library as an enterprise is also introduced.

I. Introduction

A key element of successful library management is strategic planning, which simply put provides organisational direction for the enterprise. Without a

EXPLORING THE DIGITAL FRONTIER
ADVANCES IN LIBRARIANSHIP, VOL. 32
© 2010 by Emerald Group Publishing Limited
ISSN: 0065-2830
DOI: 10.1108/S0065-2830(2010)0000032010

159

clear and coherent strategic plan, a library risks being directed by outside forces with independent motivations and perhaps more importantly, inadequate understanding of a library's broader societal role (Johnson et al., 2004; Kent, 2002). However, strategic planning is acknowledged as a challenging activity for librarians, which, at times, can be time consuming and unproductive (Linn, 2008). Furthermore, often when strategic plans do exist, they are couched in soft 'motherhood' terms, making them difficult to translate into operational plans, thus leading to ambiguous goals and objectives lacking clear measures of success. For example, a recent study that examined the strategic plans of 32 public libraries within a devolved jurisdiction of the United Kingdom, concluded that public libraries could improve not only completeness of plans (from vision statements to action plans) but also their precision, specificity, explicitness, coordination and consistency, and overall mapping to library services (Buchanan et al., 2010). Notably, the study also found digital goals broadly and generically defined and several plans to be parent local authority plans that lacked specificity to library services.

Of associated importance to a library is enterprise architecture, which strategically aligns and holistically integrates business and information system (IS) architectures, for in an era of unprecedented technological innovation and evolving user expectations and information-seeking behaviours (Brophy, 2007; Leong, 2008; Parry, 2008), solutions are often multifaceted and multiparty. For example Rogers (2007), reviewing trends in academic libraries, discusses how libraries must:

> evaluate, obtain and support products from more and more vendors whose primary clients are not libraries; participate in development and support of technology solutions with members of open source communities; (and) partner with other campus units to deliver coherent enterprise-wide information services through architectures that simplify discovery and navigation for an increasingly mobile population... (p. 375)

Brophy (2007) argues that rapid and complex technological change is where the biggest challenges lie for the library, and worryingly, suggests that librarians 'have not developed the skills to understand it, exploit it or create it' (p. 17). Whether this is true or not, there is certainly limited empirical evidence of enterprise architecture applied within the library domain, and yet without enterprise architecture, a library, like any other organisation, is at risk of technological disparity, redundancy, and obsolescence.

This chapter provides a framework for strategic planning, which, in acknowledgment of emerging digital services now increasingly common and increasingly preferred (Tonta, 2008), pays particular attention to information strategy and the relationship to enterprise architecture. The importance of a holistic approach is emphasised, with established methods and tools applicable to libraries highlighted.

II. Digital Library Services

Simply put, a digital library is a collection of digital content. However, the DELOS Network of Excellence on Digital Libraries (DELOS, 2007), describing the digital library as 'a tool at the centre of intellectual activity having no logical, conceptual, physical, temporal or personal barriers on information' (p. 15), has argued that digital libraries, in pursuit of perso- nalised interactive user experiences, have evolved from content-centric systems to person-centric systems, with the role of the digital library having 'shifted from static storage and retrieval of information to facilitation of communication, collaboration and other forms of collaboration' (p. 15). Arguably inherent within such a role is the provision of digital services, which go beyond simple provision of content.

Digital services can be considered as those services or resources accessed and/or provided through digital transaction (Williams *et al.*, 2008). Services can range from the relatively straightforward, such as provision of online tools and virtual space for collaboration, sharing of content and so on, to online reference services, and to more complex distributed and interactive systems such as digitised local archive collections purposefully linked to a local school curriculum through virtual learning environments. In the role of access provider, a digital library will also establish links to other public information providers with which it shares societal goals such as lifelong learning and health and wellbeing (e.g., across education, health and the arts), which may appear straightforward, but in practice are not so, for there are underlying information architecture implications and associated usability issues to consider, not the least of which is how to provide seamless access and interaction (Buchanan and McMenemy, 2010). However, a more significant associated challenge is that presented by dynamic and distributed multimedia content now inherent in many digital services. This, combined with rapid technological advancement and change, presents significant challenges for sustainable long-term digital preservation and access, a particular issue being how to capture and represent contextual information to preserve authenticity and integrity (Watry, 2007; Chowdhury, 2010).

Such trends and associated challenges raise a number of questions that emphasise the importance of planning strategically and designing architecturally. In particular: *what* digital services, with *who* and perhaps most challenging of all, *how*?

III. Strategy

Without strategy a library will lack organisational cohesion, shared values and common goals. Under such circumstances, library initiatives could be introduced independently of one another, encouraging division and potentially leading to disparity and duplication, particularly at the national and/or regional level and across collaborative partnerships such as those increasingly found between libraries, museums and archives. At best, the closest a library will come to exploit natural synergy and demonstrating value will be at the operational infrastructure level, but even this will be difficult to confirm without strategic direction and associated goals and measures.

A. The Components of a Strategic Plan

Although no standard definition of a strategic plan exists, often when strategy is discussed, reference is variously made to vision, mission, goals, objectives and courses of action (Koch, 2000). It is important to note that these are not synonymous terms, but discrete components of an articulated strategy:

> *Vision* is a top-level statement of what an organisation aspires to, embodying associated core values (e.g., lifelong learning). Vision statements typically set high expectations with a long-term focus, for example, Glasgow's (2006) cultural strategy aspires to 'establish ... a city of dynamic, successful, and connected communities where all forms of learning are recognised and valued'.
>
> *Mission* provides the vision statement with context. Also top-level (and often generalised to be more enduring), they provide an operational statement of what the organisation wants to do, typically focused on provision of services to particular market segments, or highlighting key activity (e.g., developing community learning hubs).
>
> *Goals* are statements about a particular end state that the organisation wishes to achieve over the medium to long term (e.g., providing a city-wide collection and catalogue). Goals are more dynamic than mission or vision statements, as they must respond to market forces and evolve to take advantage of ad hoc opportunities. They include targets and milestones.
>
> *Objectives* are specific, quantifiable and attainable short-term targets, which are used to measure the degree to which the organisation is realising its goals. Objectives are time-limited and associated with unambiguous and measurable criteria for success (e.g., increasing participation and audience development).
>
> *Courses of action* define the specific steps to be taken to realise goals and objectives, typically realised as a project plan. Action plans can be strategic (long term) or tactical (short term) but are typically short-term towards longer-term goals (e.g., developing integrated public and educational information services, creating digital heritage collections, expanding particular outreach activities).

Notwithstanding previously noted issues regarding lack of library specific plans, it is important to note that strategy can legitimately coexist at both the corporate level and unit level. Corporate level strategy, developed by the executive with input from senior management, focuses on high-level direction, mid- to long-term market position and partnerships. Unit or divisional strategy, developed by managers of the respective units, provides operational direction at the divisional level and is focused on customer service/segment and tactical responses to more dynamic and immediate market forces. Key to the existence of multiple levels of strategy is to ensure that they are hierarchical, with goals and objectives traceable back to the 'parent' strategy (e.g., the parent of an academic library strategy would be the university strategy, for a public library, the local authority strategy).

Strategic plans are also supported by policy, which provides more enduring operational guidelines, including boundaries and constraints. Focused on internal processes and procedures (e.g., collection policies for digital and repository initiatives), including legal and regulatory requirements, policy shapes and influences courses of action. Guidelines are predominantly 'hard,' motivated by legal or productivity goals, but are also influenced by 'soft' factors, such as customer expectations, and moral and ethical considerations.

B. The Strategic Planning Process

Strategic planning is typically initiated by regular planning cycle or review process (between 1 and 5 year cycles). However, dynamic market forces and new technology will continually influence and shape future directions. As a consequence, strategic planning should actually be considered a continuous process, which allows longer term plans to evolve or be revisited between cycles.

Various strategic planning processes have been proposed, but although terminology differs across authors there is underlying commonality of purpose and broad applicability. For example, Chaffey (2002), writing for e-business, proposes a four-stage process of *strategic analysis* (environmental scanning and the assessment of existing capabilities and assets), *strategic objectives* (stating the vision, mission, goals and objectives), *strategic definition* (option generation, evaluation and selection) and *strategic implementation* (planning, execution and control). Roberts and Rowley (2004), writing for information services management, propose a similar but three-stage process of *strategic analysis and audit* (external environment and internal resources), *strategic choice* (objectives, options and choices) and *strategic action and implementation* (planning, resource allocation, monitoring and control). Allison and Kaye (2005), writing for nonprofit organisations, break the planning process down into seven stages: *get ready* (setup), *articulate mission, vision and values* (strategic direction), *assess*

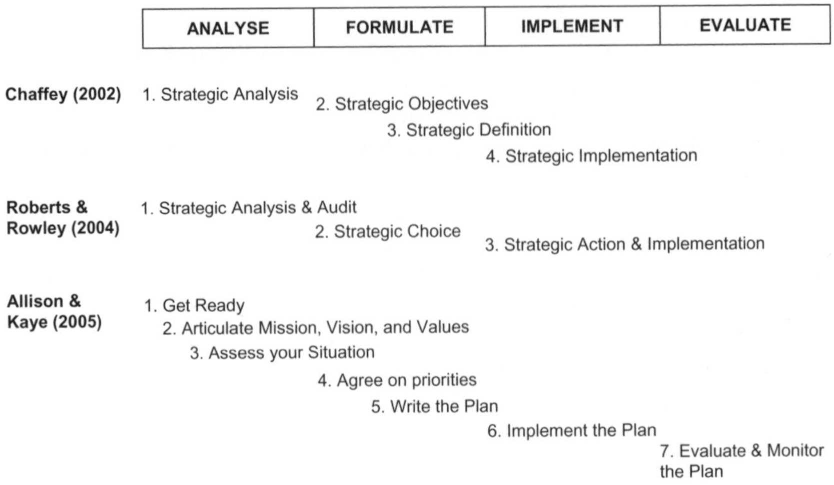

ANALYSE	FORMULATE	IMPLEMENT	EVALUATE

Chaffey (2002)   1. Strategic Analysis
                         2. Strategic Objectives
                                  3. Strategic Definition
                                            4. Strategic Implementation

Roberts &   1. Strategic Analysis & Audit
Rowley (2004)
                          2. Strategic Choice
                                  3. Strategic Action & Implementation

Allison &   1. Get Ready
Kaye (2005)
                2. Articulate Mission, Vision, and Values
                     3. Assess your Situation
                          4. Agree on priorities
                              5. Write the Plan
                                      6. Implement the Plan
                                                7. Evaluate & Monitor
                                          the Plan

Fig. 1   The strategic planning process.

your situation (internal and external analysis), *agree on priorities* (core strategies, long-term goals and objectives), *write the plan* (strategic plan), *implement the plan* (annual plan and operating guidelines) and *evaluate and monitor the strategic plan* (cyclical evaluation and revision). Through high-level comparison, a four-stage generic process of *analyse, formulate, implement* and *evaluate* can be identified (Fig. 1).

In the analyse stage, analysis of external and internal factors is undertaken to evaluate organisational performance and 'proof' new concepts/initiatives. External analysis will include evaluation of international and local trends, drivers and barriers; local market segmentation and services assessment; and opportunity analysis. Internal analysis will include organisational appraisal, including 'strategic fit' of new concepts/initiatives; and organisational readiness review, with particular regard to capability and competency, which will include infrastructure, process and resource considerations.

In the formulate stage, concepts are developed into plans, dependent on the outcome of the analyse stage (which will influence direction, budget, etc.). Formulate will typically begin with more detailed analysis and development of the value proposition, including gap analysis, vision and objectives, and options and risks. In this stage various scenarios may be explored to identify a preferred course of action. Once identified, the next step will be to specify (where applicable): target market segments, sales and distribution channels, customer management, financial implications, 'fit' within current services roadmap and key organisational factors such as process implications. This stage will also include communication of vision to gain organisational commitment and to clearly align courses of action with overall corporate strategy.

In the implement stage, the program of work/action is developed, including more detailed budget formulation and allocation. It is common to find a further budget check at this point, re-confirming costs once more detailed requirements are known/specified. Upon successful initiation of the program of work, concepts are tracked to implementation from both an operational and a strategic perspective. In simple terms, operational aligns with typical project management roles and responsibilities, while strategic ensures continued alignment with overall vision, objectives and measures.

In the evaluate stage, outcome is measured, which will involve cost–benefit analysis, market surveys and process/service benchmarking, etc. It is important to note that effective library evaluation will employ both quantitative and qualitative techniques (McMenemy et al., 2008), balancing output-oriented performance indicators (e.g., stock turnover, borrowing figures) with social audit methods extending beyond usage to social utility (e.g., personal development, social cohesion). Dependent on the initiative, the timescale for measurement will typically range from 3 to 12 months, with results forming the foundation of the learning loop, contributing to further cycles of strategic planning.

In traditional strategic planning cycles, strategy, as dictated by market goals and forces, has driven resource procurement, development and management, with associated information resources (e.g., technology, applications) often considered part of infrastructure support. However, in today's online, digital world, this relationship has evolved to become more mutually dependent, for technology can shape and influence strategy, opening up new markets and services and offering opportunity for differentiation and innovation in existing markets through enhanced offerings and additional delivery channels. Furthermore, in the digital age, information is often *the* commodity, and technology often *the* delivery process. In such circumstances, attention is drawn to the importance of information strategy.

C. Information Strategy

Information strategy provides overarching direction and operational guidance for the effective deployment and management of an organisation's information resources. Earl (1989, 2000) identifies four properties of information strategy: management, technology, systems and resources. However, Gibb et al. (2006) argue that Earl's use of the term 'information

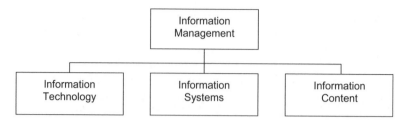

Fig. 2 The components of information strategy (adapted from Earl, 2000).

resource' is perhaps unfortunate in that there has been a long-standing use of the term information resource to refer to all the resources used to exploit information: information personnel, technology, systems and content. They propose that a more appropriate term would be 'content strategy' associated with the related activity of enterprise content management. The adapted model is illustrated in Fig. 2.

It should be emphasised that the distinctions made between these four properties to some degree represents an ideal, for in reality, the size of an organisation or its attitude to information resources may blur boundaries. However, Earl's (1989, 2000) model is important in making the distinction between the technologies needed for processing information, the applications that support or instantiate these processes, the information generated or consumed and the over-arching management of these resources.

1. Information Technology Strategy

Information technology (IT) strategy is concerned primarily with technological issues such as architecture, standards, physical security, data integrity, service availability and maintenance, support and procurement. It is therefore answering the 'how' question, for example, how will we deliver digital services? This covers desktop platforms, peripherals, networks, servers and other shared computer processing capability and repositories of data, operating systems and software tools. The key goal of the strategy is to ensure that there is a robust but flexible infrastructure that can support the range of applications required to satisfy organisational objectives. In an ideal world, it might be argued that the strategy should be to embrace the use of an agreed set of technologies to simplify management, reduce costs and provide guarantees that data can be exchanged between co-operating systems. In practice, library IT managers will have to deal with legacy issues such as new technologies for which standards may not yet be agreed, purchases that take place outside procurement guidelines and software version drift.

2. Information Systems Strategy

IS strategy is concerned with ensuring that systems development is in tune with organisational needs and identifying and prioritising applications for development. This requires a focus on service and process models, data definitions, information architectures and user needs. It is concerned with the 'what' question, for example, what application set is required to meet service objectives. The IS strategy will focus on enterprise-level application needs, in particular those systems that support and/or integrate end-to-end processes. This is particularly important for ensuring that data captured by customer-facing applications (e.g., customer request/renewal) can be instantly supported by data on, for instance, stock levels (from stock management and inter-library loan systems), lead-times (from publishers production management systems) and delivery times (from distributors supply chain management systems). It is desirable for all IS to be addressed by the IS strategy, but individual systems often justifiably exist within individual units or divisions based on local need (e.g., within collaborative partnerships). In these circumstances, clear ownership is essential.

3. Information Management Strategy

Information management strategy is concerned with identifying and specifying the roles and responsibilities necessary for the delivery, support and development of IT, IS and information content (IC) functions and activities. This involves establishing clear ownership and accountability for information activities and addresses the 'who' question (e.g., who resources, authorisers, quality assurers, tests, maintainers, controls). It should also be concerned with the co-ordination of all related information resources and establishing the appropriate controls, guidelines and procedures that are necessary to ensure the quality, availability, protection and timeliness of information. This requires a clear understanding of the implications of legislation and regulations concerned with information handling. Finally, it is concerned with identifying and ensuring that the competencies needed to deliver and exploit IS and technologies are available to the organisation. This will include in-house, contracted and outsourced activities. It will also be reflected in the need to provide appropriate training to develop and use the applications and tools.

4. Information Content Strategy

IC strategy is focused on content and its management encompassing all forms of media (e.g., paper, film, tape, disc) and all forms of information (image, sound, text and data). In addition, depending on the approach taken to knowledge management, it may include intellectual capital such as patents and copyrighted material. Earl (1989, 2000) suggests that this is about answering the 'where' question (i.e., where are we going?), but it is perhaps simpler to view it as another 'what' question: what information do our employees, suppliers and customers need in order for us to provide an effective service? IC strategy must therefore consider categorisation of information, version control, archives, documents standards, metadata for information resource description, retention and disposal policies and information quality. Categorisation is a particularly important activity as efficient and effective retrieval, and protection is predicated by effective analysis and indexing. Although libraries use standard classification systems (such as DDC or LCC) and employ cataloguing standards (e.g., MARC, ISBD, RDA), there is no single standard to which they all subscribe with differences in stock description techniques having been found to be particularly obstructive in establishing joint digital collections (Tonta, 2008; Bailey-Hainer and Urban, 2004).

D. Integrated Strategic Planning

Information strategy should not be considered as a parallel strategic planning activity, but as an integrated, and core part of the overall planning process. Earl (1989), when considering information strategy formulation, suggested that there are three approaches to analysis and planning: (a) a top-down approach that sets direction and then allocates information resource investment accordingly; (b) a bottom-up approach that evaluates current information resource capability to identify and respond to gaps in provision and (c) a two-way approach that considers both current and future needs and explores opportunity for innovation. Effective analysis and planning would encompass each of these approaches [as part of the *analyse* and *formulate* stages (see Fig. 1)], allowing a library (with particular regard to information resources) to strategically identify where it wants to be, where it currently is, and what it must provide to bridge any gaps.

Information strategy formulation is thus both strategic and architectural in perspective, with strategic plans and future digital services shaped by the potential enabling role of new technology and influenced by the limitations of existing legacy technology. A method to formally extend strategy formulation to architectural planning is provided by enterprise architecture.

IV. Enterprise Architecture

Enterprise architecture extends strategic planning to IT architecture, ensuring business and technology architectures are holistically aligned, integrated and coordinated. Beyond the strategic imperative, there are significant financial and operational benefits to be realised through an enterprise architecture, including better returns on existing IT investments, reduced new investment risk, lower development, support and maintenance costs, increased portability of applications and improved ability to address critical enterprise-wide issues (Open Group, 2006).

A. The Library as an Enterprise

Perhaps the simplest definition of an enterprise is a collection of organisational entities, which share a common goal and foundation infrastructure. The simplest example is a single organisation. However, in multi-national federated organisations, it is also valid to consider a subsidiary or division as an enterprise. It is also important to note that in today's online domain, the boundaries of an enterprise can be extended to include partners.

Across the public and private sectors, partnerships are now widely recognised, not just as a strategic option, but also in several instances as a strategic necessity (Beckett, 2005). Wildridge *et al.* (2004) argue that in a rapidly evolving and increasingly complex global society, 'partnership working is a key area for the library information professional currently, and is crucial for the profession for the future' (p. 14), and Brophy (2007, p. 212) similarly argues that 'Libraries cannot go it alone and their future strength will depend on the alliances they forge' (p. 212). Perhaps not surprisingly therefore, library collaboration is now beginning to extend beyond archives and museums to educational institutions, social services, health services, private industry and other cultural organisations, which share goals such as early learning, cultural heritage and health and wellbeing. Within the digital domain, joint initiatives such as cross-institutional digital collections and shared virtual learning environments are emerging, with libraries assuming the role of both content provider and access provider. In so doing, they are establishing the library as an enterprise, with an associated architectural requirement.

B. Elements of Enterprise Architecture

Perks and Beveridge (2003, p. 12) define enterprise architecture as 'the collection of strategic and architectural disciplines that encompass the information, business system and technical architectures' of an organisation' (p. 12). The Open Group (2006), upon which Perks and Beveridge's definition is based, further defines this as consisting of four subset architectures:

> *Business.* The strategic, governance and organisational framework and structure and the processes, functions and roles within.
>
> *Data.* Logical and physical data entities, assets and data management resources.
>
> *Application.* Individual applications, their interactions and relationship to business processes.
>
> *Technology.* The logical and physical networks, transmission media and protocols and hardware that provide the supporting infrastructure for business processes.

Similar to Earl's (1989, 2000) model, enterprise architecture distinguishes between the technology required to process information, the applications that support or instantiate processes, and the information generated or consumed. Notably, attention is also paid to business architecture, which defines the organisational processes, functions and roles supported by data, application and technology architectures.

C. Enterprise Architecture Frameworks

Two often cited architectural frameworks discussed below are the Zachmann Architectural Framework, commonly considered a founding framework (Schekkerman, 2006), and The Open Group Architectural Framework (TOGAF), an open group standard supported by the practitioner community and over 200 member organisations.

1. The Zachman Architectural Framework

The Zachman framework (Zachman, 1987) was proposed as an approach to IS architecture, which tackled the acknowledged, but then only partially addressed requirement for multiple stakeholder views of IS architecture. Zachman drew on proven architectural principles and processes from the construction, manufacturing and avionics industries, to develop a framework suitable for IS architecture. The framework provides a comprehensive and modular classification of viewpoints and models, representing and relating all stakeholder perspectives and allowing architects to focus on selected aspects of the system without losing sight of the bigger picture. In the years since its publication it has become the de facto standard for many within the IS architecture community.

The framework is a matrix of six columns and six rows providing 36 cells representing the views of IS architecture. The initial framework was made up of the first three columns (Zachman, 1987), but this was later expanded (Sowa and Zachman, 1992) to the six.

The rows represent the perspectives. They are:

Scope represents the contextual view of the planner or investor who wants an estimate of the scope of the system, what it would cost and how it would perform.

Business model represents the conceptual view of the owner who wants to understand the business model and the relationship between entities and processes.

System model represents the logical view of the designer who must determine the data elements and functions that represent business entities and processes.

Technology model represents the physical view of the builder who must adapt the IS model to the details of the programming languages, I/O devices, etc. and consider the constraints of tools, technology and resources.

Detailed representation represents the out-of-context view of the subcontractor who typically works from detailed specifications, often at the component level.

Functioning enterprise represents the operational system view.

The columns provide a set of questions, which lead to the different perspectives. They are: *what* is the system made of; *how* does the system work; *where* are the system components and connections; *who* does the work; *when* do things happen and *why* are various choices made?

Associated framework rules specify that elements (e.g., dimensions/cells) are unique, dynamically interdependent and logically recursive. There is no order of priority or sequence, but all six dimensions are needed to fully represent each perspective (the composite or integration of all cell models in one row constitutes a complete perspective).

Zachman is a logical framework, which does not prescribe or describe any particular method, representation technique, or tool. Perhaps the simplest way to view the framework is as a basic structure for providing a set of architectural representations of an organisations' enterprise architecture. The Open Group (2006) suggested that the main strength of the framework is that it provides a way of thinking about an enterprise in an organised way, so that it can be described and analysed. Abdullah and Zainab (2008), arguing that in the field of collaborative digital libraries stakeholder needs and context of use are not usually captured comprehensively, adopted the Zachman Framework as a formal framework for digital library design. They found the framework to be particularly useful for requirements specification, providing a framework for comprehensively and systematically capturing both user need and context of use via the respective perspectives and dimensions (in particular planner, owner and designer). The logic of the Zachman framework can be seen applied within other models, for example, the DELOS Digital Library Reference Model (DELOS, 2007) identifies four key views and associated actors: (a) end users who exploit digital library functionality for providing, consuming and managing content; (b) designers who define, customise and maintain the digital library; (c) system administrators who identify the necessary architectural configuration and components to implement the digital library and (d) developers who develop the components of the digital library.

2. The Open Group Architectural Framework

TOGAF is an enterprise architecture development method, which can be applied at the enterprise, multi-system or single system level of an organisation. The original version released in 1995 was based on the technical architecture framework for information management (TAFIM), developed by the U.S. Department of Defence. Since 1995 TOGAF has evolved year-on-year through extensive industry consultation and user-group feedback and involvement, with the overarching goal being to establish boundary-less information flow. The framework is freely and publicly available and has been adopted across both the public and private sector. It consists of three main parts:

> *Architectural development method (ADM).* The methodology that defines the processes required for transition from foundation architecture to organisation-specific architecture.
> *Enterprise continuum.* The virtual repository of architectural models, standards and documents.
> *Resource base.* Additional guidelines, templates, checklists and background information.

The ADM is at the core of the TOGAF model, providing a systematic step-by-step approach to enterprise architecture development. The model begins with preliminary setup tasks associated with scope, definition and management processes. The next phase continues scoping and establishing the remit of the architectural exercise, but with the emphasis now on vision, strategic alignment and organisational recognition and endorsement. The next three phases focus on systematic architectural modelling (baseline and target) of the business architecture, IS architecture (data and applications) and technology architecture. The final four phases are concerned with solution identification and implementation (viewed as parallel rather than sequential processes). The ADM is regarded as a continuous, cyclical and iterative process; with the first iteration regarded as the hardest, primarily due to it taking place at an initial stage of the enterprise continuum.

The enterprise continuum is a virtual repository of architectural artefacts and assets, which exists to enable architectural development. The continuum is expressed by TOGAF as a combination of two complementary architectural concepts: architectural continuum and solutions continuum.

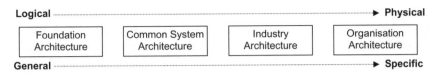

Fig. 3   The architecture continuum (adapted from TOGAF, 2002).

The architectural continuum provides a way to define and understand generic architectural rules, representations and relationships among foundation frameworks; and to discover commonality and eliminate unnecessary redundancy. Presented as an evolutionary process, which begins with the TOGAF foundation architecture, through common system architectures, and industry specific architectures, to an organisations own individual architecture (Fig. 3). This represents a progression from logical to physical and from general to specific based on adoption/leverage of reusable architectural components and building blocks.

The solutions continuum represents the implementation of the architecture at the corresponding levels of the architecture continuum (products and services, system solutions, industry solutions, organisation solutions). At each level, the solutions continuum is a population of the architecture with reference to building blocks, either purchased or built that represent a solution to organisational requirement at each respective level. A populated solution continuum can be regarded as a solution inventory or reuse library, with associated benefits.

The enterprise continuum, at the highest level, is a conceptual model providing a logical schema for architectural analysis and design, which as an example, is applicable to the previously noted digital preservation challenge. For example, Moore (2008, p. 64) has called for 'new types of storage systems, new protocols for accessing data, new data-encoding formats, and new standards for characterizing provenance' (p. 64) while Chowdhury (2010) asks:

> How do we create an environment—tools, techniques, standards and the appropriate IT infrastructure—so that the huge volume and variety of content can be taken from the past to the future, along with their specified users and the intended use, on a global scale? (p. 219)

The continuum encourages such requirements to be approached from a common perspective ensuring that solutions are industry wide. In support, TOGAF provide two sets of reference models, which provide the foundation for the continuum: firstly the foundation architecture that comprises a technical reference model (TRM) of generic services and functions (at the generic platform level) and an associated standards information base (SIB); and secondly the integrated information infrastructure reference model (III-RM), a subset of the TRM that provides a taxonomy of business applications and infrastructure applications required to provide an III (e.g., equivalent to distinguishing between the digital library system, the digital library management system and the associated development tools).

Finally, the TOGAF resource base specifies the resources required to support architectural development and management and provides a selection of guidelines, templates and background information to support the use of the TOGAF ADM, extending to contract definition. The resource base also provides a repository of case studies and includes guidelines for evaluating architectural tools.

In contrast to Zachman, the TOGAF framework provides a step-by-step method for architectural planning, development and change management. While Zachman's is simple and non-prescriptive, TOGAF is detailed and to a degree, prescriptive. However, rather than viewing the frameworks as either/or approaches, they can be considered as compatible components of an overall approach. Viewed in combination, TOGAF can provide the methodological step-by-step development process, while Zachman can guide and facilitate comprehensive visualisation and representation.

V. From Strategy to Architecture

Natural synergy between information strategy and enterprise architecture models can form the basis of an integrated approach to digital library service development, ensuring that initiatives are strategically and architecturally aligned.

A. An Integrated Framework

Buchanan and Gibb (2007) have mapped a relationship from information strategy to enterprise architecture frameworks through Earl's (1989, 2000) information strategy components, as illustrated in Fig. 4.

In Fig. 4, strategic planning is shown as a two-way process, acknowledging the iterative relationship between organisational goals, current capabilities and opportunity for technological innovation. The Zachman framework provides a method for representing the organisational and architectural entities essential to a system view, while TOGAF extends Earl's (2000) taxonomy, providing a methodology that bridges the gap between strategy formulation and architectural planning and development.

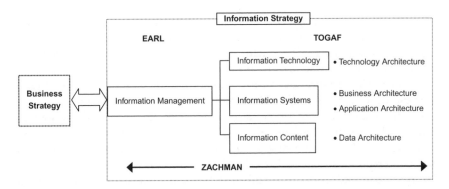

Fig. 4 Information strategy and enterprise architecture (Buchanan and Gibb, 2007).

B. The Role of the Information Audit

In support of the integrated framework illustrated in Fig. 4, Buchanan and Gibb (2007) recommend the information audit as a practical method for identifying and evaluating an organisation's information resources, which consists of five steps (Buchanan and Gibb, 1998):

> *Promote.* Communicating the benefits of the audit, establishing commitment and cooperation and conducting a preliminary survey of the organisation.
>
> *Identify.* Top-down strategic analysis of the organisation followed by identification of information resources and information flow.
>
> *Analyse.* Analysis and evaluation of identified information resources and formulation of action plans.
>
> *Account.* Cost/value analysis of information resources.
>
> *Synthesise.* Reporting on the audit and development of the organisation information strategy.

Buchanan and Gibb (2007) specify the scope of an information audit as two dimensional, with Earl's (2000) four components of information strategy the first dimension and organisational 'perspective' the second, further specified as strategic, process and resource perspectives, respectively. While process focuses on functions and associated information flow, and resource focuses on identification, classification and evaluation of information resources, strategic focuses on the realisation of strategic goals through mapping and analysis of the relationship between organisational mission and associated information resources. Typical questions to be answered by a strategic oriented information audit would include: what is our mission, how can we achieve this, what is essential to our success, what information resources do we use/require, are there any gaps or constraints, and where can we use information resources to our advantage?

The Buchanan and Gibb (1998) information audit methodology includes (as part of identify and analyse) steps to identify and define the organisations mission, environment, structure, culture, information flow and information resources and to then evaluate information resources according to strategic importance and utility and formulate action plans. Following this top-down approach allows hierarchical relationships to be mapped from mission to objectives to organisational function to information resources and enables a corresponding value to be assigned to information resources in relation to the function supported (on a scale ranging from [1] not used or has no perceived benefit to [5] critical to function). Reference is also made by Buchanan and Gibb to established business analysis tools common to strategic planning, which provide a simple, visual method by which to stimulate strategic thinking within working groups (a common and recommended approach to strategic analysis and planning). These tools can be criticised as overly simplistic, but this is largely due to inappropriate extended use. As a tool to initiate more detailed analysis and planning, they can be highly effective. For example, the Boston Consulting Group product portfolio matrix (Henderson, 1970) can be used to distinguish between low and high growth digital services relative to market/audience demand and plot position relative to alternative providers; McFarlan and McKenney's (1983) Strategic Grid to assess individual information resources, identifying their current and future strategic importance (in relation to digital services); and the Technology S-curve, derived from Rogers (1962) diffusion of innovation theory, to understand and evaluate key stages of technology adoption and diffusion (Bowden, 2004), and proactively manage technology lifecycles (e.g., e-book readers).

Undertaking an information audit as either a precursor to strategic planning or incorporated within the *review* and *formulate* stages of the planning process (Fig. 1) will assist in ensuring that a library's information resources are effectively identified and utilised in pursuit of strategic goals and that the opportunity offered by new technology is fully considered and exploited when setting these goals. Information audit output can provide direct input to the *scope*, *business model* and *system model* perspectives of the Zachman framework and establish or contribute to architectural baselines for the TOGAF ADM (Buchanan and Gibb, 2007).

C. The Role of Systems' Thinking

The relationship between strategy and architecture is complex, being interdependent and multidimensional. There are dynamic environmental factors to consider, organisational processes and procedures to understand, information resources to identify and evaluate and new technology to consider, both strategically and architecturally (in terms of organisational 'fit'). Such complexity requires a holistic perspective, as encouraged by the practice of systems' thinking.

In simple terms, a system is defined as a collection of entities linked together in a regulated set of relationships to form a complex whole. Examples could include organisational and biological systems. However, for our purposes, a system is defined as a set of logical, related components (consisting of people, technology, inputs, processes and outputs within a system boundary) brought together to accomplish a predefined organisational goal, which is achieved primarily through the processing of information.

Systems' thinking recognises that systems have emergent properties that would not exist if their component parts were not linked together (potentially transcending functional boundaries) and that any reasonably complex system will contain various sub-systems. Systems' thinking recognises that every system has a boundary, outside of which exists the system environment, where there are elements that affect the system, but which cannot be controlled by the system. The starting point for the analysis or design of a system is to determine what is inside the system and what is outside the system, but part of its environment.

Notably, within systems theory there are two perspectives regarding the fundamental nature of systems and how they should be defined, modelled and measured: a hard systems view advocated by engineering and technical professions that maintains that systems are tangible and a soft systems view advocated by social science professions that argues that systems are partly based on ideas, or models of the world, with only parts of these systems represented by objects in the physical world. In truth both perspectives provide useful insights into the processes and information flow that underpin an organisation, because effective systems must be designed and built in response to the needs of the organisation and its environment. Consequently, they must take into account complex social, economic, organisational and ergonomic requirements and relationships, as well as being technically and logically sound.

A recent evaluation of the usability and usefulness of a UK National Health Service digital library (Buchanan and Salako, 2009) illustrates this point. The digital library had been developed to provide clinicians with direct access to clinical evidence and best practice recommendations to support decision-making at the point of care and to support ongoing professional development. At the time of evaluation it had only recently been launched. Participants in the study (clinicians) found the digital library to be usable from a design standpoint, but not particularly useful, questioning its purpose in relation to existing e-library services, and more importantly, how it might be used under variable clinical conditions and settings (e.g., on ward rounds). The study highlighted the importance of cognitive and contextual considerations to system design (beyond the interface) and the importance of accounting for variable user scenarios. In a follow-on study (Buchanan and McMenemy, 2009), a systems thinking approach was adopted to demonstrate how process modelling of the clinical consultation process facilitated better understanding of activity to be supported and assisted with the identification of those environmental conditions and constraints which influence use. Such an approach not only provided the required holistic perspective, but the resultant process models could be used to inform business architecture and to guide associated data, application and technology architectures.

VI. Conclusion

In an era of unprecedented technological innovation and evolving user expectations and information seeking behaviour, we are now arguably an online society, with digital information services increasingly common and increasingly preferred. As a trusted source of information, libraries are in an advantageous position to respond, but this requires integrated strategic and architectural planning, which while challenging should be regarded as an opportunity to evolve as an enterprise in the digital age, or as a minimum, to simply keep pace with societal change and alternative service providers.

Enterprise architecture extends strategic planning to IT architecture, facilitating strategic and architectural alignment, distinguishing between low and high growth digital services, identifying current and future strategic importance of associated information resources and proactively managing technology lifecycles. Beyond the strategic imperative, there are significant financial and operational benefits to be realised, including better returns on existing IT investments; reduced new investment risk; lower development, support and maintenance costs; increased portability of applications; and improved ability to address critical enterprise-wide issues.

Strategic planning is presented as a four-stage cyclical process of *review*, *formulate*, *implement* and *evaluate*; with a relationship from strategy to enterprise architecture provided through Earl's (2000) information strategy taxonomy, which can be mapped to the four-subset architectures of TOGAF. TOGAF extends Earl's taxonomy, providing a methodology that bridges the gap between strategy formulation and architectural planning and development. The Zachman framework can assist with requirements specification, providing a framework for comprehensively and systematically capturing both user need and context of use, while the information audit can be utilised to identify and evaluate existing information resources. Systems thinking provides the necessary overarching holistic perspective.

References

Abdullah, A., and Zainab, A. N. (2008). The digital library as an enterprise: The Zachman approach. *The Electronic Library* 26(4), 446–467.

Allison, M., and Kaye, J. (2005). *Strategic Planning for Nonprofit Organizations: A Practical Guide and Workbook.* Wiley, Hoboken, NJ.

Bailey-Hainer, B., and Urban, R. (2004). The Colorado digitization program: A collaboration success story. *Library Hi Tech* 22(3), 254–262.

Beckett, R. C. (2005). Collaboration now a strategic necessity. *Handbook of Business Strategy* 6(1), 327–332.

Bowden, M. J. (2004). Moore's law and the technology s-curve. *Stevens Alliance for Technology Management* 8(1), 1–4.

Brophy, P. (2007). *The Library in the Twenty-First Century,* 2nd ed. Facet, London, England.

Buchanan, S., and Gibb, F. (1998). The information audit: An integrated strategic approach. *The International Journal of Information Management* 18(1), 29–47.

Buchanan, S., and Gibb, F. (2007). The information audit: Role and scope. *International Journal of Information Management* 27(3), 159–172.

Buchanan, S., and McMenemy, D. (2009). *Evaluating Digital Library Usefulness: Beyond the User Interface.* Paper presented at Internet Librarian International 2009, London, England.

Buchanan, S., and McMenemy, D. (2010). Towards a public library digital service taxonomy. In: Lalmas, M., Jose, J., Rauber, A., Sebastiani, F., & Frommholz, I (Eds), *Research and advanced technology for digital libraries lecture notes in computer science: Proceedings of the 14th European Conference, ECDL 2010,* Glasgow, UK (pp. 425–428).

Buchanan, S., and Salako, A. (2009). Evaluating the usability and usefulness of a digital library. *Library Review* 58(9), 38–651.

Buchanan, S., McMenemy, D., Ruthven, I., and Cousins, F. (2010). *From Strategy to Information Systems Architecture: A Review of Public Library Strategic Planning.* Poster presented at the International Conference on Conceptions of Library and Information Science (CoLIS 7), London, England.

Chaffey, D. (2002). *E-Business and E-Commerce Management.* Financial Times/Prentice Hall, Harlow, England.

Chowdhury, G. (2010). From digital libraries to digital preservation research: The importance of users and context. *Journal of Documentation* 66(2), 207–223.

DELOS (2007). *Digital Library Reference Model: Foundations for Digital Libraries Version 0.98.* Retrieved from www.delos.info/files/pdf/ReferenceModel/DELOS_DLReferenceModel_0.98.pdf.

Earl, M. J. (1989). *Management Strategies for IT.* Prentice-Hall, Englewood Cliffs, NJ.

Earl, M. J. (2000). Every business is an information business. In *Mastering Information Management* (D. Marchand, ed.), pp. 16–22, Financial Times/Prentice-Hall, London, England.

Gibb, F., Buchanan, S., and Shah, S. (2006). An integrated approach to process and service management. *International Journal of Information Management* 26(1), 44–58.

Glasgow City Council. (2006). *Glasgow's Cultural Strategy.* Retrieved from www.csglasgow.org/aboutus/Policy_Planning_Strategy/csgculturalstrategy.htm

Henderson, B. (1970). *Perspectives on the Product Portfolio.* Boston Consulting Group, Boston, MA.

Johnson, I. M., Williams, C. A., Wavell, C., and Baxter, G. (2004). Impact evaluation, professional practice, and policy making. *New Library World* 105(1/2), 33–46.

Kent, S. (2002). The public library director in the dot (.) world. *New Library World* 103(1/2), 48–54.

Koch, R. (2000). *The Financial Times Guide to Strategy: How to Create and Deliver a Useful Strategy.* Financial Times/Prentice Hall, London, England.

Leong, J. (2008). Academic reference librarians prepare for change: An Australian case study. *Library Management* 29(1–2), 77–86.

Linn, M. (2008). Library strategies: Planning strategically and strategic planning. *The Bottom Line: Managing Library Finances* 21(1), 20–23.

McFarlan, F. W., and McKenney, J. L. (1983). *Corporate Information Systems Management.* Richard D Irwin, Homewood, IL.

McMenemy, D., Buchanan, S., and Rooney-Browne, C. (2008). *Measurement of Library Services: To Quantify or Qualify?* Paper presented at Management and Marketing Section Program for the World Library and Information Congress, IFLA, Quebec City, Quebec, Canada.

Moore, R. (2008). Towards a theory of digital preservation. *The International Journal of Digital Curation* 3(1), 63–75.

Open Group. (2006). *TOGAF 8.1.1.* Retrieved from www.opengroup.org/architecture/togaf8-doc/arch/

Parry, J. (2008). Librarians do fly: Strategies for staying aloft. *Library Management* 29(1–2), 41–50.

Perks, C., and Beveridge, T. (2003). *Guide to Enterprise IT Architecture: A Strategic Approach.* Springer-Verlag, New York, NY.

Roberts, S., and Rowley, J. (2004). *Managing Information Services.* Facet, London, England.

Rogers, E. M. (1962). *Diffusion of Innovations.* Free Press, New York, NY.

Rogers, S. A. (2007). Assessing trends to cultivate new thinking in academic libraries. *Library Management* 28(6–7), 366–378.

Schekkerman, J. (2006). *How to survive in the jungle of enterprise architecture frameworks.* Trafford, Victoria, Canada.

Sowa, J. F., and Zachman, J. A. (1992). Extending and formalizing the framework for information systems architecture. *IBM Systems Journal* 31(3), 590–616.

Tonta, Y. (2008). Libraries and museums in the flat world: Are they becoming virtual destinations? *Library Collections, Acquisitions, and Technical Services* 32, 1–9.

Watry, P. (2007). Digital preservation theory and application: Transcontinental persistent archives testbed activity. *The International Journal of Digital Curation* 2(2), 41–68.

Wildridge, V., Childs, S., Cawthra, L., and Madge, B. (2004). How to create successful partnerships—A review of the literature. *Health Information and Libraries Journal* 21, 3–19.

Williams, K., Chatterjee, S., and Rossi, M. (2008). Design of emerging digital services: A taxonomy. *European Journal of Information Systems* 17(5), 505–517.

Zachman, J. A. (1987). A framework for information systems architecture. *IBM Systems Journal* 26(3), 276–292.

Recent Trends in EU Information Policy: Toward Greater Transparency in the Information Society

Debbie Rabina[a] and Scott Johnston[b]

[a]School of Information and Library Science, Pratt Institute, New York, NY, USA

[b]McPherson Library, University of Victoria, Victoria, British Columbia, Canada

Abstract

This chapter discusses recent information policy activities and initiatives in the European Union (EU). EU information policy refers to the legislation and strategies pertaining to the creation of the European information society. It is concerned with economic and industrial competitiveness, with an emphasis on the role that information and communication technologies play in revolutionizing everyday life. This discussion focuses on the information policy areas of greatest interest to information professionals. It addresses the EU's struggles with the concept of transparency with regard to the Anti-Counterfeiting Trade Agreement, the application of privacy measures to the Internet of Things, and open-access to EU-funded research.

I. Introduction

Information policy in the European Union (EU) has long been the focus of intense scrutiny as a result of the sheer scope and ambition of the undertaking. It is the goal of this chapter to provide a discussion of the major activities and initiatives in the European Information Society that have been on the European Commission's agenda during the past year as the EU struggles with the concept of transparency. Focus is on the concerns and issues of greatest interest to librarians and information professionals and

EXPLORING THE DIGITAL FRONTIER
ADVANCES IN LIBRARIANSHIP, VOL. 32
© 2010 by Emerald Group Publishing Limited
ISSN: 0065-2830
DOI: 10.1108/S0065-2830(2010)0000032011

contextualizing the analysis in a framework familiar to information professionals, particularly those practicing in the United States.

Information policy is an umbrella term for official government policies that govern the collection, storage, and dissemination of official information within a specific jurisdiction. In their definition of information policy, Hernon and Relyea (2003) emphasize the cyclical nature of the information policy process: "Information policy is ... a set of interrelated principles, laws, guidelines, rules, regulations, and procedures guiding the oversight and management of the information *life cycle*: the production, collection, distribution/dissemination, retrieval and use, and retirement, including preservation, of information" (p. 1300). At the government level, information policy is designed to be operational and is executed by a series of laws, regulations, and court cases that reflect a country's approach to information policy.

EU information policy refers to the legislation and strategies pertaining to the European policy for the creation and dissemination of information and data. This includes areas such as copyright and intellectual property, data protection and privacy, e-government, and digitization. It is also concerned with economic and industrial competitiveness, with an emphasis on the role that information and communication technologies play in revolutionizing everyday life. Information policy is viewed as contributing to the larger goals and objectives of the EU itself, particularly in relation to the European economy.

II. The European Union and European Information Society

As a supra-national body working toward peace and prosperity in Europe, the EU maintains a unique structure. It is not a federation of countries, but rather an organization in which each member state maintains its own independent governments and legislatures, while at the same time agreeing to have common institutions that make decisions on matters of joint interest to other member states. As of May, 2010, there were 27 member states as well as three candidate countries (Turkey, Croatia, and Macedonia) awaiting membership.

Information policy in the EU lacks the long tradition it has had in the United States. The term *information policy* itself is not in frequent use in the European context. It is important to note that "information policy" is a term that connotes a US perspective and attempts to understand EU information policies based on a US value and legal system. Information policy is not the preferred term of the EU policy makers, who have adopted the term "information society" to denote a broader set of issues relating to aspects of information management. The brief definition provided by the Europa glossary of the term *information society* places emphasis on information and communication technologies and their potential role in revolutionizing everyday life (Europa glossary, 2007). In this respect, it is similar to the Clinton administration's use of the term *National Information Infrastructure* (Goodwin and Spittle, 2002). The information society is a technologically driven phenomenon, and many of the efforts of the EU are devoted to developing policies centering on technological issues, specifically policies relating to market regulation, introduction of new technologies, and benefits from information and communications technologies (ICT).

Unlike the United States where information policy is piecemeal, and for the most part, reactive, information policy in the EU is preemptive. The EU views information policy as contributing to its larger goals and objectives and considers it an important part of the European economy. The role and vision of the information society has been presented as a force for economic growth: "The information society is on its way. A 'digital revolution' is triggering structural changes comparable to last century's industrial revolution with the corresponding high economic stakes. The process cannot be stopped and will lead eventually to a knowledge-based economy" (Commission of the European Communities, 1994, p. 3).

EU information policy is the result of the actions of the European Commission. Acting as the EU's executive branch, the European Commission's role is to prepare and implement legislation adopted by the European Council and the European Parliament in connection with EU policies. In 1979, the Commission issued a report that "addressed the role of networks in economic competition and the necessity of cooperation for developing new networks and services" (Schneider, 2001, p. 62).

The beginning of a comprehensive information policy for the EU can be traced back to 1994 when the European Council, recognizing the profound effect that global information and communication systems were having on European society, established a foundation for an information and communication infrastructure. The 1994 Bangemann report is often identified as the foundation of information policy for the EU. It resulted from the European Council's request for a report outlining measures and steps to be considered when laying a foundation for an information and communication infrastructure. The report recognized the profound effect that global information and communication systems were having on European society, including economic and social life. It lays out a vision for a European information society and recommends actions to achieve desired outcomes. Subsequent reports, particularly by the European Commission (1997), followed the

Bangemann report and advised the Commission on a recommended course of action. The Bangemann report was therefore advisory in nature, with implementation left to EU executives.

At the root of the EU information policy was an effort to build a legal and physical infrastructure designed to promote a global information society. The European Council's vision included a combination of free market forces and support from the regulatory system (Bangemann *et al.*, 1994) that addressed the needs of all EU citizens in an equitable way and would prevent a digital divide. The goal was for everyone to benefit from the opportunities offered by technology while controlling for its adverse effects. To curb the negative effects of an information-based society, the Bangemann report recommended that emphasis be placed on education and training. Free market forces play a major role in achieving the goals of an information society, and the Bangemann report called for ending monopolies of telecommunication operators and the system of political burdens that are inherent in them. The action plan of the report perceived the role of government as safeguarding competitive forces.

The report set out 10 areas related to ICT in which Europe needed to strengthen itself to compete in the global economy. These areas, included in chapter four of the report, were described as applications, or building blocks, of the information society. They included teleworking, distance learning, a network for universities and research centers, telematic services for small- and medium-sized enterprises, road traffic management, air traffic control, healthcare networks, electronic tendering, trans-European public administration networks, and city information highways.

In 1999, the European Commission launched an eEupore initiative to accelerate Europe's entry into the digital age. The result was *eEurope 2002*, which sought to create a cheaper, faster, and more secure Internet, to invest in people and skills, and to stimulate the use of the Internet throughout the EU (Keiser, 2003). eEurope 2002 was followed by *eEurope 2005*, and most recently i2010. i2010 is "an initiative which will provide an integrated approach to information society and audio-visual policies in the EU, covering regulation, research, and deployment and promoting cultural diversity" (Commission of the European Communities, 2005, p. 1). i2010 aims to achieve a single European information space for competitive society and media services through regulation, funding, and partnerships. It is currently the main coordinating body for European information society initiatives and implementation. i2010 actions are directed toward establishing a single European space for affordable and secure ICT in terms of diverse content and digital services. Other objectives of i2010 include developing private–public sector partnerships that promote technological innovation and providing an inclusive framework for ICT public services, particularly in the area of e-governments (Commission of the European Communities, 2005).

As the timeframe of i2010 is nearing its end, the European Parliament assessed its main achievements and on May 6, 2010, voted to pass 2015.eu, which outlines Europe's new digital agenda and Internet policy for the next five years (European Parliament Committee, 2010). 2015.eu continues the approach set forth in the earlier agenda, viewing ICT as vital for the EU's economic goals, and making recommendations to support those goals. Among the recommendations is that the European Community adopt a "European Charter of citizens' and consumers' rights in the digital environment" (European Parliament Committee, 2010, p. 8).

Within the framework of the EU, responsibility for the information society was initially that of the Commissioner for Enterprise and Information Society, but as roles expanded, so did the office, which is now known as the Commissioner for Enterprise and Industry (European Commission, Enterprise and Industry). Several important directives are included under the umbrella of Information Society legislation. These are conveniently collected and updated regularly on the EU's website (Europa. Summaries of legislation). The main areas of activity are ICT, intellectual property, data protection and pivacy, and electronic commerce. One of the main goals of the EU information policy is that of increased transparency. The past year has seen some notable developments in this pursuit. Currently on the agenda are several issues that demonstrate a shift toward policies that favor transparency and are more focused on user needs. They are the Anti-Counterfeiting Trade Agreement (ACTA); the application of privacy measures to the Internet of Things and to Social Networking; and Open-Access to EU-funded research outputs.

III. The Anti-Counterfeiting Trade Agreement

Copyright for the EU is regulated under Directive 2001/29/EC, Directive on the harmonization of certain aspects of copyright and related rights in the information society. As the word "harmonization" in the title indicates, Directive 2001/29/EC is an attempt to reconcile a variety of the member states' copyright laws and approaches stemming from different historical developments, primarily between the United Kingdom and the France. The United Kingdom saw copyright as a property right, whereas France viewed it as a natural right, with a array of EU laws addressing various aspects of the information society that predate the 2001 Directive (Bitton, 2008).

Most recently, in the area of intellectual property, the topic that has stirred greatest controversy has been the ACTA. ACTA collected enemies quickly due to the secret nature of the negotiations and its content, as parts of the Agreement was disclosed. Opposition to ACTA came from advocacy groups, government watchdogs, professional library associations, mainstream media, and from within legislating bodies.

First announced in October 2008, the ACTA is a plurilateral treaty that sets a global standard for intellectual property enforcement. Plans to negotiate ACTA were announced in October 2007 by the United States, the EU, Japan, South Korea, Mexico, New Zealand, Switzerland, and Canada. ACTA negotiations and its provision were shrouded in secrecy from the onset, prompting policy watchdogs such as the Electronic Frontier Foundation (EFF) to file a Freedom of Information Act request for the release of the treaty's draft, which was eventually denied. The official text (ACTA, 2010) of the proposed agreement was finally released by the European Commission in April, 2010, following partial and complete leaks that occurred in the preceding months.

Concerns over ACTA, as summarized by the EFF and by La Quadrature du Net, a French advocacy group, began when certain provisions of ACTA were leaked in 2008. It became clear that ACTA was not limited to monitoring counterfeit physical goods, such as medications, but also to watching over Internet piracy, specifically "Internet distribution and information technology" (European Commission. Trade, 2008, p. 4). It was viewed by its opponents as an anti file-sharing treaty that would alter the Internet by ending net neutrality. Possibly in response to this concern, the European Parliament recently called the European Commission and regulatory bodies to promote net neutrality and preserve the Internet as a "mere conduit" as established by e-commerce Directive 2000/31/EC as a way of ensuring market competition (European Parliament Committee, 2010, p. 9). ACTA, led by the world's developed economies, was set to create a new standard of intellectual property enforcement. Although the negotiating parties represented the world's developed nations, enforcement standards are to be applied globally and will affect developing countries that will be subject to enforcement, but were not part of the decision-making process.

The name of the treaty is misleading. Whereas anti-counterfeiting implies enforcement in more limited areas such as trademarks and patents, ACTA addresses a wide range of intellectual property topics. The official draft of ACTA, released on April 21, 2010, does not directly identify the scope of ACTA, but does so indirectly by saying that "intellectual property refers to all categories of intellectual property that are the subject of Sections 1 through 7 of Part II of the Agreement on Trade-Related Aspects of Intellectual Property Rights" (ACTA, 2010, p. 3). The Trade-Related Aspects of Intellectual Property Rights (TRIPS) agreements include eight areas of intellectual property, and the seven addressed by ACTA are (1) copyright and related rights, (2) trademarks, (3) geographical indications, (4) industrial design, (5) patents, (6) layout design (topographies) of integrated circuits, and (7) protection of undisclosed information (World Trade Organization, 1994).

The ACTA provision that caused the most concern was the one that would direct Internet Service Providers (ISP) to turn over information regarding copyright infringers to law enforcement without a warrant. *La Quadrature* identified one of the major faults of ACTA was responding to, and enforcing measures against all type of infringements equally, whether they involve life-endangering drugs or minor copyright infringements, and operating under a presumption of infringement. Health Action International (HAI)-Europe, a nonprofit advocacy group for health policy, released a statement expressing concern that the broad definitions and scope of enforcement of ACTA would create damaging confusion between counterfeit drugs and generic drugs and could potentially prevent developing countries from obtaining essential drugs by advancing a wider intellectual property monopoly enforcement. HAI's main concern was that ACTA could chill generic competition and threaten the generics industry (HAI-Europe, 2010). *La Quadrature* described the procedure under which ACTA was negotiated as policy laundering, in that the negotiations circumvented democratic procedures and debates by elected bodies (the European Parliament or the United States Congress), leaving only an all or nothing option of adoption (La Quadrature du Net, 2009). The International Federation of Library Associations (IFLA) also released a statement describing its position on ACTA, pointing to the secret nature of the negotiations and to the lack of transparency in the process as a main threat to the balance of copyright. IFLA expressed concern, on behalf of the world's library community, that ACTA could hinder equitable access to information and cultural expression (IFLA, 2010).

Responding to the mounting criticism, the European Commission published several documents summarizing key elements of ACTA to address public concern. This was all done without making the draft of the agreement public or providing minutes or any additional information about the negotiations. In November 2008, the European Commission released a fact sheet explaining some of the main provisions in the area of enforcement of intellectual property rights (European Commission. Trade, 2008). In April 2009, the Commission published a document that summarized the key elements of ACTA (European Commission. Trade, 2009).

The European Parliament took the extraordinary measure of voting against ACTA before the release of the official version, based only on the leaked document. In the March 10, 2010 vote (663 to 13) and subsequent resolution, the European Parliament called for the European Commission to reject ACTA, threatening to take the matter up before the European Court of Justice unless support of ACTA was withdrawn. The ACTA provision that received the most attention was one that would allow cutting off users from the Internet for copyright infringements that included downloading of copyrighted content, known as the "three-strikes" provision. The three-strikes provision allows ISPs to cut off Internet service from households upon the third copyright infringement (European Parliament resolution of March 10, 2010).

Several weeks later, the European Parliament reiterated its call for increased transparency in ACTA negotiations and supported shifting the negotiations to the World Intellectual Property Organization (WIPO) (European Parliament resolution of May 5, 2010). Members of the European Parliament wrote representative of the World Trade Organization (WTO) and WIPO requesting their involvement in ACTA negotiations (Albrecht *et al.*, 2010, April 15). Pascal Lamy, Director General of the WTO, responded on May 4 by saying that the WTO has no standing in the ACTA negotiations (Lamy, 2010) but encouraged keeping an open channel of communication between the European Parliament and the WTO. Correspondence between the two continues with the Parliament emphasizing the need for transparency (Albrecht *et al.*, 2010, May 26). All of the stakeholders are now awaiting the next round of ACTA negotiations scheduled to place during June, 2010, in Switzerland.[1]

IV. Privacy Protection in the Internet of Things

The strong protection of personal information of and about EU citizens is a result of the EU Database Directive. The Directive views privacy as a human right and provides strong government regulations to safeguard personal information. Even these protections, and the enforcement of the EU standards on non-EU bodies handling information on EU citizens, are under threat of erosion in the face of technological advances and social ways in which information is shared and exchanged. The EU often finds itself helpless after privacy violations occur, such as in the recent admission by

---

[1]The deadline for submission of this chapter preceded the beginning of the ACTA negotiations.

Google that it systematically collected personal information as part of its Street View photo archive (O'Brien, 2010).

Recently, the European Commission has focused its attention on two areas that have the potential of infringing on personal property rights: The Internet of Things and Social Networking. It has released several position papers and press releases on the subject (European Commission. RFID, 2010; European Commission. Social Networking Sites, 2010; Europa RAPID Press Releases, 2009; Europa RAPID Press Releases, 2010).

The first concern addresses the process that occurs when information shifts from being something abstract intangible item into an object. The objectification of information is usually referred to as the Internet of Things, a term attributed to Kevin Ashton who used the phrase in 1999 to describe the increasing proliferation of Radio Frequency Identification Tags (RFID) that bring real-time updated information to otherwise dumb objects (Ashton, 2009). The Internet of Things is a result of the integration of hardware, software, and services in wired and wireless networks that facilitate data and information from real and sensed environment and allow objects to communicate, particularly in public spaces. Some examples include smart phone applications that read another phone's information or identify a song; RFID tags on library books that contain book information; microchips implanted in dogs that contain medical information; and smart passports. As the Internet of Things depends on information based on identity, there is a heightened need to protect personally identifiable information. Consistent with the EU approach to ICT, these technologies are highly regarded for their potential to propel the economy and the expectation is that they will affect areas such a transportation, environment, energy efficiency, and health (Commission of the European Communities, 2008).

The 2008 Commission paper acknowledges a possible undermining of privacy as a result of the Internet of Things, but approaches this problem not by seeking the best way to protect policy values, but rather by seeking ways to institute policies that will promote public trust of the Internet of Things (Commission of the European Communities, 2008). The Commission favors a pragmatic market perspective over an information policy values perspective. The report's first two recommendations discuss the policy challenges brought on by the use of RFID tags to build awareness among stakeholders and to make the Internet of Things affordable and accessible to all. Only the third point addresses the fundamental right of individuals to privacy (Commission of the European Communities, 2008).

Following this report, the Commission issued recommendations to address the problems tied to data protection in RFID-enabled applications (Commission of the European Communities, 2009). The Commission recommended that they extend the same protections to guarantee the fundamental right to privacy as available in the Database Directive (Directive 95/46/EC, 1995), but with a decisively economic objective in mind. The justification for the recommendation of the Treaty of Rome was found, which ensures "the proper functioning and development of the common market" (Treaty, 1992, article 211). Further evidence of the importance of the economic factor in the 2009 recommendation is the use of RFID tags in retail (Commission of the European Communities, 2009, pp. 7–8) and the specific need for follow-up in the retail section. The retail section encourages EU industry to collaborate with civil society stakeholders to develop a RFID data privacy framework within 6 months (Commission of the European Communities, 2009, p. 9). The European Parliament held its most recent meeting on the Internet of Things on March 17, 2010, to discuss the Commission's 2009 report *Internet of Things—An action plan for Europe* and reasserted that public trust in the safety of their personal data is vital for the continuing role of the Internet of Things in the European information society (European Parliament, 2010, March 17).

An attempt to predict future areas of development for the Internet of Things identifies expectant applications in the area of social networking services (SNS) (Botterman, 2009). This coincided with the publication of the *Opinion 5/2009 on Online Social Networking* by the Article 29 Working Party (Opinion 5/2009, 2009). The Article 29 Working Party is an independent European advisory body that serves as a watchdog and provides opinions to the European Commission on questions of data protection. It was set up under Article 29 of Directive 95/46/EC (1995). While the Opinion encourages users of SNS to exercise caution when establishing privacy settings on sites such as Facebook, it determined that service providers and users of SNS are subject to the protections of the Data Protection Directive (Opinion 5/2009, 2009, p. 5), although it recognizes some exceptions, mainly the Household Exemption, which excludes individuals who process personal data "in the course of a purely personal or household activity" from the responsibilities of a data controller (Opinion 5/2009, 2009, p. 5).

In practical terms, applying the household exemption to SNS means that SNS are considered data controllers. They are thus accountable for applying Directive 95/46/EC (1995) to the information of EU citizens, even if the SNS is not located in the EU. The SNS are required to set the default privacy settings to ensure that a minimal amount of information is shared and that all information remains under the control of the user as household information. When the user expands access to personal information, responsibility for protections shifts to the SNS. However, as the ways in which individuals use SNS shifts from personal entertainment to activities more closely resembling that of a data controller, the household exemption may begin to exclude individuals using SNS in ways that can no longer be considered personal and thus will not be eligible for the household exemption. Some examples provided in the Opinion 5/2009 (2009) include using SNS to advance commercial, political, or charitable causes. The *Working Group Opinion* calls for operators of SNS to make default privacy settings that protect users (Opinion 5/2009, 2009, p. 6). As the differences between data users and data controllers on SNS blur, the Article 29 Data Protection Working Party addressed the question of who is a data controller. They recently published Opinion 1/2010 (2010) clarifying the concept of a data controller (Opinion 1/2010, 2010). This concept is a key to the implementation of the EU Database Directive, which instructs data controllers to protect the personal data they collect and process and makes them responsible and accountable for safeguarding information they collect, hold, and process.

The Working Group opinion is an attempt to prevent a situation where ambiguity regarding who is responsible for safeguarding data results in no one taking responsibility. The Working Group's interest is to promote application of and compliance with personal data protection as described in Directive 95/46/EC (1995). If through the use of SNS individuals are assuming roles of SNS, the responsibilities they carry becomes greater and more legally binding to them. Although Opinion 1/2010 (2010) does not change the definition of data controller and data processer provided in Directive 95/46/EC (1995), it does clarify them and provides examples and relevant context from recent data uses in the area of SNS. Article 2(d) of Directive 95/46/EC (1995) defines a Data Controller as "the natural or legal person, public authority, agency or any other body which alone or jointly with others **determines** the purposes and means of the processing of personal data" [emphasis added].

Opinion 1/2010 (2010) clarifies that "determines" should be looked at from a factual point of view and ask "why is this processing taking place? Who initiated it?" "[A] body which has neither legal nor factual influence to determine how personal data are processed cannot be considered as a controller" (Opinion 1/2010, 2010, p. 8). Opinion 1/2010(2010) makes clear that SNS are considered data controllers: "Social network service providers provide online communication platforms which enable individuals to publish and exchange information with other users. These service providers are data controllers, since they determine both the purposes and the means of the processing of such information. The users of such networks, uploading personal data also of third parties, would qualify as controllers provided that

their activities are not subject to the so-called 'household exception.'"
(Opinion 1/2010, 2010, p. 21).

V. Open Access Policies

Steps toward open access publishing in Europe have taken place mostly on the
national level rather than by the EU as a whole and have been driven by policy
rather than by legislation. Research activities for the EU are overseen by the
European Commission's Research Directorate-General whose main goal is to
work on the European Research Area (ERA). The Research Directorate-
General works jointly with European Research Council (ERC) and the Seventh
Research Framework Programme (FP7) on European basic research policy
(European Basic Research Policy, 2006). Together, they have published studies
and initiated projects to examine, understand, and test open access policies and
models that will suit the needs of the European research community.

The ERC, a grant funding body established in February, 2007, by the
European Commission, has been engaged in open access publishing and
policies as a think tank, contributing studies and expert opinion. The
ERC's open access policy regarding ERC-funded research requires that all
peer-reviewed publications and primary data sets be deposited in open
access research repositories (where available) within 6 months of publication
(ERC, 2007).

The FP7 began an open access pilot project in 2008 (expected to run
through 2013) providing open access to articles resulting from European-
funded research (European Commission. Research. *Open access pilot in FP7*).
FP7 covers research in the areas of energy, environment, health, information
and communication technologies, research infrastructures, science in society,
socioeconomic sciences, and humanities. Any research receiving grants in
these areas will be required, as part of the terms of their grant, to deposit
articles resulting from the research into an institutional or subject repository
within 6 months, or in the case or science in society, socioeconomics and
humanities, within 12 months (COM, 2008, 4408).

In 2006, the Research Directorate-General published a study examining
the economic and technical evaluation of the scientific publication markets in
Europe (European Commission. Directorate General-Research, 2006). The
study resulted from concern about a lack of access to and dissemination of
scientific research of the EU (European Commission. Directorate General-
Research, 2006, p. 5). Of the eight recommendations for actions outlined in
the study, only the first recommendation, to, "guarantee public access to
publicly-funded research results shortly after publication" (European

Commission. Directorate General-Research, 2006, p. 87), was adopted by the ERC in their open access policy. Thus, this recommendation speaks to the heart of open access policies.

FP7 is engaged in two large-scale projects in the area of open access publishing. FP7 is funding the Study of Open Access Publishing (SOAP). Running from March 2009 to 28 February 2011, SOAP brings together some of the stakeholders studied under the Directorate General-Research study Europe (European Commission. Directorate General-Research, 2006). SOAP collaborates on open access business models necessitated by the transition from print to digital documents and advises the European Commission and the stakeholders on best practices for the transition (Project SOAP, 2009). In addition, FP7 is also behind the Open Access Infrastructure for Research in Europe (OpenAIRE). OpenAIRE is a project intended to provide bibliographic control over FP7 and ERC-funded research. It will, in effect, be a registry of research outputs in any form, including articles, conference proceedings, primary datasets, and any additional materials that can result from research, regardless of the repository where the research is deposited. In cases where the research is not in a depository, OpenAIRE will provide archiving services as well. OpenAIRE will serve mainly as a portal to peer-reviewed publications that will be deposited in institutional and subject repositories (OpenAIRE, 2010).

VI. Conclusion

In a recent overview of information policy in the EU, the authors described the development of, and approach to, information policy taken by the EU, and identified the major areas of the European Information Society as ICT; intellectual property; electronic commerce; and data protection (Rabina and Johnston, 2010). This discussion has focused on three initiatives in the European Information Society, which have been on the European Commission's agenda in the past year, ACTA, the application of privacy measures to the Internet of Things and to Social Networking, and open access to EU-funded research results.

Although many of the proposed measures and legislation in these areas are still under ongoing negotiations, the United States and the EU continue to pursue measures consistent with their existing policy perspectives. The EU Parliament continues to question both the content of ACTA and the conduct of negotiations, whereas the US copyright office recently defended the content of ACTA and dismissed concerns about the negotiations (Future of Music Colation, 2010). The differences between the EU and the United

States are starkest in approaches to privacy and data protection. In its approach to the Internet of Things and Social Networking sites, the EU has continued to increase regulation and legislation, whereas the United States has continued to leave individual privacy protection up to market forces. The EU and the United States maintain their respective approaches in the area of open access as well. The United States mandates open access through legislation in an attempt to guarantee dissemination of public-funded research to the public. The EU encourages but does not enforce open access practices, using policies and initiatives rather than legislation.

All three of these issues discussed here reveal the struggle that is going on within the EU to address greater transparency. The EU, for reasons both historical and pragmatic, focuses more efforts on execution than on vision. Although its member institutions are democratic, and increased transparency continues to be one of the EU's main goals, the EU is not in the purest sense a democratic institution because the Parliament, whose members are elected directly by the citizens of member states, has limited ability to exercise control over the European Commission. If past actions are any guide, transparency and access to information will continue to be a challenge for the EU, in spite of the adoption of a code of conduct regulating information practices.

References

Albrecht, J. P., Delli, K., Schlyter, C., Keller, S., Sargentini, J., Engstrom, J., Bélier, S., Greens/EFA in the European Parliament. (2010, April 15). *Letter to Pascal Lamy, Director General World Trade Organization and Others Regarding European Parliament Resolution of 10 March, 2010 on Transparency and State of Play of the Anti-Counterfeiting Trade Agreement (ACTA)*. Retrieved from http://www.erikjosefsson.eu/sites/default/files/WTO-letter-from-Greens-EFA.html

Albrecht, J. P., Delli, K., Schlyter, C., Keller, S., Sargentini, J., Engstrom, J., Bélier, S., Greens/EFA in the European Parliament. (2010, May 26). *Letter to Pascal Lamy, Director General World Trade Organization and Others*. Retrieved from http://www.erikjosefsson.eu/sites/default/files/Follow_up_letter_on_ACTA.html

Anti-Counterfeiting Trade Agreement (ACTA). (2010, April). *Consolidated Text Prepared for Public Release*. Retrieved from http://www.ustr.gov/acta.

Ashton, K. (2009, June 22). The 'Internet of Things' thing: In the real world, things matter more than ideas. *RFID Journal*. Retrieved from http://www.rfidjournal.com/article/articleview/4986/1/82/

Bangemann, M., Cabral da Fonseca, E., Davis, P., de Benedetti, C., Gyllenhammar, P., Hunsel, L., *et al.* (1994). *Europe and the Global Information Society: Bangemann Report Recommendations to the European Council*. Retrieved from http://www.umic.pt/images/stories/publicacoes200801/raport_Bangemanna_1994.pdf

Bitton, M. (2008). Exploring European Union copyright policy through the lens of the Database Directive. *Berkeley Technology Law Journal* 23(4), 1411–1470.

Botterman, M. (2009, May 10). *Internet of Things: An early reality of the future Internet.* Prepared for the European Commission, Information Society and Media Directorate General, Networked Enterprise & RFID Unit (D4). Retrieved from http://www.future-internet.eu/fileadmin/documents/reports/FI-content/IoT_Prague_Workshop_report_vFinal__060709.pdf

COM. (2008) *Commission of the European Communities. Commission Decision on the Adoption and a Modification of Special Clauses Applicable to the Model Grant Agreement.* Retrieved on April 10, 2007 from http://ec.europa.eu/research/press/2008/pdf/decision_grant_agreement.pdf

Commission of the European Communities. (1994, July 19). *Europe's Way to the Information Society: An Action Plan.* [Communication from the Commission to the Council, the European Parliament, the Economic and Social Committee and the Committee of the Regions, COM (94) 347 final]. Commission of the European Communities: Brussels, Belgium. Retrieved from http://aei.pitt.edu/947/01/info_socieity_action_plan_COM_94_347.pdf

Commission of the European Communities. (2005). *i2010—A European Information Society for Growth and Employment.* [COM (2005) 229 final]. Retrieved from http://eur-lex.europa.eu/LexUriServ/LexUriServ.do?uri = COM:2005:0229:FIN:EN:PDF.

Commission of the European Communities. (2008, September 29). *Future Networks and the Internet Early Challenges Regarding the "Internet of Things."* [Commission staff working document. Accompanying document to the Communication form the Commission to the European Parliament, The Council, the European and Social Committee and the Committee of the Regions]. Retrieved from http://ec.europa.eu/information_society/eeurope/i2010/docs/future_internet/swp_internet_things.pdf

Commission of the European Communities. (2009, May 12). *Commission Recommendations of 12.5.2009 on the Implementation of Privacy and Data Protection Principles in Applications Supported by Radio-Frequency Identification.* C (2009) 3200 final. Retrieved from http://ec.europa.eu/information_society/policy/rfid/documents/recommendationonrfid2009.pdf

Directive 95/46/EC (1995). *Directive 95/46/EC of the European Parliament and of the Council of 24 October 1995 on the protection of individuals with regard to the processing of personal data and on the free movement of such data.* Retrieved from http://ec.europa.eu/justice_home/fsj/privacy/law/index_en.htm.

European Research Council. Scientific Council (2007, December 17). *ERC Scientific Council Guidelines for Open Access.* Retrieved from http://erc.europa.eu/pdf/ScC_Guidelines_Open_Access_revised_Dec07_FINAL.pdf

Europa glossary. (2007). Retrieved from http://europa.eu/scadplus/glossary/full_en.htm

Europa RAPID Press Releases. (2009, April 14). *Citizens' Privacy must Become Priority in Digital Age, Says EU Commissioner Reding* [Press release]. Retrieved from http://europa.eu/rapid/pressReleasesAction.do?reference = IP/09/571&format = HTML&aged = 0&language = EN&guiLanguage = en

Europa RAPID Press Releases. (2010, February 9). *European Commission Calls on Social Networking Companies to Improve Child Safety Policies* [Press release]. Retrieved from http://europa.eu/rapid/pressReleasesAction.do?reference = IP/10/144&format = HTML&aged = 0&language = EN&guiLanguage = en

Europa. *Summaries of legislation—Information society.* Retrieved from http://europa.eu/legislation_summaries/information_society/index_en.htm

European basic research policy. (2006, May 17). *Stimulating the Creativity for Basic Research.* Retrieved from http://ec.europa.eu/research/future/basic_research/index_en.html

European Commission. *Enterprise and Industry.* Retrieved from http://ec.europa.eu/enterprise/index_en.htm.

European Commission. *Research. Open access pilot in FP7.* Retrieved from http://ec.europa.eu/research/science-society/index.cfm?fuseaction=public.topic&id=1680.

European Commission. Directorate General-Research. (2006). *Study on the Economic and Technical Evaluation of the Scientific Publication Markets in Europe.* Retrieved from http://ec.europa.eu/research/science-society/pdf/scientific-publication-study_en.pdf

European Commission. (1997, April). Directorate-General for Employment, Industrial Relations and Social Affairs. *Building the European Information Society for Us All: Final Policy Report of the High Level Expert Group.* Retrieved from http://aei.pitt.edu/8692/

European Commission. RFID (2010). *Radio Frequency Identification and the Internet of Things.* Retrieved from http://ec.europa.eu/information_society/policy/rfid/index_en.htm

European Commission. Social Networking Sites (2010). *Making the Most of Social Networking.* Retrieved from http://ec.europa.eu/information_society/activities/social_networking/index_en.htm

European Commission. Trade (2008, November). *The Anti-Counterfeiting Trade Agreement (ACTA) fact sheet.* Retrieved from http://trade.ec.europa.eu/doclib/docs/2008/october/tradoc_140836.11.08.pdf

European Commission. Trade (2009, April). The Anti-Counterfeiting Trade Agreement (ACTA). *The Anti-Counterfeiting Trade Agreement-Summary of Key Elements under Discussion.* Retrieved from http://trade.ec.europa.eu/doclib/docs/2009/november/tradoc_145271.pdf

European Parliament. (2010, March 17). Committee on Industry, Research and Energy. *Meeting Agenda.* Retrieved from http://www.europarl.europa.eu/meetdocs/2009_2014/organes/itre/itre_20100317_0900.htm

European Parliament. (2010, March 25). Committee on Industry, Research and Energy. *Report on a New Digital Agenda for Europe: 2015*.eu (2009/2225(INI)). Retrieved from http://www.europarl.europa.eu/sides/getDoc.do?pubRef=-//EP//TEXT+REPORT+A7-2010-0066+0+DOC+XML+V0//EN

European Parliament resolution of 10 March. (2010). *European Parliament resolution of 10 March on the Transparency and State of Play of the ACTA Negotiations.* Text adopted P7_TA (2010)0058. Retrieved from http://www.europarl.europa.eu/sides/getDoc.do?type=TA&reference=P7-TA-2010-0058&language=EN&ring=P7-RC-2010-0154

European Parliament resolution of 5 May. (2010). *European Parliament resolution on the Upcoming EU-Canada Summit on 5 May 2010.* Retrieved from http://www.europarl.europa.eu/sides/getDoc.do?type=MOTION&reference=B7-2010-0233&language=EN

Future of Music Colation. (2010, May 25). *DC Policy Day 2010 Panel.* Retrieved from http://www.ustream.tv/recorded/7200032

Goodwin, I., and Spittle, S. (2002). The European Union and the information society: Discourse, power and policy. *New Media and Society* 4(2), 225–249.

HAI-Europe. (2010, March 22). *Comments on ACTA Stakeholder Consultation.* Retrieved from http://www.haiweb.org/22032010/DGTradeConsultationACTA. pdf

Hernon, P., and Relyea, H. C. (2003). Information policy. In *Encyclopedia of Library and Information Science* (M. Drake, ed.), Vol. 2, 2nd ed., pp. 1300–1315, Marcel Dekker, New York.

IFLA. (2010, March 26). *IFLA Position on the Anti-Counterfeiting Trade Agreement.* Retrieved from http://www.ifla.org/en/publications/ifla-position-on-the-anti-counterfeiting-trade-agreement

Keiser, K. (2003). *EU Guide to the Digital Economy.* EU Committee of the American Chamber of Commerce, Brussels, Belgium.

Lamy, P. (2010, May 4). *Letter in Response to Resolution of the European Parliament on Transparency and State of Play of the Anti-Counterfeiting Trade Agreement (ACTA).* Retrieved from http://keionline.org/node/838

La Quadrature du Net. (2009). *ACTA.* Retrieved from http://www.laquadrature.net/en/ACTA

O'Brien, K. J. (2010, May 15). Google data admission angers Europe. *The New York Times.* Retrieved from http://www.nytimes.com/2010/05/16/technology/16 google.html?hpw

OpenAIRE. (2010). *About the project: Fact sheet.* Retrieved from http://www.openaire. eu/en/about-openaire/general-information/fact-sheet.html

Opinion 5/2009. (2009). *Opinion 5/2009 on Online Social Networking, Adopted on 12 June 2009 (WP 163).* Retrieved from http://ec.europa.eu/justice_home/fsj/ privacy/docs/wpdocs/2009/wp163_en.pdf

Opinion 1/2010 (2010). *Opinion 1/2010 on Concepts of "Controller" and "Processor", Adopted on 16 February. 2010 (WP 169).* Retrieved from http://ec.europa.eu/ justice_home/fsj/privacy/docs/wpdocs/2010/wp169_en.pdf.

Project SOAP. (2009). *The Study of Open Access Publishing.* Retrieved from http:// project-soap.eu/

Rabina, D., and Johnston, S. (2010). Information policy: European Union. In *Encyclopedia of Library and Information Sciences* (M. Bates, Ed.), 3rd ed., 2009 CRC Press Taylor & Francis Group, Boca Raton, FL. DOI: 10.1081/E-ELIS3-120044551.

Schneider, V. (2001). Institutional reform in telecommunications: The European Union in transitional policy diffusion. In *Transforming Europe: Europeanization and Domestic Change* (M. G. Cowels, J. Caporaso and T. Riesse, eds.), pp. 60–78, Cornell University Press, Ithaca, NY.

Treaty Establishing the European Community (1992, February 7). *1 C.M.L.R. 573.* Retrieved from http://eur-lex.europa.eu/en/treaties/dat/12002E/htm/C_2002325 EN.003301.html

World Trade Organization (1994). *Trade-Related Aspects of Intellectual Property Rights (TRIPS).* Retrieved from http://www.wto.org/english/docs_e/legal_e/27-trips_ 01_e.htm

Author Index

Subject Index

Page numbers followed by f and t indicate figures and tables, respectively.